THE ULTIMATE OBJECTIVES OF ARTIFICIAL INTELLIGENCE

Theoretical and Research Foundations, Philosophical and Psychological Implications

Morton Wagman

 PRAEGER

Westport, Connecticut
London

Library of Congress Cataloging-in-Publication Data

Wagman, Morton.
    The ultimate objectives of artificial intelligence : theoretical
and research foundations, philosophical and psychological
implications / Morton Wagman.
      p. cm.
    Includes bibliographical references and indexes.
    ISBN 0–275–95910–4 (alk. paper)
    1. Artificial intelligence. I. Title.
Q335.W344 1998
006.3'01—dc21   97–28884

British Library Cataloguing in Publication Data is available.

Library of Congress Catalog Card Number: 97–28884
ISBN: 0–275–95910–4

First published in 1998

Praeger Publishers, 88 Post Road West, Westport, CT 06881
An imprint of Greenwood Publishing Group, Inc.

Printed in the United States of America

The paper used in this book complies with the
Permanent Paper Standard issued by the National
Information Standards Organization (Z39.48–1984).

10 9 8 7 6 5 4 3 2 1

Copyright Acknowledgments

The author and publisher gratefully acknowledge permission to use extracts from the following materials.

Achinstein, P. (1965). Theoretical models. *The British Journal for the Philosophy of Science, 16(62)*, 102–120. Reprinted with the permission of Oxford University Press.

Brooks, R. A. (1991). Intelligence without representation. *Artificial Intelligence, 47*, 139–159. Reprinted with the permission of Elsevier Science Publishers.

Elio, R. and Scharf, P. B. (1990). Modeling novice-to-expert shifts in problem solving strategy and knowledge organization. *Cognitive Science, 14*, 579–639. Reprinted with the permission of the Ablex Publishing Corporation.

Hall, R. P. (1989). Computational approaches to analogical reasoning: A comparative analysis. *Artificial Intelligence, 39*, 39–120. Reprinted with the permission of Elsevier Science Publishers.

Holyoak, K. J. and Thagard, P. (1989). Analogical mapping by constraint satisfaction. *Cognitive Science, 13*, 295–355. Reprinted with the permission of the Ablex Publishing Corporation.

Horgan, J. (1993). The death of proof. *Scientific American, 269*, 93–103. Reprinted with the permission of *Scientific American*.

Hovy, E. H. (1990). Pragmatics and natural language generation. *Artificial Intelligence, 43*, 153–197. Reprinted with the permission of Elsevier Science Publishers.

Keyes, R. W. (1993). The future of the transistor. *Scientific American, 268*, 70–78. Reprinted with the permission of *Scientific American*.

Kirsh, D. (1991). Foundations of AI: The big issues. *Artificial Intelligence, 47*, 3–30. Reprinted with the permission of Elsevier Science Publishers.

Kulkarni, D. and Simon, H. A. (1988). The processes of scientific discovery: The strategy of experimentation. *Cognitive Science, 12*, 139–175. Reprinted with the permission of the Ablex Publishing Corporation.

Kurzwell, R. (1990). *The age of intelligent machines*. Cambridge, MA: The MIT Press. Reprinted with the permission of the MIT Press.

Langley, P. (1981). Data-driven discovery of physical laws. *Cognitive Science, 5*, 50. Reprinted with the permission of the Ablex Publishing Corporation.

Lehnert, W. (1983). BORIS—An expert in in-depth understanding of narratives. *Artificial Intelligence, 20*, 15–61. Reprinted with the permission of Elsevier Science Publishers.

Lenat, D. B., and Feigenbaum, E. A. (1991). On the thresholds of knowledge. *Artificial Intelligence, 47*, 185–250. Reprinted with the permission of Elsevier Science Publishers.

Rosenbloom, P. S., Laird, J. E., Newell, A., and McCarl, R. (1991). A preliminary analysis of the SOAR architecture as a basis for general intelligence. *Artificial Intelligence, 47*, 289–325. Reprinted with the permission of Elsevier Science Publishers.

Thagard, P. (1989). Explanatory coherence. *Behavioral and Brain Sciences, 12*, 435–502. Reprinted with the permission of Cambridge University Press.

Wagman, M. (1983). A factor analytic study of the psychological implications of the computer for the individual and society. *Behavior Research Methods and Instrumentation, 15*, 413–419. Reprinted with the permission of the Psychonomic Society, Inc.

Wagman, M. (1991). *Cognitive Science and Concepts of Mind: Toward a General Theory of Human and Artificial Intelligence*. Westport, CT: Praeger. Reprinted with the permission of Praeger Publishers, an imprint of Greenwood Publishing Group, Inc., Westport, CT.

Wagman, M. (1993). *Cognitive Psychology and Artificial Intelligence: Theory and Research in Cognitive Science*. Westport, CT: Praeger. Reprinted with the permission of Praeger Publishers, an imprint of Greenwood Publishing Group, Inc., Westport, CT.

Wagman, M. (1995). *The Sciences of Cognition: Theory and Research in Psychology and Artificial Intelligence*. Westport, CT: Praeger. Reprinted with the permission of Praeger Publishers, an imprint of Greenwood Publishing Group, Inc., Westport, CT.

Wagman, M. (1996). *Human Intellect and Cognitive Science: Toward a General Unified Theory of Intelligence*. Westport, CT: Praeger. Reprinted with the permission of Praeger Publishers, an imprint of Greenwood Publishing Group, Inc., Westport, CT.

Winston, P. H. (1980). Learning and reasoning by analogy. *Communications of the ACM, 23(12)*, 689–703. Reprinted with the permission of the Association of Computing Machinery.

Contents

Illustrations

TABLES

FIGURES

Preface

The field of artificial intelligence possesses an open-ended character in its theory, research, and objectives.

This book discusses the advancing intellectual developments in artificial intelligence. In focusing on theory and research, the book is distinguished from applications type and futurist books. In considering philosophical and psychological implications that derive directly from current theory and research, this book is distinguished from speculative books lacking in intellectual grounding.

In the first chapter, artificial intelligence and its objectives are considered. The technical objective of achieving the continuous augmentation of computer intelligence is distinguished from the intellectual objective of developing an abstract science of general intelligence inclusive of humans, computers, and animals. In the second part of the chapter, artificial intelligence and theoretical psychology are discussed. The abstract mathematical universal Turing machine and its input/output (I/O) functions are described, and the Turing thesis of correspondences in the input/output functions of computers and humans is examined in depth. Turing-based computational psychology is compared with empirical cognitive psychology.

In the second chapter, symbolic and connectionist models of the brain are considered. The information-processing paradigm thesis that the brain is a problem-solving system that employs heuristics to process symbolic representations of problem states is described. The neural network thesis that the brain is a massively parallel, hard-wired connection of simple neuronal or mathematical units with changes in connection weights coordinated to learning is discussed. Major differences in the two paradigms are detailed in a summary table. In the

second part of the chapter, hybrid symbolic-connectionist paradigms are examined. The integration of the paradigms within specific and unified architectures is considered, and the relevance of this integration for a theoretical account
of the human cognitive system is discussed. The chapter concludes with a detailed examination of the philosophical and psychological implications of the
parallel processing paradigm, including its cognitive validity and appropriate
level of analysis.

In the third chapter, Newell's unified theory of cognition and its embodiment
in the SOAR research project are discussed in depth. Following an account of
SOAR's theoretical background and methodological assumptions, the structure
of SOAR, including its memory, decision, and goal levels, are set forth; its
learning, problem-solving, and other cognitive abilities are highlighted; and its
scope and limits are delineated. The chapter concludes with a consideration of
the philosophical and psychological implications contained in SOAR's ambitious research objective of capturing the full range of general human intelligence.

In the fourth chapter, major research programs in artificial intelligence are
compared with respect to their theoretical positions on central conceptual assumptions. Four research programs (logicism, connectionism, SOAR, and roboticism) are discussed with respect to their positions on each of five
fundamental assumptions. A summary table that facilitates the comparisons is
presented. The chapter concludes with a consideration of the philosophical and
psychological implications of the differing perspectives for the nature of intelligence and intelligent systems.

In the fifth chapter, the ten-year CYC research project is discussed in depth.
CYC, designated to be completed in 1994, has the artificial intelligence research
objective of emulating, by means of an immense declarative and procedural
knowledge base, the full range of human knowledge and eventually surpassing
it. The philosophical and psychological implications of this research program
are critically examined. In the second part of the chapter, the theory of explanatory coherence and its embodiment in the ECHO system are described. ECHO
performs high-level intellectual integration and consistency tests of the coherence of competing scientific explanations and hypotheses.

In the sixth chapter, artificial intelligence and the processes of scientific discovery are discussed. The seriality of biochemical hypotheses and experiments
executed by the KEKADA program is described. KEKADA's success in redis-
covering the ornithine effect is demonstrated to model closely the creative processes used by Hans Krebs to establish the original discovery. In the second
part of the chapter, the philosophical and psychological implications of the
KEKADA system as a general simulator of the scientific discovery process are
critically examined. The chapter concludes with a summary analysis of the extent to which computational discovery systems can emulate a set of ten types
of scientific problems, ranging from theory formation to experimentation and
data analysis.

In the seventh chapter, theory and research concerned with the interrelationship of strategic approach and knowledge organization learning and problem solving are examined. The theory is embodied in the EUREKA system that updates its knowledge organization as it learns to solve progressively more difficult physics problems. Experimental protocols demonstrate EUREKA's progress from novice to expert problem solver. The chapter concludes with a consideration of the philosophical and psychological implications of the EUREKA system for the nature of complex adaptive systems.

In the eighth chapter, the development of intelligent robots is discussed. The thesis is advanced that the ultimate objective of a robot that can make its autonomous way in the world is constrained by the subset of world attributes that frame the robot's behavior and delimit the problem faced by the designer of robotic systems. Following a brief description of the range of current robotic applications, the highly sophisticated computer musician, Wabot-2, that comprehends and performs musical scores is presented in detail. In the next part of the chapter, the Brook's thesis that mobile robot intelligence can be engineered without regard to the traditional artificial intelligence methods of symbolic or conceptual representation is discussed in depth, and the Brook's research project for the development of automous robotic agents is described and critically assessed. The chapter concludes with a consideration of the philosophical and psychological implications of the creation of intelligent robots.

In the ninth chapter, artificial intelligence approaches to language comprehension and language generation are discussed. In the first part of the chapter, the characteristics and limitations of language comprehension systems—including the ELIZA system for psychotherapeutic comprehension, the SHRDLU system for microworld comprehension, a system for the comprehension of Shakespearian plays, the BORIS system for narrative comprehension, and a massively parallel processing system for the comprehension of language—are described in depth. In the second part of the chapter, the general logic, principles, features, behavioral examples, and limitations of PAULINE, an artificial intelligence system for pragmatic language generation, are described. The theory underlying PAULINE, particularly the principles of rhetorical strategy and of interleaving of generation processes, inclusive of both humans and computers, are critically examined, and PAULINE's pragmatic ability to adapt its language-generation style so as to achieve different intentionalities for different audiences, circumstances, and settings is highlighted. The chapter concludes with a consideration of the philosophical and psychological implications of computational language systems for a general theory of intelligence.

In the tenth chapter, artificial intelligence and analogical reasoning are discussed. In the first part of the chapter, a theory of the conceptual components of analogical reasoning, inclusive of computers and humans, is presented and an account is given of the recognition, elaboration, evaluation, and consolidation componential processes. In the second part of the chapter, the ACME model of analogical mapping, its logic of parallel constraint satisfaction, and its wide application to numerous domains from formal mathematical analogies to classical literary metaphors are examined in depth. The chapter concludes with a consideration of the philosophical and psychological implications of computational analogy systems for the nature of analogical thought.

In the eleventh chapter, limitations of artificial intelligence are discussed. In the first part of the chapter, limits in physics are considered. The quantum computer is discussed as the ultimate computational device, and the power and limits of the transistor are described. In the second part of the chapter, limits in logic are considered. The essential concepts of fuzzy logic are presented. The implications of Gödel's theorem for the ultimate logical foundations of artificial intelligence are examined. A discussion of the philosophical and psychological implications of the limitations of artificial intelligence concludes the chapter.

In the twelfth chapter, the epilogue, general philosophical and psychological implications of artificial intelligence and its objectives discussed in the book are examined in depth. The chapter concludes with a discussion of the abstract validity of logical and mathematical structures and their bearing on the ultimate nature of cognition.

Appendix A presents a conception of the characteristics of a general theory of intelligence that includes symbolic, finite, discrete, and autonomous characteristics. Appendix B presents research concerned with the Cybernetics Attitude Scale and its application in a factor analytic study of the psychological implications of the computer for the individual and society.

The book is intended for scholars and professionals in psychology, artificial intelligence, and cognitive science. Graduate and advanced undergraduate students in these and related disciplines will also find the book useful.

ACKNOWLEDGMENTS

I am grateful to LaDonna Wilson for her assistance in the preparation of all aspects of the manuscript. I thank Amy Osheck for excellent typing of portions of the manuscript.

1

Prologue

ARTIFICIAL INTELLIGENCE AND ITS OBJECTIVES

The field of artificial intelligence (AI), a specialized discipline within general computer science, is directed toward the continuous augmentation of computer intelligence. The augmentation of intelligence in computers may be achieved by two general methods or by a combination of the methods.

In the first general method, the computer models the cognitive processes of human intellect. Augmentation of computer intelligence through this method requires the continuous expansion of reliable and valid knowledge concerning human cognitive processes.

In the second general method, the intelligence of the computer models formal logical structures and processes. Augmentation of computer intelligence through this method requires the continuous expansion of reliable and valid knowledge concerning the theory and application of systems of logic and coordinated sets of programming languages.

These two general methods of augmenting computer intelligence depend for their physical realization on the continuous expansion of knowledge in the field of computer engineering. Improvements in computer engineering design and materials (e.g., from serial to parallel processing, from electronic to optical circuitry) optimize the results of the application of the two general methods of artificial intelligence.

In addition to the engineering objective of the augmentation of the intelligence of computers, the field of artificial intelligence also has a scientific objective concerned with the development of a general theory of intelligence. This abstract science of intelligence would systematically establish the general principles, commonalities, and singularities of human, animal, and computer intelligence.

ARTIFICIAL INTELLIGENCE AND THEORETICAL PSYCHOLOGY

The Nature of Computational Psychology

The computational theory of psychology finds its model in artificial intelligence, the science that holds that computers, by virtue of their mathematical structure, can reason. Artificial intelligence does not require the computer to understand what it is reasoning about.

The reasoning mechanism is a calculus indifferent to its content. In contrast, the calculus of human thought is, as demonstrated in the psychoanalytic theory of psychology, distinctly responsive to the content and import of personal ideation. Thus artificial intelligence is limited to modeling only the mechanics of human reasoning and human problem solving.

The mathematical descriptions of human thought and computer thought may approach an identical form. Such a universal mathematical description of reasoning and problem solving can be valuable for both human psychology and artificial intelligence. Advances in knowledge of the mechanisms of thought in one domain benefit the other domain as well.

Just as mathematical description is a language expressing the essentiality of relationships between theoretical variables, so symbolic logic in the language of the propositional and predicate calculus expresses the essentiality of the structures or architecture of thought; and just as mathematical symbols can be manipulated in place of physical reality, so the logical calculus can be manipulated in place of cognitive reality. The language of mathematics is to physical reality as the language of the predicate calculus is to cognitive reality.

The Universal Turing Machine

The abstract mathematical universal Turing machine (Turing, 1939) possesses input/output functions that can map or imitate input/output functions of any formally specifiable intelligent system, computer, or human. Turing (1950) proposed a test of his theory of the universal Turing machine that would establish correspondences in the input/output functions of computers and humans. Where an interrogator addressing questions to computers and people could not distinguish between their outputs, the theory of the universal Turing machine would be confirmed. Ultimately, human cognition is a subset of universal computation.

Turing's Thesis and Empirical Cognitive Psychology

The Turing thesis, however, is a mathematical abstraction, a formal description of cognition, just as the wave equation is a formal description of electricity, light, and sound. While all are waves, they have different constituents and different properties. In an analogous fashion, the formal description of the human cognitive system as an instantiation of the universal Turing machine possessing corresponding input/output functions does not *ipso facto* establish the detailed properties and constituents of human cognitive processes. The finding that computers could regularly pass the Turing test would not prove that the internal processes between the input and output functions have properties and constituents that were identical in both the computer system and the system of the mind.

The formal equivalence of input/output functions of the mind and computation requires, if there is to be a psychology of cognition as well as a formal computational mapping of cognition, an empirical theory that would describe the cognitive operations that permit the intelligent behavior seen in reasoning or problem solving. At the empirical level, then, the computer becomes a model of thought whose program can be modified to yield a succession of prototypes as experimental data produce confirmation or refutation of hypotheses.

This empirical investigation requires the description of the naive experience of thought that can be given by verbal reports of subjects responding to an experimental task that involves reasoning, problem solving, or some other aspect of cognition. Protocols of these verbal reports, together with observations of the experimental subject and reaction time measures, are now regularly used in cognitive psychology. An example is the series of investigations by Just and Carpenter (1980, 1987) concerning the cognitive processes involved in the psychology of reading and the comprehension of texts.

Computer Programs as Theoretical Models

Computer programs function as theoretical models in cognitive research. As theoretical models, programs possess one or more of the following characteristics typical of theoretical models in science:

A theoretical model is

1. A set of assumptions about some object or system
2. A description of a type of object or system which attributes to it what might be called an inner structure, composition, or mechanism, reference to which is intended to explain various properties exhibited by that object or system
3. Treated as a simplified approximation useful for certain purposes
4. Proposed within the broader framework of some more basic theory or theories

5. Often formulated, developed, and even named on the basis of an analogy between the object or system described in the model and some different object or system (Achinstein, 1965, pp. 112–116)

In the above list, characteristic 2 is descriptive of the computer program KEKADA, which models both the biochemical knowledge and cognitive processes of an outstanding scientist.

Unitary Theory of Cognition

The mapping of cognitive reality in a general programming language that would accommodate the general structure or architecture of thought has been attempted by a number of cognitive scientists. An important example is John Anderson's unitary theory of cognition:

INTERLISP (Teitleman, 1976) . . . is *general-purpose*, that is, one can use the same data structures and processes in programs for language and for problem solving. Individual programs can be created that do language and problem solving as special cases. In analogy to INTERLISP, I claim that a single set of principles underlies all of cognition and that there are no principled differences or separations of faculties. It is in this sense that the theory is unitary. (Anderson, 1983, p. 5)

General Unified Theory of Intelligence

A different, more abstract, and inclusive general unified theory of intelligence can be formulated on the basis of the logic of implication. This *fundamental theorem of intelligence* would hold that the logic of implication (if *p*, then *q*) subsumes both the formal structure of human reasoning and problem solving and the formal structure of artificial intelligence. The logic of implication is foundational to mathematical and scientific reasoning and to the reasoning of everyday behavior as well (Wagman, 1978, 1984a) and is foundational to programming logic and knowledge-representation formalisms in artificial intelligence systems (Wagman, 1980b, 1988, 1991a, 1991b).

The Production System Formalism

The principal mechanism for problem solving in artificial intelligence is the production system (Hunt, 1989; Nilsson, 1980; Rolston, 1988). The production system has its conceptual source in the mathematical logic of E. L. Post (1943) and its derived application in the information-processing theory of Newell and Simon (1972).

The production system was one of those happy events, though in minor key, that historians of science often talk about: a rather well-prepared formalism, sitting in wait for a scientific mission. Production systems have a long and diverse history. Their use of symbolic logic starts with Post (1943), from whom the name is taken. They also show up as Markov algorithms (1954). Their use in linguistics, where they are also called rewrite rules, dates from Chomsky (1957). As with so many other notions in computer science, they really entered into wide currency when they became operationalised in programming languages. (Newell and Simon, 1972, p. 889)

The production system consists of three modular elements: a global data base, a set of production rules, and a set of control structures. The modularity of the elements allows for their modification without any complicating interaction effects. The content of the elements consists of encoded knowledge in a given problem domain. Production rules are composed of condition-action pairs. Satisfaction by the data base of the conditions of production rules instigates their operation. The determination of the specific sequence of production rules in a cycle of operations is a major function of the control structures.

In applying production systems to problem solving, pathways through the problem space (the set of possible problem states) are searched until the goal state is achieved. The sequence of operations of the production system directs a search trajectory. Trajectories are mapped onto a search three structure consisting of nodes that represent problem states and directed arcs that represent production rules.

2

Modeling of the Human Brain

MAJOR PARADIGMS IN PSYCHOLOGY AND ARTIFICIAL INTELLIGENCE: SYMBOLIC SYSTEMS (INFORMATION PROCESSING) AND CONNECTIONISM (NEURAL NETWORKS)

Symbolic Systems (Information Processing)

The classical and, for several decades, unchallenged paradigm for theories of the cognitive processes has been the doctrine of symbol systems as exemplified in the concepts and methods of the logic theorists and the general problem-solver programs of Newell and Simon (1972). The centrality of symbol systems and their manifestations in programming languages such as LISP (McCarthy, 1960) and PROLOG (Sterling and Shapiro, 1986) are, from the standpoint of intellectual history, continuous with the Platonist and Cartesian philosophical world views that assign a special status to the mind and to mathematical and logical representations of reality. In this view, symbolic structures and symbolic operations constitute the descriptive language of intelligence.

—*The human brain is an information-processing system* whose memories hold interrelated symbol structures and whose sensory and motor connections receive encoded symbols from the outside via sensory organs and send encoded symbols to motor organs. *It accomplishes its thinking* by copying and reorganizing symbols in memory, receiving and outputting symbols, and comparing symbol structures for identity and difference.

—*The brain solves problems by creating a symbolic representation of the problem* (called the problem space) that is capable of expressing initial, intermediate, and final problem situations as well as the whole range of concepts employed in the solution process, and using the operators that are contained in the definition of the problem space to modify the symbol structures that describe the problem situation (thereby conducting a *mental search* for a solution through the problem space).

—The search for a problem solution is not carried on by trial and error, but is selective. It is guided in the direction of a goal situation (or symbolic expressions describing a goal) by rules of thumb, called heuristics. Heuristics make use of information extracted from the problem definitions and the states already explored in the problem space to identify promising paths for search. Thus, for problem solving *we postulate an information processing system* that creates problem representations and searches selectively through trees of intermediate situations, seeking the goal situation and using heuristics to guide its search. (Langley et al., 1987, pp. 7–8; italics added)

Connectionism (Neural Networks)

In contrast to the symbol system paradigm, the doctrine of connectionism has as its intellectual heritage the Newtonian world view which construes the mind and mental phenomena as the physical processes of the brain. A network of neuronal or mathematical units and their connections constitutes knowledge, and changes in the weights of the connections account for sensory, motor, and, ultimately, cognitive processes. The language of connectionism is differential equations rather than mathematical logic. Major features of neural-network models are given in the following account.

A neural-network model is composed of several components (Rumelhart, Hinton, and McClelland, 1986):

1. A set of processing units, referred to as ''nodes'' or ''cognitive units.'' They are similar to neurons, but not nearly as complicated. The only thing a node can do is to take on some level of activation.

2. A state of activation. Nodes can be activated to varying degrees. If some nodes are activated beyond some threshold, we are conscious of whatever they code. The set of these activated nodes corresponds to the contents of consciousness. The most activated nodes represent whatever is being attended to at that moment. Other nodes, such as those dealing with much of motor behavior, operate outside of conscious awareness.

3. A pattern of connections among nodes. Nodes are connected to one another by either excitatory or inhibitory connections that differ in strength. The strength of these connections constitutes long-term memory for associations between whatever the nodes represent. All long-term memories are coded in this way.

4. Activation rules for the nodes. These rules specify such things as exactly how a node ''adds up'' its inputs, how it combines inputs with its current state of activation, the rate at which its activation decays and so on.

5. Output functions for the nodes. How does the output of a node relate to its activation? If the output of a node were exactly the same as its input, the node wouldn't be good for much of anything. If we assign thresholds or make output a nonlinear function of the node's activation, we get useful results. (Martindale, 1990, pp. 12–13)

HYBRID SYMBOLIC-CONNECTIONIST PARADIGMS

A general unified theory of intelligence would need to be inclusive of a dual typology of human cognition and a dual typology of computational models. Deliberative human thought, as represented by reasoning, problem solving, planning, judgment, and decision making, is distinguished from automatic human memory, as represented by retrieval and recognition processes. The first set of cognitive activities is best modeled by symbolic computational models, the second by connectionist computational models. A complete account of cognition will require an integration of the symbolic and connectionist architectures. In the general unified theory of intelligence, both the cognition and the models have their ultimate foundation in the logic of implication.

Holyoak and Spellman (1993) provide a useful account of integrated symbolic-connectionist architectures.

The fact that human cognition has both symbolic and subsymbolic aspects encourages various attempts to integrate the approaches. A number of suggestions for hybrid "symbolic-connectionist" models have been offered (e.g., Dyer, 1991; Holyoak, 1991; Minsky, 1991). These models can be divided roughly into two classes. One class of models maintains a core of "traditional" symbolic machinery (e.g., discrete propositions and rules) to represent relation structures, while adding connectionist-style mechanisms for "soft" constraint satisfaction. The second class of models seeks to develop connectionist representations of relation structures by introducing techniques for handling the binding of objects to roles. We review examples of each of these approaches to integrating the two theoretical perspectives.

Soft Constraint Satisfaction in Reasoning

The generation and evaluation of beliefs—the central task of induction—has a holistic quality that has posed grave difficulty for theoretical treatments. Tweney (1990) identified the complex interrelatedness of hypotheses as a major challenge for computational theories of scientific reasoning. Fodor (1983) has taken the pessimistic position that little progress is to be expected in understanding central cognition because the facts relevant to any belief cannot be circumscribed (i.e., we do not operate within a closed world) and the degree of confirmation of any hypothesis evaluation (Holland et al., 1986).

One mechanism with the requisite properties is parallel constraint satisfaction, a basic capability of connectionist models. In a connectionist network, local computations involving individual units interact to generate stable global patterns of activity over the entire network. Models that perform "soft" constraint satisfaction over units corresponding to relation structures can attempt to capitalize on the complementary strengths of symbolic representation and connectionist processing. Such symbolic-connectionist models can make inferences based on incomplete information, which standard symbolic systems are often unable to do, using knowledge that distributed connectionist systems cannot readily represent. Models of this sort have been used to account for psychological data concerning text comprehension, analogical reasoning, and evaluation of explanations.

Kintsch (1988) has developed a symbolic-connectionist model to deal with the resolution of ambiguities during text comprehension. His "construction-integration" model has four main components:

1. initial parallel activation of memory concepts corresponding to words in the text, together with formation of propositions by parsing rules;
2. spreading of activation to a small number of close associates of the text concepts;
3. inferring additional propositions by inference rules; and
4. creating excitatory and inhibitory links, with associated weights, between units representing activated concepts and propositions, and allowing the network to settle.

The entire process is iterative. A small portion of text is processed, the units active after the settling process are maintained, and then the cycle is repeated with the next portion of text. In addition to accounting for psycho-linguistic data on text comprehension, the construction-integration model has been extended to simulate levels of expertise in planning routine computing tasks (Mannes & Kintsch, 1991).

Symbolic-connectionist models have been developed to account for two of the basic processes in analogical reasoning—retrieving useful analogs from memory and mapping the elements of a known situation (the source analog) and a new situation (the target analog) to identify useful correspondences. Because analogical mapping requires finding correspondences on the basis of relation structure, most distributed connectionist models lack the requisite representational tools to do it. Purely symbolic models have difficulty avoiding combinatorial explosion when searching for possible analogs in a large memory store and when searching for optimal mappings between two analogs. The two symbolic-connectionist models—the ACME model of Holyoak and Thagard (1989), which does analogical mapping, and the ARCS model of Thagard et al. (1990), which does analogical retrieval—operate by taking symbolic, predicate-calculus-style representations of situations as inputs, applying a small set of abstract constraints to build a network of units representing possible mappings between elements of two analogs, and then allowing parallel constraint satisfaction to settle the network into a stable state in which asymptotic activations of units reflect degree of confidence in possible mappings. The constraints on mapping lead to preferences for sets of mapping hypotheses that yield isomorphic correspondences, link similar elements, and map elements of special importance. These same constraints (with differing relative impacts) operate in both the mapping and retrieval models. The mapping model has been applied successfully to model human judgments about complex naturalistic analogies (Spellman & Holyoak, 1992) and has been extended to account for data concerning analogical transfer in mathematical problem solving (Holyoak, Novick, and Melz, 1993).

Thagard (1989, 1992) has shown that the problem of evaluating competing explanations can be addressed by a symbolic-connectionist model of explanatory coherence, ECHO. The model takes as inputs symbolic representations of basic explanatory relations between propositions corresponding to data and explanatory hypotheses. The system then builds a constraint network linking units representing the propositions, using a small number of very general constraints that support explanations with greater explanatory breadth (more links to data), greater simplicity (fewer constituent assumptions), and greater correspondence to analogous explanations of other phenomena.

Relations of mutual coherence (modeled by symmetrical excitatory links) hold between hypotheses and the data they explain; relations of competition (inhibitory links) hold between rival hypotheses. Parallel constraint satisfaction settles the network into an asymptotic state in which units representing the most mutually coherent hypotheses and data are active and units representing inconsistent rivals are deactivated. Thagard (1989) showed that ECHO can model a number of realistic cases of explanation evaluation in both scientific and legal contexts; Schank & Ranney (1991, 1992; Ranney, 1993) have used the model to account for student belief revision in the context of physics problems; and Read & Marcus-Newhall (1993) have applied the model to the evaluation of explanations of everyday events.

Reflexive Reasoning Using Dynamic Binding

Whereas the models discussed above involve hybridizations of connectionist processing mechanisms and symbolic representations, a second class of models attempts to provide pure connectionist-style representations of complex relational knowledge. . . . Shastri & Ajjanagadde (1993) have developed a detailed computational model that uses temporal dynamics to code the relation structure of propositions and rules. Dynamic bindings in working memory are represented by units firing in phase. Consider a proposition such as "John gave the book to Mary." On a single phase, the unit representing the object John will fire in synchrony with a unit representing the "giver" role; in a different phase the unit for Mary will fire in synchrony with a unit for the "recipient" role. The system is object-based, in the sense that each time a slice is occupied by the firing of a single active object unit together with units for all the argument roles that the object fills. Bindings are systematically propagated to make inferences by means of links between units for argument slots. For example, in a rule stating that "If someone receives something, then they own it," the "recipient" role in the antecedent of the rule will be connected to the "owner" role in the consequent. Accordingly, if Mary is dynamically bound to the "recipient" role (by phase locking firing of the "Mary" and "recipient" units), then Mary will become bound to the "owner" role as well (i.e., the unit for Mary will fire in phase with units for *both* relevant roles). Shastri and Ajjanagadde show that their model can answer questions based on inference rules in time that is linear with the length of the inference chain but independent of the number of rules in memory—the most efficient performance pattern theoretically possible.

Shastri & Ajjanagadde (1993) note a number of interesting psychological implications of their dynamic binding model. In particular, they distinguish between two forms of reasoning, which they term "reflexive" and "reflective." Reflexive reasoning is based on spontaneous and efficient inferences drawn in the course of everyday understanding, whereas reflective reasoning is the deliberate and effortful deliberation required in conscious planning and problem solving. It is intriguing that humans are far better at text comprehension than, for example, syllogistic reasoning, even though the formal logical complexity of the former task is much greater than that of the latter (Stenning & Oaksford, 1993). In terms of the Shastri & Ajjanagadde model, text comprehension mainly involves reflexive reasoning, whereas syllogistic inference requires reflective reasoning. Fluent comprehension draws upon a rich network of stored rules, which are used in conjunction with the input to establish a coherent, elaborated model of the situation. Reflexive reasoning of the sort involved in ordinary comprehension relies on dynamic binding of objects to argument slots in preexisting rules. These rules have been encoded into long-term memory, with appropriate interconnections between their arguments. In contrast, reflective reasoning requires manipulation of knowledge in absence of relevant pre-stored rules. An arbitrary deductive syllogism (e.g., "If all artists are beekeepers, and some beekeepers are chemists, what follows?") is unrelated to any stored rules; rather, understanding the premises requires setting up de novo "rules" (e.g., "If someone is an artist, then that person is a beekeeper") for each problem.

Shastri & Ajjanagadde's model predicts that reflexive reasoning will be constrained by limits on the number of multiply-instantiated predicates, as well as by patterns of variable repetition across the arguments of a rule. The model also makes predictions about the limits of the information that can be active simultaneously in working memory. Although the number of active argument units is potentially unlimited, the number of objects that can be reasoned about in a single session is limited to the number of distinct phases available (because only one object unit may fire in a single phase). Given plausible assumptions about the speed of neural activity, this limit on the number of active objects can be calculated as being five or fewer. This figure is strikingly similar to Miller's (1956) estimate of short-term memory capacity and is consistent with work by Halford & Wilson (1980) indicating that adults cannot simultaneously represent relations involving more than four elements. For example, recent empirical evidence (described by Halford et al., 1993) confirms a limit that will be recognized by anyone who has worked with statistical interactions: The most complex statistical relation that people can deal with in working memory is a 3-way interaction (which involves three independent variables and one dependent variable, for a total of four dimensions). Experimental studies of people's memory for bindings between individuals and properties have revealed similar capacity limits, as well as error patterns consistent with distributed representations of bindings (Stenning & Levy, 1988; Stenning, 1988). Recent work has extended the temporal-synchrony approach to other forms of reasoning. Hummel & Holyoak (1992) have shown that the principles embodied in Holyoak & Thagard's (1989) ACME model of analogical mapping can be captured by a model that encodes propositional structure by temporal synchrony.

An interesting feature of the synchrony approach is that the need to minimize "cross talk" between the constituents of relation structures encourages postulating specific types of serial processing at the "micro" level of temporal phases. For example, in the Shastri & Ajjanagadde model only one object is allowed to fire in each time slice. It is also noteworthy that their model combines localist representations of concepts with distributed control and, thus, exemplifies a theoretical "middle ground" between traditional production systems and fully distributed connectionist networks. It is possible that attempts to develop connectionist models of symbol systems will cast new light on the limits of parallel information processing. In addition, connectionist models may provide more effective implementations of the flexible recognition processes based on long-term memory that appear crucial to expertise (Chase & Simon, 1973). More generally, the confluence of the symbolic and connectionist paradigms seems likely to deepen our understanding of the kinds of computations that constitute human thinking. (Holyoak and Spellman, 1993, pp. 272–277)

PHILOSOPHICAL AND PSYCHOLOGICAL IMPLICATIONS OF PARALLEL DISTRIBUTED PROCESSING

Parallel distributed processing represents the research implementation of a theory of cognition with classical origins in the writings of Lucretius (95–53 B.C.) that has been aptly described from an introspective point of view by the mathematician Henri Poincaré (1854–1912):

The privileged unconscious phenomena, those susceptible of becoming conscious, are those which . . . affect most profoundly our emotional sensibility. . . . Now, what are the mathematic entities to which we attribute this character of beauty and elegance? . . . They are those whose elements are harmoniously disposed so that the mind without effort can embrace their totality while realizing the details. This harmony is at once a satisfaction of our esthetic needs and an aid to the mind, sustaining and guiding. . . . *Figure the future elements of our combinations as something like the unhooked atoms of Epicurus. . . . They flash in every direction through the space . . . like the molecules of a gas in the kinematic theory of gases. Then their mutual impacts may produce new combinations.* (Poincaré, 1913, p. 35; italics added)

The combinatory emergence of complex cognition from the convergent interaction of numerous simple elements constitutes the central concept in Rumelhart and McClelland's research into the microstructure of cognition:

The idea of parallel distributed processing—the notion that intelligence emerges from the interactions of large numbers of simple processing units—has come and gone before. . . . Symbol-processing machines . . . had failed to provide a framework for representing knowledge in a way that allowed it to be accessed by content and effectively combined with other knowledge to produce useful automatic syntheses that would allow intelligence to be productive. (Rumelhart, McClelland and the PDP Research Group, 1986, pp. ix–x; italics added)

The Microstructure of Cognition

Problem solving, planning, reasoning, and other forms of deliberative thought typically involve sequential states of cognition. The sequential states have been computationally modeled by the serial processing formalisms (Newell and Simon, 1972). Rumelhart and McClelland (Rumelhart, McClelland and the PDP Research Group, 1986) assert that a microanalysis of states of cognition will disclose an internal structure for each state consisting of a network of simple interconnected units, acting in a nonserial fashion and giving rise, emergently and interactively, to the cognitive state, and that such a microanalysis provides advantages of precision and flexibility compared with classical serial processing models:

Parallel distributed processing models offer alternatives to serial models of the micro-structure of cognition. . . . In general, from the PDP point of view, the objects referred to in macrostructural models of cognitive processing are seen as approximate descriptions of emergent properties of the microstructure. Sometimes these approximate descriptions may be sufficiently accurate to capture a process or mechanism well enough; but many times . . . they fail to provide sufficiently elegant or tractable accounts that capture the . . . flexibility and open-endedness of cognition. (Rumelhart and McClelland, 1986, pp. 12–13)

PDP Models and Cognitive Science

Rumelhart and McClelland (1986) discuss the implications of their parallel distributed processing (PDP) models for a set of issues in cognitive science. The issues constitute a constellation of frequent objections made to PDP models. Each issue will be presented briefly.

The Cognitive Quality of PDP Models

Classical computational approaches to the modeling of cognition have de-pended on explicitly formulated production rules that stipulate relationships be-tween conditions to be met and actions to be taken. Can cognition be modeled in the absence of explicitly formulated rules? Rumelhart and McClelland (1986) respond:

Some have viewed our argument against explicit rules as an argument against the cog-nitive approach to psychology. We do not agree. We believe that we are studying the mechanisms to cognition. The application of a rule (e.g., the firing of a production) is neither more nor less cognitive than the activation of our units. The real character of cognitive science is the attempt to explain mental phenomena through an understanding of the mechanisms which underlie those phenomena. (Rumelhart and McClelland, 1986, pp. 120–121)

Level of Analysis in PDP Models

The scientific analysis of cognition can take place at several levels of de-scription: the level of formal analysis, the levels of specific procedures or al-gorithms, and the level of physiological or neural implementation (see Table 2.1). PDP theories have sometimes been criticized (e.g., Broadbent, 1985; Fodor and Pylyshyn, 1988) for not centering on the psychological level, that is, on the procedural or algorithmic level. Are PDP models at the wrong level? Rumelhart and McClelland reply:

David Marr (1982) has provided an influential analysis of the issue of levels in cognitive science . . . [Table 2.1] gives a description of Marr's three levels. *We believe that PDP models are generally stated at the algorithmic level and are primarily aimed at specifying*

Table 2.1
The Three Levels at which Any Machine, Carrying Out Information-Processing Tasks, Must Be Understood

Computational Theory	Representation and Algorithm	Hardware Implementation
What is the goal of the computation, why is it appropriate, and what is the logic of the strategy by which it can be carried out?	How can this computational theory be implemented? In particular, what is the representation for the input and output, and what is the algorithm for the transformation?	How can the representation and algorithm be realized physically?

Source: Marr (1982), p. 25.

the representation of information and the processes or procedures involved in cognition.
... There is an implicit computational theory in PDP models as well as an appeal to certain implementational (physiological) considerations. (Rumelhart and McClelland, 1986, pp. 122–124; italics added)

3

Modeling Human Cognitive Processes

THEORIES OF UNIFIED COGNITION

Newell's Unified Theory and the SOAR Research Project

In the following passage from his theoretical and research volume, *Unified Theories of Cognition*, Newell (1990) presents his position on the unitary nature of cognition as derivative from a small set of basic mechanisms:

Psychology has arrived at the possibility of unified theories of cognition—theories that gain their power by having a single system of mechanisms that operate together to produce the full range of cognition.

I do not say they are here. But they are within reach and we should strive to attain them. (Newell, 1990, p. 1)

The "single system of mechanisms" is a central objective of the SOAR research program (Rosenbloom et al., 1991)

Theoretical Background of SOAR

Rosenbloom et al. (1991) discuss the general theoretical background of the SOAR system and its relationship to human and artificial intelligence.

The central scientific problem of artificial intelligence (AI) is to understand what constitutes intelligent action and what processing organizations are capable of such action. Human intelligence—which stands before us like a holy grail—shows to first observation what can only be termed general intelligence. A single human exhibits a bewildering diversity of intelligent behavior. The types of goals that humans can set for themselves or accept from the environment seem boundless. Further observation, of course, shows limits to this capacity in any individual—problems range from easy to hard, and problems can always be found that are too hard to be solved. But the general point is still compelling.

Work in AI has already contributed substantially to our knowledge of what functions are required to produce general intelligence. There is substantial, though certainly not unanimous, agreement about some functions that need to be supported: symbols and goal structures, for example. Less agreement exists about what mechanisms are appropriate to support these functions, in large part because such matters depend strongly on the rest of the system and on cost-benefit tradeoffs. Much of this work has been done under the rubric of AI tools and languages, rather than AI systems themselves. However, it takes only a slight shift of viewpoint to change from what is an aid for the programmer to what is structure for the intelligent system itself. Not all features survive this transformation, but enough do to make the development of AI languages as much substantial research as tool building. These proposals provide substantial ground on which to build.

The SOAR project has been building on this foundation in an attempt to understand the functionality required to support general intelligence. Our current understanding is embodied in the SOAR architecture. (Laird, 1986; Laird, Newell, and Rosenbloom, 1987) (Rosenbloom et al., 1991, pp. 289–290; italics added)

General Intelligence and Levels of Description

Rosenbloom et al. (1991) analyze general intelligence at several levels of description, employing the concepts of cognitive, neural, and logical bands:

The idea of analyzing systems in terms of multiple levels of description is a familiar one in computer science. In one version, computer systems are described as a sequence of levels that starts at the bottom with the device level and works up through the circuit level, the logic level, and then one or more program levels. Each level provides a description of the system at some level of abstraction. The sequence is built up by defining each higher level in terms of the structure provided at the lower levels. This idea has also recently been used to analyze human cognition in terms of levels of description (Newell, 1990). Each level corresponds to a particular time scale, such as 100 msec. and 1 sec., with a new level occurring for each new order of magnitude. *The four levels between 10 msec. and 10 sec. comprise the cognitive band (See Figure 3.1).* The lowest cognitive level—at 10 msec.—is the symbol-accessing level, where the knowledge referred to by symbols is retrievable. The second cognitive level—at 100 msec.—is the level at which elementary deliberate operations occur; that is, the level at which encoded knowledge is brought to bear, and the most elementary choices are made. The third and fourth cognitive levels—at 1 sec. and 10 sec.—are the simple-operator-composition and goal-attainment levels. At these levels, sequences of deliberations can be composed to achieve goals. *Above the cognitive band is the rational band, at which the system can be described as being goal-oriented, knowledge-based, and strongly adaptive. Below the cognitive band is the neural band.*

[We] describe SOAR as a sequence of three cognitive levels: the memory level, at which symbol accessing occurs; the decision level, at which elementary deliberate operations occur; and the goal level, at which goals are set and achieved via sequences of

Figure 3.1
Partial Hierarchy of Time Scales in Human Cognition

The Soar architecture as a basis for general intelligence

Rational Band   . . .

	$\sim$ 10 sec.	Goal attainment
Cognitive Band	$\sim$ 1 sec.	Simple operator composition
	$\sim$ 100 msec.	Elementary deliberate operations
	$\sim$ 10 msec.	Symbol accessing

Neural Band   . . .

Source: Rosenbloom et al. (1991). Reprinted with the permission of Elsevier Science Publishers.

decisions. The goal level is an amalgamation of the top two cognitive levels from the analysis of human cognition.

In this description we will often have call to describe mechanisms that are built into the architecture of the SOAR. *The architecture consists of all of the fixed structure of the SOAR system. According to the levels analysis, the correct view to be taken of this fixed structure is that it comprises the set of mechanisms provided by the levels underneath the cognitive band. For human cognition this is the neural band. For artificial cognition, this may be a connectionist band, though it need not be. This view notwithstanding, it should be remembered that it is the SOAR architecture which is primary in our research. The use of the levels viewpoint is simply an attempt at imposing a particular, hopefully illuminating, theoretical structure on top of the existing architecture.* (Rosenbloom et al., 1991, pp. 290–291; italics added)

SOAR: The First Methodological Assumption

The development of SOAR rests on four methodological assumptions (see Table 3.1). The first of these four assumptions is described in the following section:

The first assumption is the utility of focusing on the cognitive band, as opposed to the neural or rational bands. This is a view that has traditionally been shared by a large segment of the cognitive science community; it is not, however, shared by the connectionist community, which focuses on the neural band (plus the lower levels of the cognitive band), or by the logicist and expert-systems communities, which focus on the rational band. This assumption is not meant to be exclusionary, as a complete under-

Table 3.1
SOAR's Methodological Assumptions

---

1.   General intelligence comprises neural, cognitive, and rational levels or bands. SOAR concentrates on the cognitive band.

2.   A theory of general intelligence embraces both human and artificial intelligence.

3.   The intelligence of SOAR results from a small set of mechanisms.

4.   Research should utilize SOAR's existing mechanisms in exploring new areas of application rather than adding new mechanisms.

---

standing of general intelligence requires the understanding of all these descriptive bands (Investigations of the relationship of SOAR to the neural and rational bands can be found in Newell, 1990; Rosenbloom, 1989; and Newell and Laird, 1990). Instead the assumption is that there is important work to be done by focussing on the cognitive band. One reason is that, as just mentioned, a complete model of general intelligence will require a model of the cognitive band. A second reason is that an understanding of the cognitive band can constrain models of the neural and rational bands. A third, more applied reason, is that a model of the cognitive band is required in order to be able to build practical intelligence systems. Neural-band models need the higher levels of organization that are provided by the cognitive band in order to reach complex task performance. Rational-band models need the heuristic adequacy provided by the cognitive band in order to be computationally feasible. *A fourth reason is that there is a wealth of both psychological and AI data about the cognitive band that can be used as the basis for elucidating the structure of its levels. This data can help us understand what type of symbolic architecture is required to support general intelligence.* (Rosenbloom et al., 1991, pp. 291–292; italics added)

SOAR: The Second Methodological Assumption

The second methodological assumption concerns the benefits that accrue from a conception of general intelligence that includes both human and artificial intelligence.

The second assumption is that general intelligence can most usefully be studied by not making a distinction between human and artificial intelligence. The advantage of this assumption is that it allows wider ranges of research methodologies and data to be brought to bear to mutually constrain the structure of the system. Our research methodology includes a mixture of experimental data, theoretical justifications, and comparative studies in both artificial intelligence and cognitive psychology. Human experiments provide data about performance universals and limitations that may reflect the structure of the architecture. For example, the ubiquitous power law of practice—the time to perform a task is a power-law function of the number of times the task has been performed—was used to generate a model of human practice (Newell and Rosenbloom, 1981; Rosenbloom and Newell, 1986), which later converted into a proposal for a general artificial learning mechanism (Laird, Rosenbloom, and Newell, 1984, 1986; Steier et al., 1987). Artificial experiments—the application of implemented systems to a variety of tasks requiring intelligence—provide sufficient feedback about the mechanisms embodied in the architecture and their interactions (Hsu, Prietula, and Steier, 1988; Rosenbloom et al., 1985; Steier, 1987; Steier and Newell, 1988; Washington and Rosenbloom, 1988). Theoretical justifications attempt to provide an abstract analysis of the requirements of intelligence, and of how various architectural mechanisms fulfill those requirements (Newell, 1990; Newell, Rosenbloom, and Laird, 1989; Rosenbloom, 1989; Rosenbloom, Laird, and Newell, 1988; Rosenbloom, Newell, and Laird, 1990). Comparative studies, pitting one system against another, provide an evaluation of how well the respective systems perform, as well as insight about how the capabilities of one of the systems can be incorporated in the other (Etzioni and Mitchell, 1989; Rosenbloom and Laird, 1986). (Rosenbloom et al., 1991, p. 292; italics added)

SOAR: The Third Methodological Assumption

The third methodological assumption posits a small set of mechanisms to be sufficient for the SOAR architecture to function intelligently:

The third assumption is that the architecture should consist of a small set of orthogonal mechanisms. All intelligent behaviors should involve all, or nearly all, of these basic mechanisms. This assumption biases the development of SOAR strongly in the direction of uniformity and simplicity, and away from modularity (Fodor, 1983) and toolkit approaches. When attempting to achieve a new functionality in SOAR, the first step is to determine in what ways the existing mechanisms can already provide the functionality. This can force the development of new solutions to old problems, and reveal new connections—through the common underlying mechanisms—among previously distinct capabilities (Rosenbloom, Laird, and Newell, 1988). Only if there is no appropriate way to achieve the new functionality are new mechanisms considered. (Rosenbloom et al., 1991, p. 293; italics added)

SOAR: The Fourth Methodological Assumption

The fourth methodological assumption is that the SOAR system should be maximally stretched to expand its range of intelligent performance.

The fourth assumption is that architectures should be pushed to the extreme to evaluate how much of general intelligence they can cover. A serious attempt at evaluating the coverage of an architecture involves a long-term commitment by an extensive research group. Much of the research involves the apparently mundane activity of replicating classical results within the architecture. Sometimes these demonstrations will by necessity be strict replications, but often the architecture will reveal novel approaches, provide a deeper understanding of the result and its relationship to other results, or provide the means of going beyond what was done in the classical work. *As these results accumulate over time, along with other more novel results, the system gradually approaches the ultimate goal of general intelligence.* (Rosenbloom et al., 1991, p. 293; italics added)

Structure of SOAR: Memory Level

SOAR's declarative, procedural, control, and episodic knowledge are stored in a long-term memory production and can be retrieved for processing in working memory.

Long-Term Memory

Major characteristics of SOAR's long-term memory are described in the following account.

A general intelligence requires a memory with a large capacity for the storage of knowledge. A variety of types of knowledge must be stored, including declarative knowledge (facts about the world, including facts about actions that can be performed), procedural knowledge (facts about how to perform actions, and control knowledge about which actions to perform when), and episodic knowledge (which actions were done when). Any particular task will require some subset of the knowledge stored in the memory. Memory access is the process by which this subset is retrieved for use in task performance.

The lowest level of the SOAR architecture is the level at which these memory phenomena occur. *All of SOAR's long-term knowledge is stored in a single production memory. Whether a piece of knowledge represents procedural, declarative, or episodic knowledge, it is stored in one or more productions.* Each production is a condition-action structure that performs its actions when its conditions are met. Memory access consists of the execution of these productions. During the execution of a production, variables in its actions are instantiated with values. Action variables that existed in the conditions are instantiated with the values bound in the conditions. Action variables that did not exist in the conditions act as generators of new symbols. (Rosenbloom et al., 1991, pp. 293–294; italics added)

Working Memory

Important features and functions of SOAR's working memory are summarized in the following section:

The result of memory access is the retrieval of information into a global working memory. The working memory is a temporary memory that contains all of SOAR's short-term processing context. Working memory consists of an interrelated set of objects with attribute-value pairs. For example, an object representing a green cat named Fred might look like (objecto025 name fred type cat color green). The symbol o025 is the identifier of the object, a short-term symbol for the object that exists only as long as the object is in working memory. Objects are related by using the identifiers of some objects as attributes and values of other objects.

There is one special type of working memory structure, the preference. Preferences encode control knowledge about the acceptability and desirability of actions, according to a fixed semantics of preference types. Acceptability preferences determine which actions should be considered as candidates. Desirability preferences define a partial ordering on the candidate actions. For example, a better (or alternatively, worse) preference can be used to represent the knowledge that one action is more (or less) desirable than another action, and a best (or worst) preference can be used to represent the knowledge that an action is at least as good (or bad) as every other action. (Rosenbloom et al., 1991, p. 294; italics added)

Memory and Productions

The retrieval operations of SOAR's productions are set forth in the following account:

In a traditional production-system architecture, each production is a problem-solving operator (see, for example, [Nilsson, 1980]). The right-hand side of the production represents some action to be performed, and the left-hand side represents the preconditions for correct application of the action (plus possibly some desirability conditions). One consequence of this view of productions is that the productions must also be the locus of behavioral control. If productions are going to act, it must be possible to control which one executes at each moment; a process known as conflict resolution. In a logic architecture, each production is a logical implication. The meaning of such a production is that if the left-hand side (the antecedent) is true, then so is the right-hand side (the consequent). (The directionality of the implication is reversed in logic programming languages such as Prolog, but the point still holds.) SOAR's productions are neither operators nor implications. Instead, SOAR's productions perform (parallel) memory retrieval. Each production is a retrieval structure for an item in long-term memory. The right-hand side of the rule represents a long-term datum, and the left-hand side represents the situations in which it is appropriate to retrieve that datum into working memory. The traditional production-system and logic notions of action, control, and truth are not directly applicable to SOAR's productions. All control in SOAR is performed at the decision level. *Thus, there is no conflict resolution process in the SOAR production system, and all productions execute in parallel. This all flows directly from the production system being a long-term memory. SOAR separates the retrieval of long-term information from the control of which act to perform next.* (Rosenbloom et al., 1991, pp. 294–295; italics added)

Encoding Knowledge in Productions

The rationale for SOAR's method of encoding declarative and procedural knowledge in productions is given in the following passage:

Of course it is possible to encode knowledge of operators and logical implications in the production memory. For example, the knowledge about how to implement a typical operator can be stored procedurally as a set of productions which retrieve the state resulting from the operator's application. The productions' conditions determine when the state is to be retrieved—for example, when the operator is being applied and its preconditions are met. An alternative way to store operator implementation knowledge is declaratively as a set of structures that are completely contained in the actions of one or more productions. The structures describe not only the results of the operator, but also its preconditions. The productions' conditions determine when to retrieve this declarative operator description into working memory. A retrieved operator description must be interpreted by other productions to actually have an affect.

In general, there are these two distinct ways to encode knowledge in the production memory: procedurally and declaratively. If the knowledge is procedurally encoded, then the execution of the production reflects the knowledge, but does not actually retrieve it into working memory—it only retrieves the structures encoded in the actions. On the other hand, if a piece of knowledge is encoded declaratively in the actions of a production, then it is retrievable in its entirety. *This distinction between procedural and declarative encodings of knowledge is distinct from whether the knowledge is declarative (represents facts about the world) or procedural (represents facts about procedures). Moreover, each production can be viewed in either way, either as a procedure which implicitly represents conditional information, or as the indexed storage of declarative structures.* (Rosenbloom et al., 1991, p. 295; italics added)

Structure of SOAR: Decision Level

The capacity to execute an appropriate course of action depends on its decision structures and functions as described in the following account:

In addition to a memory, a general intelligence requires the ability to generate and/or select a course of action that is responsive to the current situation. The second level of the SOAR architecture, the decision level, is the level at which this processing is performed. The decision level is based on the memory level plus an architecturally provided, fixed, decision procedure. The decision level proceeds in a two phase elaborate-decide cycle. During elaboration, the memory is accessed repeatedly, in parallel, until quiescence is reached; that is, until no more productions can execute. This results in the retrieval into working memory of all of the accessible knowledge that is relevant to the current decision. This may include a variety of types of information, but most direct relevance here is knowledge about actions that can be performed and preference knowledge about what actions are acceptable and desirable. After quiescence has occurred, the decision procedure selects one of the retrieved actions based on the preferences that were retrieved into working memory and their fixed semantics.

The decision level is open both with respect to the consideration of arbitrary actions, and with respect to the utilization of arbitrary knowledge in making a selection. This openness allows SOAR to behave in both plan-following and reactive fashions. SOAR is following a plan when a decision is primarily based on previously generated knowledge about what to do. SOAR is being reactive when a decision is based primarily on knowledge about the current situation (as reflected in the working memory). (Rosenbloom et al., 1991, pp. 295–296; italics added)

Structure of SOAR: Goal Level

The nature of goal setting and goal processing is described in the following section;

In addition to being able to make decisions, a general intelligence must also be able to direct this behavior towards some end; that is, it must be able to set and work towards goals. The third level of the SOAR architecture, the goal level, is the level at which goals are processed. This level is based on the decision level. Goals are set whenever a decision cannot be made; that is, when the decision procedure reaches an impasse. Impasses occur when there are no alternatives that can be selected (*no-change* and *rejection* impasses) or when there are multiple alternatives that can be selected, but insufficient discriminating preferences exist to allow a choice to be made among them (*tie* and *conflict* impasses). Whenever an impasse occurs, the architecture generates the goal of resolving the impasse. Along with this goal, a new *performance context* is created. The creation of a new context allows decisions to continue to be made in the service of achieving the goal of resolving the impasse—nothing can be done in the original context because it is at an impasse. If an impasse now occurs in this subgoal, another new subgoal and performance context are created. This leads to a goal (and context) stack in which the top-level goal is to perform some task, and lower-level goals are to resolve impasses in problem solving. A subgoal is terminated when either its impasse is resolved, or some higher impasse in the stack is resolved (making the subgoal superfluous). (Rosenbloom et al., 1991, p. 296; italics added)

Goals and Problem Spaces

Goal activities are processed in problem spaces, as described in the following account;

In SOAR, all symbolic goal-oriented tasks are formulated in problem spaces. A problem space consists of a set of states and a set of operators. The states represent situations, and the operators represent actions which when applied to states yield other states. Each performance context consists of a goal, plus roles for a problem state, a state, and an operator. Problem solving is driven by decisions that result in the selection of problem spaces, states, and operators for their respective context roles. Given a goal, a problem space should be selected in which goal achievement can be pursued. Then an initial state should be selected that represents the initial situation. Then an operator should be selected for application to the initial state. Then another state should be selected (most likely the result of applying the operator to the previous state). This process continues until a sequence of operators has been discovered that transforms the initial state into a state in which the goal has been achieved. One subtle consequence of the use of problem spaces is that each one implicitly defines a set of constraints on how the task is to be performed. For example, if the Eight Puzzle is attempted in a problem space containing only a slide-tile operator, all solution paths maintain the constraint that the tiles are never picked up off the board. Thus, such conditions need not be tested explicitly in desired states.

Each problem solving decision—the selection of a problem space, a state, or an operator—is based on the knowledge accessible in the production memory. If the knowledge is both correct and sufficient, SOAR exhibits highly controlled behavior each decision point the right alternative is selected. Such behavior is accurately described as being algorithmic or knowledge-intensive. However, for a general intelligence faced with a broad array of unpredictable tasks, situations will arise—inevitably and indeed frequently—in which the accessible knowledge is either incorrect or insufficient. It is possible that correct decisions will fortuitously be made, but it is more likely that either incorrect decisions will be made or an impasse will occur. If an incorrect decision is made, the system must eventually recover and get itself back on a path to a goal, for example, by backtracking. If instead an impasse occurs, the system must execute a sequence of problem space operators in the resulting subgoal to find (or generate) the information that will allow a decision to be made. This processing may itself be highly algorithmic, if enough control knowledge is available to uniquely determine what to do, or it may involve a large amount of further search.

As described earlier, operator implementation knowledge can be represented procedurally in the production memory, enabling operator implementation to be performed directly by memory retrieval. When the operator is selected, a set of productions execute that collectively build up the representation of the result state by combining data from long-term memory and the previous state. This type of implementation is comparable to the conventional implementation of an operator as a fixed piece of code. However, if operator implementation knowledge is stored declaratively, or if no operator implementation knowledge is stored, then a subgoal occurs, and the operator must be implemented by the execution of a sequence of problem space operators in the subgoal. If a declarative description of the to-be-implemented operator is available, then these lower operations may implement the operator by interpreting its declarative description (as was demonstrated in work on task acquisition in SOAR [Steier et al., 1987]). Otherwise the operator can be implemented by decomposing it into a set of simpler operators for which operator implementation knowledge is available, or which can in turn be decomposed further.

When an operator is implemented in a subgoal, the combination of the operator and the subgoal correspond to the type of deliberately created subgoal common in AI problem solvers. The operator specifies a task to be performed, while the subgoal indicates that accomplishing the task should be treated as a goal for further problem solving. In complex problems, like computer configuration, it is common for there to be complex high-level operators, such as *Configure-computer* which are implemented by selecting problem spaces in which they can be decomposed into simpler tasks. Many of the traditional goal management issues—such as conjunction, conflict, and selection—show up as operator management issues in SOAR. For example, a set of conjunctive subgoals can be ordered by ordering operators that later lead to impasses (and subgoals).

As described in [Rosenbloom, Laird, and Newell, 1988], a subgoal not only represents a subtask to be performed, but it also represents an introspective act that allows unlimited amounts of meta-level problem-space processing to be performed. The entire working memory—the goal stack and all information linked to it—is available for examination and augmentation in a subgoal. At any time a production can examine and augment any part of the goal stack. Likewise, a decision can be made at any time for any of the goals in the hierarchy. This allows subgoal problem solving to analyze the situation that led to the impasse, and even to change the subgoal, should it be appropriate. One not uncommon occurrence is for information to be generated within a subgoal that instead of satisfying the subgoal, causes the subgoal to become irrelevant and consequently to disappear. Processing tends to focus on the bottom-most goal because all of the others have reached impasses. However, the processing is completely opportunistic, so that when appropriate information becomes available at a higher level, processing at that level continues immediately and all lower subgoals are terminated. (Rosenbloom et al., 1991, pp. 297–298; italics added)

Learning in SOAR

The concept of chunks, their nature, content, and role in learning are summarized in the following account:

All learning occurs by the acquisition of chunks—productions that summarize the problem solving that occurs in subgoals [Laird, Rosenbloom, and Newell, 1986]. The actions of a chunk represent the knowledge generated during the subgoal: that is, the results of the subgoal. The conditions of the chunk represent an access path to this knowledge, consisting of those elements of the parent goals upon which the results depended. The results of the subgoal are determined by finding the elements generated in the subgoal that are available for use in subgoals—an element is a result of a subgoal precisely because it is available to processes outside of the subgoal. The access path is computed by analyzing the traces of the productions that fired in the subgoal—each production trace effectively states that its actions depended on its conditions. This dependency analysis yields a set of conditions that have been implicitly generalized to ignore irrelevant aspects of the situation. The resulting generality allows chunks to transfer to situations other than the one in which it was learned. The primary system-wide effect of chunking is to move SOAR along the space-time trade-off by allowing relevantly similar future decisions to be based on direct retrieval of information from memory rather than on problem solving within a subgoal. If the chunk is used, an impasse will not occur, because the required information is already available.

Care must be taken to not confuse the power of chunking as a learning mechanism with the power of SOAR as a learning system. Chunking is a simple goal-based, dependency-tracing, caching scheme, analogous to explanation-based learning (DeJong and Mooney, 1986; Mitchell, Keller, and Kedar-Cabelli, 1986; Rosenbloom and Laird, 1986) and a variety of other schemes (Rosenbloom and Newell, 1986). *What allows SOAR to exhibit a wide variety of learning behaviors are the variations in the types of subgoals that are chunked; the types of problem solving, in conjunction with the types and sources of knowledge, used in the subgoals; and the ways the chunks are used in later problem solving. The role that a chunk will play is determined by the type of subgoal for which it was learned.* State-no-change, operator-tie, and operator-no-change subgoals lead respectively to state augmentation, operator selection, and operator implementation productions. *The content of a chunk is determined by the types of problem solving and knowledge used in the subgoal. A chunk can lead to skill acquisition if it is used as a more efficient means of generating an already generatable result. A chunk can lead to knowledge acquisition (or knowledge level learning (Dietterich, 1986)) if it is used to make old/new judgements; that is, to distinguish what has been learned from what has not been learned (Rosenbloom, Laird, and Newell, 1987, 1988, 1990).* (Rosenbloom et al., 1991, pp. 298–299; italics added)

Perception and Motor Control in SOAR

The perceptual-motor interface and its relationship to working memory are described in the following section:

One of the most recent functional additions to the SOAR architecture is a perceptual-motor interface (Weismeyer, 1988, 1989). All perceptual and motor behavior is mediated through working memory; specifically, through the state in the top problem solving context. Each distinct perceptual field has a designated attribute of this state to which it adds its information. Likewise, each distinct motor field has a designated attribute of the state from which it takes its commands. The perceptual and motor systems are autonomous with respect to each other and the cognitive system.

Encoding and decoding productions can be used to convert between the high-level structures used by the cognitive system, and the low-level structures used by the perceptual and motor systems. These productions are like ordinary productions, except that they examine only the perceptual and motor fields, and not any of the rest of the context stack. This autonomy from the context stack is critical, because it allows the decision procedure to proceed without waiting for quiescence among the encoding and decoding productions, which may never happen in a rapidly changing environment. (Rosenbloom et al., 1991, pp. 299–300)

Default Knowledge in SOAR

The default knowledge in SOAR permits it to resolve impasses in its operations.

SOAR has a set of productions (55 in all) that provide default responses to each of the possible impasses that can arise, and thus prevent the system from dropping into a bottomless pit in which it generates an unbounded number of content-free performance contexts.... This allows another candidate operator to be selected, if there is one, or for a different impasse to arise if there are no additional candidates. This default response, as with all of them, can be overridden by additional knowledge if it is available.

One large part of the default knowledge (10 productions) is responsible for setting up large operator subgoaling as the default response to no-change impasses on operators. That is, it attempts to find some other state in the problem space to which the selected operators can be applied. This is accomplished by generating acceptable and worst preferences in the subgoal for the parent problem space. If another problem space is suggested, possibly for implementing the operator, it will be selected. Otherwise, the selection of the parent problem space in the subgoal enables operator subgoaling. A sequence of operators is then applied in the subgoal until a state is generated that satisfies the preconditions of an operator higher in the goal stack.

Another large part of the default knowledge (33 productions) is responsible for setting up lookahead search as the default response to tie impasses. This is accomplished by generating acceptable and worst preferences for the *selection* problem space. The selection problem space consists of operators that evaluate the tied alternatives. Based on the evaluations produced by these operators, default productions create preferences that break the tie and resolve the impasse. In order to apply the evaluation operators, domain knowledge must exist that can create an evaluation. If no such knowledge is available, a second impasse arises—a no-change on the evaluation operator. As mentioned earlier, the default response to an operator no-change impasse is to perform operator subgoaling. However, for a no-change impasse on an evaluation operator this is overridden and a lookahead search is performed instead. The results of the lookahead search are used to evaluate the tied alternatives.

As SOAR is developed, it is expected that more and more knowledge will be included as part of the basic system about how to deal with a variety of situations. For example, one area on which we are currently working is the provision of SOAR with a basic arithmetical capability, including problem spaces for addition, multiplication, subtraction, division, and comparison. One way of looking at existing default knowledge is as the tip of this large iceberg of background knowledge. However, another way to look at the default knowledge is as part of the architecture itself. Some of the default knowledge—how much is still unclear—must be innate rather than learned. The rest of the system's knowledge, such as the arithmetic spaces, should then be learnable from there. (Rosenbloom et al., 1991, pp. 300–301; italics added)

SOAR: Task Achievements

SOAR's achievements in search-based tasks are summarized in the following section (see [Table 3.2].

Various versions of SOAR have been demonstrated to be able to perform over 30 different search methods (Laird, 1986; Laird and Newell, 1983; Laird, Newell, and Rosenbloom, 1987). SOAR can also exhibit hybrid methods—such as a combination of hill-climbing and depth-first search or of operator subgoaling and depth-first search—and use different search methods for different problem spaces within the same problem (Rosenbloom et al., 1991, p. 310).

SOAR's achievements with knowledge-based tasks are indicated in the following section:

Several knowledge-based tasks have been implemented in SOAR, including the R1-SOAR computer configuration system ([Rosenbloom, Laird, and Newell,] 1987), the Cypress-SOAR and Designer-SOAR algorithm design systems (Steier, 1987; Steier and Newell, 1988), the Neomycin-SOAR medical diagnosis system (Washington and Rosenbloom, 1988), and the Merl-SOAR job-shop scheduling system (Hsu, Prietula, and Steier, 1988). (Rosenbloom et al., 1991, pp. 310–311)

SOAR's achievements with learning tasks are discussed in the following section:

The architecture directly supports a form of experimental learning in which chunking compiles goal-level problem solving into memory-level productions. Execution of the productions should have the same effect as the problem solving would have had, just more quickly. The varieties of subgoals for which chunks are learned lead to varieties

Table 3.2
Examples of SOAR's Task Achievements

Tasks	Examples
Search Based	Broad variety of search methods; hill-climbing and depth-first search (singly and combined); operator subgoaling and depth-first search (singly and combined); range of search methods appropriate for range of problem spaces.
Knowledge based	R1-SOAR computer configuration system; the Cypress-SOAR design system; the Neomycin SOAR medical diagnosis system.
Learning	Learning from success; learning from failure; transfer of learned knowledge in trials and across problems; learning from a variety of sources.

Source: Rosenbloom et al. (1991). Reprinted with the permission of Elsevier Science Publishers.

in types of productions learned: problem space creation and selection; state creation and selection; and operator creation, selection, and execution. An alternative classification for this same set of behaviors is that it covers procedural, episodic and declarative knowledge [Rosenbloom, Newell, and Laird, 1990]. The variations in goal outcomes lead to both learning from success and learning from failure. The ability to learn about all subgoal results leads to learning about important intermediate results, in addition to learning about goal success and failure. The implicit generalization of chunks leads to transfer of learned knowledge to other subtasks within the same problem (within-trial transfer), other instances of the same problems (across-trial transfer), and other problems (across-task transfer). Variations in the types of problems performed in SOAR lead to chunking in knowledge-based tasks, search-based, and robotic tasks. Variations in sources of knowledge lead to learning from both internal and external knowledge sources. A summary of many of the types of learning that have so far been demonstrated in SOAR can be found in [Steier, et al., 1988]. (Rosenbloom, et al., 1991, p. 311).

SOAR: Source of Its Power

The reasons for SOAR's effectiveness and efficiency are discussed in the following section (see [Table 3.3]):

SOAR's power and flexibility arise from at least four identifiable sources. The first source of power is the universality of the architecture. While it may seem that this should go without saying, it is in fact a crucial factor, and thus important to mention explicitly.

Table 3.3
Sources of SOAR's Power and Flexibility

I. Universality of its architecture

II. Uniformity of its architecture

    A.   Single type of memory structure
    B.   Single type of task representation: problem spaces
    C.   Single type of decision procedure

III. Specific mechanisms built into its architecture

    A.   Production memory
    B.   Working memory
    C.   Decision procedures and controls
    D.   Subgoals
    E.   Problem spaces
    F.   Chunking
    G.   Perceptual motor system

IV. The coordination of methods and mechanisms within a unified system

    A.   The combining of weak methods and learning mechanisms
    B.   The combining of strong methods (knowledge) and weak methods (search)

Universality provides the primitive capability to perform any computable task, but does not by itself explain why SOAR is more appropriate than any other universal architecture for knowledge-based, search-based, learning, and robotic tasks.

The second source of power is the uniformity of the architecture. Having only one type of long-term memory structure allows a single, relatively simple, learning mechanism to behave as a general learning mechanism. Having only one type of task representation (problem spaces) allows SOAR to move continuously from one extreme of brute-force search to the other extreme of knowledge-intensive (or procedural) behavior without having to make any representational decisions. Having only one type of decision procedure allows a single, relatively simple, subgoal mechanism to generate all of the types of subgoals needed by the system.

The traditional downside of uniformity is weakness and inefficiency. If instead the system were built up as a set of specialized modules or agents, as proposed in [Fodor, 1983; Minsky, 1986], then each of the modules could be optimized for its own narrow task. Our approach to this issue in SOAR has been to go strongly with uniformity—for all of the benefits listed above—but to achieve efficiency (power) through the addition of knowledge. This knowledge can either be added by hand (programming) or by chunking.

The third source of power is the specific mechanisms incorporated into the architecture. The production memory provides pattern-directed access to large amounts of knowledge; provides the ability to use strong problem solving methods; and provides a memory structure with a small-grained modularity. The working memory allows global access to processing state. The decision procedure provides an open control loop that can react immediately to new situations and knowledge; contributes to the modularity of the memory by allowing access to proceed in an uncontrolled fashion (conflict resolution was a major source of nonmodularity in earlier production systems); provides a flexible control language (preferences); and provides a notion of impasse that is used as the basis for the generation of subgoals. Subgoals focus the system's resources on situations where the accessible knowledge is inadequate; and allow flexible meta-level processing. Problem spaces separate control from action, allowing them (control and action) to be reasoned about independently; provide a constrained context within which the search for a desired state can occur; provide the ability to use weak problem solving methods; and provide for straightforward responses to uncertainty and error (search and backtracking). Chunking acquires long-term knowledge from experience; compiles interpreted procedures into non-interpreted ones; and provides generalization and transfer. The perceptual-motor system provides the ability to observe and affect the external world in parallel with the cognitive activity.

The fourth source of power is the interaction effects that result from the integration of all of the capabilities within a single system. The most compelling results generated so far come about from these interactions. One example comes from the mixture of weak methods, strong methods, and learning that is found in systems like R1-SOAR. Strong methods are based on having knowledge about what to do at each step. Because strong methods tend to be efficient and to produce high-quality solutions, they should be used whenever possible. Weak methods are based on searching to make up for lack of knowledge about what should be done. Such methods contribute robustness and scope by providing the system with a fall-back approach for situations in which the available strong methods do not work. Learning results in the addition of knowledge, turning weak methods into strong ones. For example, in R1-SOAR it was demonstrated how computer configuration could be cast as a search problem, how strong methods (knowledge) could be used to reduce search, how weak methods (subgoals and search) could be used to make up for a lack of knowledge, and how learning could add knowledge as the result of search.

Another interesting interaction effect comes from work on abstraction planning, in which a difficult problem is solved by first learning a plan for an abstract version of the problem, and then using the abstract plan to aid in finding a plan to the full problem [Newell and Simon, 1972; Sacerdoti, 1974; Unruh, Rosenbloom, and Laird, 1987; Unruh and Rosenbloom, 1989]. Chunking helps the abstraction planning process by recording the abstract plan as a set of operator-selection productions, and by acquiring other productions that reduce the amount of search required in generating a plan. Abstraction helps the learning process by allowing chunks to be learned more quickly—abstract searches tend to be shorter than normal ones. Abstraction also helps learning by enabling chunks to be more general than they would otherwise be—the chunks ignore the details that were abstracted away—thus allowing more transfer and potentially decreasing the cost of matching the chunks (because there are now fewer conditions). (Rosenbloom et al., 1991, pp. 313–314; italics added).

SOAR: Scope and Limits

Rosenbloom et al. (1991) evaluate SOAR's progress and prospects in the following detailed discussion:

The original work on SOAR demonstrated its capabilities as a general problem solver that could use any of the weak methods when appropriate, across a wide range of tasks. Later we came to understand how to use SOAR as the basis for knowledge-based systems, and how to incorporate appropriate learning and perceptual-motor capabilities into the architecture. These developments increased SOAR's scope considerably beyond its origins as a weak-method problem solver. Our ultimate goal has always been to develop the system to the point where its scope includes everything required of a general intelligence. In this section we examine how far SOAR has come from its relatively limited initial demonstrations towards its relatively unlimited goal. This discussion is divided up according to the major components of the SOAR architecture, . . . memory, decisions, goals, learning, and perception and motor control.

Level 1: Memory

The scope of SOAR's memory level can be evaluated in terms of the amount of knowledge that can be stored, the types of knowledge that can be represented, and the organization of the knowledge.

Amount of Knowledge. Using current technology, SOAR's production memory can support the storage of thousands of independent chunks of knowledge. The size is primarily limited by the cost of processing larger numbers of productions. Faster machines, improved match algorithms and parallel implementations [Gupta and Tambe, 1988; Tambe, Acharya, and Gupta, 1989; Tambe et al., 1988] may raise this effective limit by several orders of magnitude over the next several years.

Types of Knowledge. The representation of procedural and propositional declarative knowledge is well developed in SOAR. However, we don't have well worked-out approaches to many other knowledge-representation problems, such as the representation of quantified, uncertain, temporal, and episodic knowledge. The critical question is whether architectural support is required to adequately represent these types of knowledge, or whether such knowledge can be adequately treated as additional objects and/or attributes. Preliminary work on quantified [Polk and Newell, 1988] and episodic [Rosenbloom, Newell, and Laird, 1990] knowledge is looking promising.

Memory Organization. An issue that often gets raised with respect to the organization of SOAR's memory, and with respect to the organization of production memories in general, is the apparent lack of higher-order memory organization. There are no scripts [Schank and Ableson, 1977], frames [Minsky, 1975], or schemas [Bartlett, 1932] to tie fragments of related memory together. Nor are there any obvious hierarchical structures which limit what sets of knowledge will be retrieved at any point in time. However, SOAR's memory does have an organization, which is derived from the structure of productions, objects, and working memory (especially the context hierarchy).

What corresponds to a schema in SOAR is an object, or a structured collection of objects. Such a structure can be stored entirely in the actions of a single production, or it can be stored in a piecemeal fashion across multiple productions. If multiple productions are used, the schema as a unit only come into existence when the pieces are all retrieved contemporaneously into working memory. The advantage of this approach is that it allows novel schemas to be created from fragments of separately learned ones. The disadvantage is that it may not be possible to determine whether a set of fragments all originated from a single schema.

What corresponds to a hierarchy of retrieval contexts in SOAR are the production conditions. Each combination of conditions implicitly defines a retrieval context, with a hierarchical structure induced by the subset relationship among the combinations. The contents of working memory determines which retrieval contexts are currently in force. For example, problem spaces are used extensively as retrieval contexts. Whenever there is a problem solving context that has a particular problem space selected within it, productions that test for other problem space names are not eligible to fire in that context. This approach has worked quite well for procedural knowledge, where it is clear when the knowledge is needed. We have just begun to work on appropriate organizational schemes for episodic and declarative knowledge, where it is much less clear when the knowledge should be retrieved. Our initial approach has been based on the incremental construction, via chunking, of multi-production discrimination networks [Rosenbloom, Laird, and Newell, 1988; Rosenbloom, Newell, and Laird, 1990]. Though this work is too premature for a thorough evaluation in the context of SOAR, the effectiveness of discrimination networks in systems like Epam [Feigenbaum and Simon, 1984] and Cyrus [Kolodner, 1983b] bodes well.

Level 2: Decisions

The scope of SOAR's decision level can be evaluated in terms of its speed, the knowledge brought to bear, and the language of control.

Speed. SOAR currently runs approximately 10 decisions/second on current workstations such as a Sun4/280. This is adequate for most of the types of tasks we currently implement, but it is too slow for tasks requiring large amounts of search or very large knowledge bases (the number of decisions per second would even get smaller than it is now). The principle bottleneck is the speed of memory access, which is a function of two factors: the cost of processing individually expensive productions (the *expensive chunks* problem) [Tambe and Newell, 1988], and the cost of processing a large number of productions (the *average growth effect* problem) [Tambe, 1988]. We now have a solution to the problem of expensive chunks which can guarantee that all productions will be cheap—the match cost of a production is at worst linear in the number of conditions [Tambe and Rosenbloom, 1989]—and are working on other potential solutions. Parallelism looks to be an effective solution to the average growth effect problem [Tambe, 1988].

Bringing Knowledge to Bear. Iterated, parallel, indexed access to the contents of long-term memory has proven to be an effective means of bringing knowledge to bear on the decision process. The limited power provided by this process is offset by the ability to use subgoals when the accessible knowledge is inadequate. The issue of devising good access paths for episodic and declarative knowledge is also relevant here.

Control Language. Preferences have proven to be a flexible means of specifying a partial order among contending objects. However, we cannot yet state with certainty that the set of preference types embodied in SOAR is complete with respect to all the types of information which ultimately may need to be communicated to the decision procedure.

Level 3: Goals

The scope of SOAR's goal level can be evaluated in terms of the types of goals that can be generated and the types of problem solving that can be performed in goals. SOAR's subgoaling mechanism has been demonstrated to be able to create subgoals for all of the types of difficulties that can arise in problem solving in problem spaces (Laird, 1986). This leaves three areas open. The first area is how top-level goals are generated; that is, how the top level task is picked. Currently this is done by the programmer, but a general intelligence must clearly have grounds—that is, motivations—for selecting tasks on its own. The second area is how goal interactions are handled. Goal interactions show up in SOAR as operator interactions, and are normally dealt with by adding explicit knowledge to avoid them, or by backtracking (with learning) when they happen. It is not yet clear the extent to which SOAR could easily make use of more sophisticated approaches, such as non-linear planning (Chapman, 1987). The third area is the sufficiency of impasse-driven subgoaling as a means for determining when meta-level processing is needed. Two of the activities that might fall under this area are goal tests and monitoring. Both of these activities can be performed at the memory or decision level, but when they are complicated activities it may be necessary to perform them by problem solving at the goal level. Either activity can be called for explicitly by selecting a "monitor" or "goal-test" operator, which can then lead to the generation of a subgoal. However, goals for these tasks do not arise automatically, without deliberations. Should they? It is not completely clear.

The scope of the problem solving that can be performed in goals can itself be evaluated in terms of whether problem spaces cover all of the types of performance required, the limits on the ability of subgoal-based problem solving to access and modify aspects of the system, and whether parallelism is possible. These points are addressed in the next three paragraphs.

Problem Space Scope. Problem spaces are a very general performance model. They have been hypothesized to underlie all human, symbolic, goal-oriented behavior [Newell, 1980]. The breadth of tasks that have so far been represented in problem spaces over the whole field of AI attests to this generality. One way of pushing this evaluation further is to ask how well problem spaces account for the types of problem solving performed by two of the principal competing paradigms: planning [Chapman, 1987] and case-based reasoning [Kolodner, 1988]. Both of these paradigms involve the creation (or retrieval) and use of a data structure that represents a sequence of actions. In planning, the data structure represents the sequence of actions that the system expects to use for the current problem. In case-based reasoning, the data structure represents the sequence of actions used on some previous, presumably related, problem. In both, the data structure is used to decide what sequence of actions to perform in the current problem. SOAR straightforwardly performs procedural analogues of these two processes. When it performs a lookahead search to determine what operator to apply to a particular state, it acquires (by chunking) a set of search control productions which collectively tell it which operator should be applied to each subsequent state. This set of chunks forms a procedural plan for the current problem. When a search control chunk transfers between tasks, a form of procedural case-based reasoning is occurring.

Simple forms of declarative planning and case-based reasoning have also been demonstrated in SOAR in the context of an expert system that designs floor systems (Reich, 1988). When this system discovers, via lookahead search, a sequence of operators that achieves a goal, it creates a declarative structure representing the sequence and returns it as a subgoal result (plan creation). This plan can then be used interpretively to guide performance on the immediate problem (plan following). The plan can also be retrieved during later problems and used to guide the selection of operators (case-based reasoning). This research does not demonstrate the variety of operations one could conceivably use to modify a partial or complete plan, but it does demonstrate the basics.

Meta-Level Access. Subgoal-based problem solving has access to all of the information in working memory—including the goal stack, problem spaces, states, operators, preferences, and other faces that have been retrieved or generated—plus any of the other knowledge in long-term memory that it can access. It does not have direct access to the productions, or to any of the data structures internal to the architecture. Nonetheless, it should be able to indirectly examine the contents of any productions that were acquired by chunking, which in the long run should be just about all of them. The idea is to reconstruct the contents of the production by going down into a subgoal and retracing the problem solving that was done when the chunk was learned. In this way it should be possible to determine what knowledge the production cached. This idea has not yet been explicitly demonstrated in SOAR, but research on the recovery from incorrect knowledge has used a closely related approach [Laird, 1988].

The effects of problem solving are limited to the addition of information to working memory. Detection of working memory elements is accomplished by a garbage collector provided by the architecture. Productions are added by chunking, rather than by problem solving, and are never deleted by the system. The limitation on production creation— that it only occurs via chunking—is dealt with by varying the nature of the problem solving over which chunking occurs [Rosenbloom, Newell, and Laird, 1990]. The limitation on production deletion is dealt with by learning new productions which overcome the effects of old ones [Laird, 1988].

Parallelism. Two principal sources of parallelism in SOAR are at the memory level: production match and execution. On each cycle of elaboration, all productions are matched in parallel to the working memory, and then all of the successful instantiations are executed in parallel. This lets tasks that can be performed at the memory level proceed in parallel, but not so for decision-level and goal-level tasks.

Another principal source of parallelism is provided by the motor systems. All motor systems behave in parallel with respect to each other, and with respect to the cognitive system. This enables one form of task-level parallelism in which non-interfering external tasks can be performed in parallel. To enable further research on task-level parallelism we have added the experimental ability to simultaneously select multiple problem space operators within a single problem solving context. Each of these operators can then proceed to execute in parallel, yielding parallel subgoals, and ultimately an entire tree of problem solving contexts in which all of the branches are being processed in parallel. We do not yet have enough experience with this capability to evaluate its scope and limits.

Despite all of these forms of parallelism embodied in SOAR, most implementations of the architecture have been on serial machines, with the parallelism being simulated. However, there is an active research effort to implement SOAR on parallel computers. A parallelized version of the production match has been successfully implemented on an Encore Multimax, which has a small number (2–20) of large-grained processors [Tambe et al., 1988], and unsuccessfully implemented on a Connection Machine [Hillis, 1985], which has a large number (16K–64K) of small-grained processors [Flynn, 1988]. The

Connection Machine implementation failed primarily because a complete parallelization of the current match algorithm can lead to exponential space requirements. Research on restricted match algorithms may fix this problem in the future. Work is also in progress toward implementing SOAR on message-passing computers [Tambe, Acharya, and Gupta, 1989].

Learning. In [Steier et al., 1987] we broke down the problem of evaluating the scope of SOAR's learning capabilities into four parts: when can the architecture learn; from what can the architecture learn; what can the architecture learn; and when can the architecture apply learned knowledge. . . .

One important additional issue is whether SOAR acquires knowledge that is at the appropriate level of generalization or specialization. Chunking provides a level of generality that is determined by a combination of the representation used and the problem solving performed. Under varying circumstances, this can lead to both over generalization [Laird, Rosenbloom, and Newell, 1986] and overspecialization. The acquisition of over-general knowledge implies that the system must be able to recover from any errors caused by its use. One solution to this problem that has been implemented in SOAR involves detecting that a performance error has occurred, determining what should have been done instead, and acquiring a new chunk which leads to correct performance in the future [Laird, 1988]. This is accomplished without examining or modifying the over-general production; instead it goes back down into the subgoals for which the over-general productions were learned.

One way to deal with overspecialization is to patch the resulting knowledge gaps with additional knowledge. This is what SOAR does constantly—if a production is over-specialized, it doesn't fire in circumstances when it should, causing an impasse to occur, and providing the opportunity to learn an additional chunk that covers the missing case (and possibly other cases). Another way to deal with overspecialized knowledge is to work towards acquiring more general productions. A standard approach is to induce general rules from a sequence of positive and negative examples [Mitchell, 1982; Quinlan, 1986]. This form of generalization must occur in SOAR by search in problem spaces, and though there has been some initial work on doing this [Rosenbloom, 1988; Saul, 1984], we have not yet provided SOAR with a set of problem spaces that will allow it to generate appropriate generalizations from a variety of sets of examples. So, SOAR cannot yet be described as a system of choice for doing induction from multiple examples. On the other hand, SOAR does generalize quite naturally and effectively when abstraction occurs [Unruh and Rosenbloom, 1989]. The learned rules reflect whatever abstraction was made during problem solving.

Learning behaviors that have not yet been attempted in SOAR include the construction of a model of the environment from experimentation in it [Rajamoney, DeJong, and Faltings, 1985], scientific discovery and theory formation [Langley et al., 1987], and conceptual clustering [Fisher and Langley, 1985].

Perception and Motor Control. The scope of SOAR's perception and motor control can be evaluated in terms of both its low-level I/O mechanisms and its high-level language capabilities. Both of these capabilities are quite new, so the evaluation must be even more tentative than for the preceding components.

At the low-level, SOAR can be hooked up to multiple perceptual modalities (and multiple fields within each modality) and can control multiple effectors. The critical low-level aspects of perception and motor control are currently done in a standard procedural language outside of the cognitive system. The resulting system appears to be an effective testbed for research on high-level aspects of perception and motor-control. It also appears to be an effective testbed for research on the interactions of perception and motor control with other cognitive capabilities, such as memory, problem solving, and learning. However, it does finesse many of the hard issues in perception and motor control, such as selective attention, shape determination, object identification, and temporal coordination. Work is actively in progress on selective attention [Wiesmeyer, 1988].

At the high end of I/O capabilities is the processing of natural language. An early attempt to implement a semantic grammar parser in SOAR was only a limited success [Powell, 1984]. It worked, but it did not appear to be the right long-term solution to language understanding in SOAR. More recent work on NL-SOAR has focussed on the incremental construction of a model of the situation by applying comprehension operators to each incoming word [Lewis, Newell, and Polk, 1989]. Comprehension operators iteratively augment and refine the situation model, setting up expectations for the part of the utterance still to be seen, and satisfying earlier expectations. As a side effect of constructing the situation model, an utterance model is constructed to represent the linguistic structure of the sentence. This approach to language understanding has been successfully applied to acquiring task-specific problem spaces for three immediate reasoning tasks: relational reasoning [Johnson-Laird, 1988], categorical syllogisms, and sentence verification [Clark and Chase, 1972]. It has also been used to process the input for these tasks as they are performed. Though NL-SOAR is still far from providing a general linguistic capability, the approach has proven promising. (Rosenbloom et al., 1991, pp. 314–321; italics added)

PHILOSOPHICAL AND PSYCHOLOGICAL IMPLICATIONS OF COMPUTATIONAL COGNITION

SOAR is, at once, an advanced artificial intelligence system directed toward the emulation of human cognition; a theoretical and research tool for testing and integrating the data of experimental cognitive psychology; an empirical research program with foundations resting on the basic concepts contained in the physical symbol system hypothesis; a methodology that draws upon the concepts, techniques, and data of cognitive science; and, ultimately, a unified theory of human and artificial cognition.

SOAR's central value is that it provides theoretical and research instrumentation for the long-term conceptual integration of the numerous diverse findings of experimental studies in cognitive psychology and artificial intelligence.

4

Developing a General and Versatile Computer Intelligence

INTRODUCTION

How general and versatile can computer intelligence be? According to the Church-Turing thesis (Church, 1936; Turing, 1937), computer intelligence can solve any problem that human intelligence can solve. The thesis would be inclusive of the proposing of problems, the application of known solution methods, and the creation of original solutions. No matter how broad, flexible, and creative the level of human intelligence, it can be matched, in every respect, by the algorithms of computation. The Church-Turing thesis has inspired the intellectual foundations of artificial intelligence. The most significant theories in artificial intelligence will be described and compared in the following chapter.

FOUNDATIONAL PROBLEMS OF ARTIFICIAL INTELLIGENCE

As is true of any science, it is important to inquire into the conceptual foundations of artificial intelligence. Kirsh (1991) provides a critical inquiry into the foundational assumptions of artificial intelligence.

The Foundational Assumptions of Artificial Intelligence: Overview

Kirsh (1991) has identified five far-reaching general assumptions that lie at the foundations of artificial intelligence research. These assumptions and the theoretical positions taken on them by various research programs are discussed in the following section:

The objective of research in the foundations of AI is to address . . . basic questions of method, theory, and orientation. It is to self-consciously reappraise what AI is all about.

The pursuit of AI does not occur in isolation. Fields such as philosophy, linguistics, psychophysics and theoretical computer science have exercised a historical influence over the field and today there is as much dialogue as ever, particularly with the new field of cognitive science. One consequence of dialogue is that criticisms of positions held in one discipline frequently apply to positions held in other disciplines.

In this . . . essay, my objective is to bring together a variety of these arguments both for and against the dominant research programs of AI.

It is impossible, of course, to explore carefully all of these arguments in a single paper. . . . *It may be of use, though, to stand back and consider several of the most abstract assumptions underlying the competing visions of intelligence. These assumptions—whether explicitly named by theorists or not—identify issues which have become focal points of debate and serve as dividing lines of positions.*

Of these, five stand out as particularly fundamental:

—*Preeminence of knowledge and conceptualization:* Intelligence that transcends insect-level intelligence requires declarative knowledge and some form of reasoning-like computation—call this cognition. Core AI is the study of the conceptualizations of the world presupposed and used by intelligent systems during cognition.

—*Disembodiment:* Cognition and the knowledge it presupposes can be studied largely in abstraction from the details of perception and motor control.

—*Kinematics of cognition are language-like:* It is possible to describe the trajectory of knowledge states or informational states created during cognition using a vocabulary very much like English or some regimented logico-mathematical version of English.

—*Learning can be added later:* The kinematics of cognition and the domain knowledge needed for cognition can be studied separately from the study of concept learning, psychological development, and evolutionary change.

—*Uniform architecture:* There is a single architecture underlying virtually all cognition.

Different research programs are based, more or less, on a mixture of these assumptions plus corollaries.

Logicism [Hobbs and Moore, 1985; Newell and Simon, 1972] as typified by formal theorists of the common-sense world, formal theorists of language and formal theorists of belief [Konolige, 1985; Levesque, 1986], presupposes almost all of these assumptions. Logicism, as we know it today, is predicated on the pre-eminence of reasoning-like processes and conceptualization, the legitimacy of disembodied analysis, on interpreting rational kinematics as propositional, and the possibility of separating thought and learning. It remains neutral on the uniformity of the underlying architecture.

Other research programs make a virtue of denying one or more of those assumptions.

SOAR, [Newell, 1990; Rosenbloom et al., 1991] for instance, differs from logicism in according learning a vital role in the basic theory and in assuming that all of cognition can be explained as processes occurring in a single uniform architecture. Rational kinematics in SOAR are virtually propositional but differ slightly in containing control markers—preferences—to bias transitions. In other respects, SOAR shares with logicism the assumption that reasoning-like processes and conceptualization are central, and that it is methodologically acceptable to treat central processes in abstraction from perceptual and motor processes.

Connectionists [Rumelhart, McClelland, and the PDP Research Group, 1986; Mc-Clelland, Rumelhart, and the PDP Research Group, 1986], by contrast, deny that reasoning-like processes are pre-eminent in cognition, that core AI is the study of the concepts underpinning domain understanding, and that rational kinematics is language-like. Yet like SOAR, connectionists emphasize the centrality of learning in the study of cognition, and like logicists they remain agnostic about the uniformity of the underlying architecture. They are divided on the assumption of disembodiment.

Mobotists [Brooks, 1991] take the most extreme stance and deny reasoning, conceptualization, rational kinematics, disembodiment, uniformity of architecture and the separability of knowledge and learning (more precisely evolution). Part of what is attractive in the mobotics approach is precisely its radicalness.

Similar profiles can be offered for Lenat and Feigenbaum's position [Lenat and Feigenbaum, 1991], Minsky's society of mind theory [Minsky, 1986], Schank's anti-formalist approach [Schank, 1985; Schank and Reisbeck, 1981] and Hewitt and Gasser's accounts [Gasser, 1991; Hewitt, 1991] of much of distributed AI research. (Kirsh, 1991, pp. 3–5, italics added)

To facilitate comparisons of theoretical positions of various research programs on the foundational assumptions discussed by Kirsh (1991, pp. 3–4), I have constructed Table 4.1, which indicates the position (denied, affirmed, neutral) of each of four research programs/theories (logicism, connectionism, SOAR, roboticism) on each of the five assumptions.

First Assumption: Essentiality of Knowledge, Conceptualization, and Reasoning-Like Computation

In general, artificial intelligence theorists and researchers (with the exception of roboticists and connectionists) agree on the canonical necessity of knowledge and inference. Knowledge can be declarative or compiled, and inference can be explicit or implicit.

In accepting the priority of knowledge level theories, one is not committed to supposing that knowledge is explicitly encoded declaratively and deployed in explicitly inferential processes, although frequently knowledge will be. One's commitment is that knowledge and conceptualization lie at the heart of AI: that a major goal in the field is to discover the basic knowledge units of cognition (of intelligent skills).

What are these knowledge units? In the case of qualitative theories of the common-sense world, and in the case of Lenat's CBC project [Lenat and Guha, 1989; Lenat and

Table 4.1
Comparison of Theoretical Positions of Logicism, Connectionism, SOAR, and Roboticism on Foundational Assumptions in Artificial Intelligence

Theoretical Positions	The essentiality of knowledge, conceptualization, and reasoning-like computation processes	The separateness of cognition from perceptual-motor processes	The adequacy of English or symbolic languages to describe cognition	The separateness of cognition from learning	The uniformity of cognitive architecture
Logicism [Hobbs & Moore, 1985; Newell & Simon, 1972]	Affirmed	Affirmed	Affirmed	Affirmed	Neutral
Connectionism [McClelland & Rumelhart, 1986; Rumelhart, McClelland, & the PDP Research Group, 1986]	Denied	Divided	Denied	Denied	Neutral
SOAR [Newell; Rosenbloom et al., 1991]	Affirmed	Affirmed	Affirmed	Denied	Affirmed
Roboticism [Brooks, 1991]	Denied	Denied	Denied	Denied	Denied

Note: The indicated theoretical positions are general and modal.
Source: Based on Kirsh (1991).

Feigenbaum, 1991], these basic knowledge units are the conceptual units of *consensus reality*—the core concepts underpinning "the millions of things that we all know and that we assume everyone else knows" [Lenat and Guha, 1989, p. 4]. Not surprisingly, these concepts are often familiar ideas with familiar names—though sometimes they will be theoretical ideas, having a technical meaning internal to the theory. . . .

The basic idea that knowledge and conceptualization lie at the heart of AI stems from the seductive view that cognition is inference. Intelligent skills, an old truism of AI runs, are composed of two parts: a declarative knowledge base and an inference engine.

The inference engine is relatively uncomplicated; it is a domain-independent program that takes as input a set of statements about the current situation plus a fragment of the declarative knowledge base, it produces as output a stream of inferred declaratives culminating in the case of decision making and routine activity, in directives for appropriate action.

In contrast to the inference engine, the knowledge base is domain-specific and is as complicated as a cognitive skill requires. Domain knowledge is what distinguishes the ability to troubleshoot a circuit from the ability to understand the meaning of a sentence. Both require knowledge but of different domains. It follows that the heart of the AI problem is to discover what the agent knows about the world that permits success. This idea, *in one form or another*, has been endorsed by logicists, by Lenat and Feigenbaum [Lenat and Feigenbaum, 1991], Chomsky [Chomsky, 1986], Montague [Montague, 1974], and with variations by Schank [Schank and Riesbeck, 1981], and Newell and Simon [Newell and Simon, 1972].

The qualification *in one form or another* is significant. As mentioned, a commitment to theorizing about knowledge and knowledge units is not in itself a commitment to large amounts of on-line logical reasoning or explicit representation of domain knowledge. It is well known that not all skills that require intelligent control require an *explicit* knowledge base. So it is a further thesis that declarative knowledge and logical inference are actually deployed in most cognitive skills. In such cases we still may say that cognition is inference, but we no longer expect to find explicit inference rules or even complete trajectories of inferential steps. In the source code of cognition we would find instructions for inferential processes throughout. But knowledge can be compiled into procedures or designed into control systems which have no distinct inference engines. So often our account of cognition is more of the form "The system is acting *as if* it were inferring. . . ."

Knowledge Compilation. One question of considerable interest among theorists who accept the centrality of knowledge and the virtue of knowledge level theories, is "How far can this knowledge compilation go?"

According to Nilsson there are severe limits on this compilation. Overt declaratives have special virtues.

> The most versatile intelligent machines will represent much of their knowledge about their environment declaratively . . . [A declarative can] be used by the machine even for purposes unforeseen by the machine's designer, it [can] more easily be modified than could knowledge embodied in programs, and it facilitate[s] communication between machine and other machines and humans. [Nilsson, 1991]

For Nilsson, the theory of what is known is a good approximation of what is actually represented declaratively. He suggests that some reactions to situations and some useful inferences may be compiled. But storage and indexing cost militate against compiling knowledge overmuch. Real flexibility requires explicit declarative representation of knowledge. No doubt, it is an empirical question just how much of a cognitive skill can be compiled. But as long as a system uses some explicit declaratives, the apparatus of declarative representation must be in place, making it possible, when time permits, to control action through run time interference. . . .

[Rosenschein and Kaebling, 1986] see the inflexibility of knowledge compilation as far less constraining. On their view, a significant range of tasks connected with adaptive response to the environment can be compiled. To determine the appropriate set of re-actions to build into a machine, a designer performs the relevant knowledge level logical reasoning at compile time so that the results will be available at run time. Again, it is an empirical matter how many cognitive skills can be completely automatized in this fashion. But the research program of situated automata is to push the envelope as far as possible.

A similar line of thought applies to the work of Chomsky and Montague. When they claim to be offering a theory about the knowledge deployed in parsing and speech pro-duction it does not follow they require on-line inference. By offering their theories in the format of ''here's the knowledge base use the obvious inference engine'' they estab-lish the effectiveness of their knowledge specification: it is a condition on their theory that when conjoined with the obvious inference engine it should generate all and only syntactic strings (or some specified fragment of that set). That is why their theories are called *generative*. But to date no one has offered a satisfactory account of how the theory is to be effectively implemented. Parsing *may* involve considerable inference, but equally it may consist of highly automated retrieval processes where structures or fragments of structures previously found acceptable are recognized. To be sure, some theorists say that recognition in itself is a type of inference: that recognizing a string of words *as* an NP involves inference. Hence even parsing construed as constraint satisfaction or as schema retrieval (instantiation) and so forth, is itself inferential at bottom. But this is not the dominant view. Whatever the answer, though, there are no *a priori* grounds for assuming that statements of linguistic principle are encoded explicitly in declaratives and operated on by explicit inference rules.

Whether knowledge be explicit or compiled, the view that cognition is inference and that theorizing at the knowledge level is at least the starting place of scientific AI is endorsed by a large fragment of the community.

Opposition. In stark contrast is the position held by Rod Brooks. According to Brooks [1991,] a theory in AI is not an account of the knowledge units of cognition. Most tasks that seem to involve considerable world knowledge may yet be achievable without appeal to declaratives, to concepts, or to basic knowledge units, even at compile time. Knowl-edge level theories, he argues, too often chase fictions. If AI's overarching goal is to understand intelligent control of action, then if it turns out to be true, as Brooks be-lieves it will, that most intelligent behaviour can be produced by a system of carefully tuned control systems interconnected in a simple but often ad hoc manner, then why study knowledge? A methodology more like experimental engineering is what is required.

If Brooks is right, intelligent control systems can be designed before a designer has an articulated conceptualization of the task environment. Moreover, the system itself can succeed without operating on a conceptualization in any interesting sense. New behav-iours can be grown onto older behaviours in an evolutionary fashion that makes otiose the task of conceptualizing the world. The result is a system that, for a large class of tasks, might match the versatility of action achievable with declaratives, yet it never calls on the type of capacities we associate with having knowledge of a conceptualization and symbolic representation of the basic world elements. (Kirsh, 1991, pp. 6–9; italics added)

The Second Assumption: The Separateness of Cognition from Perceptual-Motor Processes

The distinction between formal knowledge level theories and perceptual-motor theories is a distinction that belongs to the context of the designer of systems. The distinction does not belong to the system except where the system is a human system and a separation arises because conscious knowledge and symbolization are separated from neural structures that automatically accomplish perceptual-motor action and the adaptation of the system to the environment. The distinction between the conscious knowledge level and the autonomic knowledge level, between cognitive processes and sensory-motor processes, will gradually fade as research discloses more and more about the details of neural structures and functions that support both types of knowledge and of their interrelationships. The viewpoint that I have just expressed is in contrast with that taken by Kirsh (1991), as well as that of Brooks on robotic systems and those of Gibson on animal and human systems. The views of these theorists, together with those of Kirsh, are included in the following section:

I have been presenting a justification for the view that, in the main, intelligence can be fruitfully studied on the assumption that the problems and tasks facing intelligent agents can be formally specified, and so pursued abstractly at the knowledge or conceptual level. For analytic purposes we can ask questions about cognitive skills using symbolic characterizations of the environment as input and symbolic characterizations of motor activity as output. Concerns about how conceptual knowledge is *grounded* in perceptual-motor skills can be addressed separately. These questions can be bracketed because what differentiates cognitive skills is not so much the perceptual-motor parameters of a task but the knowledge of the task domain which directs action in that domain. This is the methodological assumption of disembodiment. What are the arguments against it?

In his attack on core AI, Brooks identifies three assumptions related to disembodiment which, in his opinion, dangerously bias the way cognitive skills are studied:

—The output of vision is conceptualized and so the interface between perception and "central cognition" is clean and neatly characterizable in the language of the predicate calculus, or some other language with terms denoting objects and terms denoting properties.

—Whenever we exercise our intelligence we call on a central representation of the world state where some substantial fraction of the world state is represented and regularly updated perceptually or by inference.

—When we seem to be pursuing our tasks in an organized fashion our actions have been planned in advance by envisioning outcomes and choosing a sequence that best achieves the agent's goals.

The error in each of these assumptions, Brooks contends, is to suppose that the real world is somehow simple enough, sufficiently decomposable into concept-sized bites, that we can represent it, in real time, in all the detailed respects that might matter to achieving our goals. It is not. Even if we had enough concepts to cover its relevant aspects we would never be able to compute an updated world model in real time. Moreover, we don't need to. Real success in a causally dense world is achieved by tuning the perceptual system to *action-relevant* changes.

To take an example from J. J. Gibson, an earlier theorist who held similar views, if a creature's goals are to avoid obstacles on its path to a target, it is not necessary for it to constantly judge its distance from obstacles, update a world model with itself at the origin, and recalculate a trajectory given velocity projections. It can instead exploit the invariant relation between its current velocity and instantaneous time to contact obstacles in order to determine a new trajectory directly. It adapts its actions to changes in time to contact. If the environment is perceived in terms of actions that are *afforded* rather than in terms of objects and relations, the otherwise computationally intensive task is drastically simplified.

Now this is nothing short of a Ptolemaic revolution. If the world is always sensed from a perspective which views the environment as a *space of possibilities for actions*, then every time an agent performs an action which changes the action potentials which the world affords it, it changes the world as it perceives it. In the last example, this occurs because as the agent changes its instantaneous speed and direction it may perceive significant changes in environmental affordances despite being in almost the same spatial relations to objects in the environment. Even slight actions can change the way a creature perceives the world. If these changes in perception regularly simplify the problem of attaining goals, then traditional accounts of the environment as a static structure composed of objects, relations and functions, may completely misstate the actual computational problems faced by creatures acting in the world. The real problem must be defined relative to the world-for-the-agent. The world-for-the-agent changes despite the world-in-itself remaining constant.

To take another example of how action and perception are intertwined, and so must be considered when stating the computational problems facing agents, consider the problems of grasp planning. Traditionally the problem is defined as follows: Given a target object, an initial configuration of hand joints and free space between hand and target, find a trajectory of joint changes that results in a stable grasp. At one time it was thought that to solve this problem it was necessary to compute the 3D shape of the target, the final configuration of joints, and the trajectory of joint changes between initial and final configurations—a substantial amount of computation by anyone's measure. Yet this is not the problem if we allow compliance. Instead we simply need locate a rough center of mass of the target, send the palm of the hand to that point with the instruction to close on contact, and rely on the hand to comply with the object. The problem is elegantly simplified. No longer must we know the shape of the object, the mapping relation between 3D shape and joint configuration, or the constraints on joint closure. The original definition of the grasp planning problem was a mis-statement. It led us to believe that certain subproblems and certain elements of knowledge would be required, when in fact they are not. Compliance changes everything. It alters the way the world should be interpreted.

The point is that the possibility of complying with shapes restructures the world. A creature with a compliant hand confronts a different world than a creature without. Accordingly, a knowledge level account of grasping which did not accommodate the simplifications due to compliance would be false. It would be working with an incorrect set of assumptions about the manipulator.

By analogy, one cardinal idea of the embodied approach to cognition, is that the hardware of the body—in particular, the details of the sensori-motor system—when taken in conjunction with an environment and goals shape the kinds of problems facing an agent. These problems in turn shape the cognitive skills agents have. Consequently, to specify these skills correctly it is necessary to pay close attention to the agent's interactions with its environment—to the actions it does and can do at any point. Disembodied approaches do not interpret the environment of action in this dynamic manner, and so inevitably give rise to false problems and false solutions. They tend to define problems in terms of task environments specified in the abstract perspective independent language of objects and relations.

Now this argument, it seems to me, is sound. But how far does it go? It serves as a reminder to knowledge level theorists that they may easily misspecify a cognitive skill, and that to reliably theorize at the knowledge level one should often have a model of the agent's sensori-motor capabilities. But it is an empirical question just how often hardware biases the definition of a cognitive problem. *A priori* one would expect a continuum of problems from the most situated—where the cognitive task cannot be correctly defined without a careful analysis of the possible compliances and possible agent environment invariants—to highly abstract problems, such as word problems, number problems, puzzles, and so forth, where the task is essentially abstract, and its implementation in the world is largely irrelevant to performance.

Ultimately, Brook's rejection of disembodied AI is an empirical challenge: for a large class of problems facing an acting creature the only reliable method of discovering how they can succeed, and hence what their true cognitive skills are, is to study them *in situ*.

Frequently this is the way of foundational questions. One theorist argues that many of the assumptions underpinning the prevailing methodology are false. He then proposes a new methodology and looks for empirical support.

But occasionally it is possible to offer, in addition to empirical support, a set of purely philosophical arguments against a methodology.

Philosophical Objections to Disembodied AI

At the top level we may distinguish two philosophical objections: first, that knowledge level accounts which leave out a theory of the body are too incomplete to serve the purpose for which they were proposed. Second, that axiomatic knowledge accounts fail to capture all the knowledge an agent has about a domain. Let us consider each in turn.

Why We Need a Theory of the Body. The adequacy of a theory, whether in physics or AI, depends on the purpose it is meant to serve. It is possible to identify three rather different purposes AI theorists have in mind when they postulate a formal theory of the commonsense world. An axiomatic theory T of domain D is:

(1) adequate for *robotics* if it can be used by an acting perceiving machine to achieve its goals when operating in D;

(2) adequate for a *disembodied rational planner* if it entails all and only the intuitive truths of D as expressed in the language of the user of the planner;

(3) adequate for *cognitive science* if it effectively captures the knowledge of D which actual agents have.

The philosophical arguments I will now present are meant to show that a formal theory of D, unless accompanied by a theory about the sensori-motor capacities of the creature using the theory, will fail no matter which purpose a theorist has in mind. Theories of conceptualization alone are inadequate, they require theories of embodiment.

Inadequacy for robotics. According to Nilsson, the touchstone of adequacy of a logicist theory is that it marks the necessary domain distinctions and makes the necessary domain predictions for an acting perceiving machine to achieve its goals. Theoretical adequacy is a function of four variables: D: the actual subject-independent properties of a domain; P: the creature's perceptual capacities; A: the creature's action repertoire; and G: the creature's goals. In principle a change in any one of these can affect the theoretical adequacy of an axiomatization. For changes in perceptual abilities, no less than changes in action abilities or goals may render domain distinctions worthless, invisible to a creature.

If axioms are adequate only relative to (D P A G) then formal theories are strictly speaking untestable without an account of (D P A G). We can never know whether a given axiom set captures the distinctions and relations which a particular robot will need for coping with D. We cannot just assume that T is adequate if it satisfies our own intuitions of the useful distinctions inherent in a domain. The intuitions we ourselves have about the domain will be relative to our own action repertoire, perceptual capacities, and goals. Nor will appeal to model theory help. Model theoretic interpretations only establish consistency. They say nothing about the appropriateness, truth or utility of axiom sets for a given creature.

Moreover, this need to explicitly state A, P, and G is not restricted to robots or creatures having substantially different perceptual-motor capacities to our own. There is always the danger that between any two humans there are substantive differences about the intuitively useful distinctions inherent in the domain. The chemist, for instance, who wishes to axiomatize the knowledge a robot needs to cope with the many liquids it may encounter, has by dint of study refined his observational capacities to the point where he or she can notice theoretical properties of the liquid which remain invisible to the rest of us. She will use in her axiomatizations primitive terms that she believes are observational. For most of us they are not. We require axiomatic connections to tie those terms to more directly observational ones. As a result, there is in all probability a continuum of formal theories of the commonsense world ranging from ones understandable by novices to those understandable only by experts. Without an account of the observational capacities presupposed by a theory, however, it is an open question just which level of expertise a given T represents.

It may be objected that an account of the observational capacities supposed by a theory is not actually part of the theory but of the metatheory of use—the theory that explains how to *apply* the theory. But this difference is in name alone. The domain knowledge that is required to tie a predicate to the observational conditions that are relevant to it is itself substantial. If a novice is to use the expert's theory he will have to know how to make all things considered judgements about whether a given phenomenon is an A-type event or B-type event. Similarly if the expert is to use the novice's theory he must likewise consult the novice's theory to decide the best way to collapse observational distinctions he notices. In either case, it is arbitrary where we say these world linking axioms are to be found. They are part and parcel of domain knowledge. But they form the basis for a theory of embodiment. (Kirsh, 1991, pp. 18–19)

The Third Assumption: The Adequacy of English or Symbolic Languages to Describe Cognitive Processes

In the following section, Kirsh (1991) questions whether computational languages are adequate to capture all varieties of cognition. In addition, Kirsh (1991) warns against the theorist's attribution to the machine of understanding the machine's language in the same way that the theorist understands the language.

I have been arguing that there are grave problems with the methodological assumption that cognitive skills can be studied in abstraction from the sensing and motor apparatus of the bodies that incorporate them. Both empirical and philosophical arguments can be presented to show that the body shows through. This does not vitiate the program of knowledge level theorists, but it does raise doubts about the probability of correctly modelling all cognitive skills on the knowledge-base/inference-engine model.

A further assumption related to disembodied AI is that we can use logic or English to track the trajectory of informational states a system creates as it processes a cognitive task. That is, either the predicate calculus or English can serve as a useful semantics for tracking the type of computation that goes on in cognition. They are helpful metalanguages.

From the logicist's point of view, when an agent computes its next behavior it creates a trajectory of informational states that are *about* the objects, functions and relations designated in the designer's conceptualization of the environment. This language is, of course, a logical language. Hence the transitions between these informational states can be described as *rational transitions* or inferences in that logical language. If English is the semantic metalanguage, then rational transitions between sentences will be less well-defined, but ought nonetheless to make sense as reasonable.

There are two defects with this approach. First, that it is parochial: that in fact there are many types of computation which are not amenable to characterization in a logical metalanguage, but which still count as cognition. Second, because it is easy for a designer to mistake his own conceptualization for a machine's conceptualization there is a tendency to misinterpret the machine's information trajectory, often attributing to the machine a deeper grasp of the world than is proper.

Argument 1. Consider the second objection first. As mentioned earlier, it is necessary to distinguish those cases where:

(1) the designer uses concepts to describe the environment which the machine does not understand and perhaps could not;

(2) the designer uses only those concepts which the machine grasps, but the two represent those concepts differently;

(3) both designer and machine use the same concepts and encode them in the same way.

The first two cases concern the appropriate metalanguage of design, the last the object language of processing. *Our goal as scientists is to represent a creature's cognition as accurately as possible, both so we can certify what it is doing, hence debug it better, and so we can design it better from the outset.*

The trouble that regularly arises, though, is that the designer has a conceptualization of the task environment that is quite distinct from that of the system. There is always more than one way of *specifying* an ability, and more than one way of specifying an environment of action. Choice of a metalanguage should be made on pragmatic grounds: which formalism most simplifies the designer's task? *But lurking in the background is the worry that if the designer uses a metalanguage that invokes concepts the system simply does not or could not have, then he may propose mistaken designs which he later verifies as correct using the same incorrect metalanguage. . . .*

For example, suppose we wish to design a procedure controlling a manipulator able to draw a circle on a crumpled piece of paper. The naive procedure will not produce a curve whose distance on the crumpled surface is equidistant. Its design works for flat surfaces, not for arbitrary surfaces. Yet if a system did have concepts for equidistance, locus and points it ought to be *adaptive* enough to accommodate deformations in the surface topology. To be sure such a machine would have to have some way of sensing topology. That by itself is not enough, though. It is its dispositions to behave in possible worlds that matters. This is shown by the old comment that whether I have the concept *chordate* (creature having a heart) or *renate* (creature having kidneys) cannot be determined by studying my normal behaviour alone [Quine, 1960]. In normal worlds, chordates are renates. Only in counterfactual worlds—where it is possible to come across viable creatures with hearts but no kidneys—could we display our individuating dispositions. *The upshot is that a designer cannot assume that his characterization of the informational trajectory of a creature is correct, unless he confirms certain claims about the creature's dispositions to behave in a range of further contexts. Sometimes these contexts lie outside the narrow task he is building a cognitive skill for.*

None of the above establishes that English is inadequate. It just shows that it is easy to make false attributions of content. The criticism that logic and natural language are not adequate metalanguages arises as soon as we ask whether they are expressive enough to describe some of the bizarre concepts systems which funny dispositions will have. *In principle, both logic and English are expressive enough to capture any comprehensible concept. But the resulting characterization may be so long and confusing that it will be virtually incomprehensible.* For instance, if we try to identify what I have been calling the implicit concepts of the compass controller we will be stymied. If the system could talk what would it say to the question: Can a *circle* be drawn in a space measured with a non-Euclidean metric? What nascent idea of equidistance does it have? *Its inferences would be so idiosyncratic that finding an English sentence or reasonable axiomatic account would be out of the question. English and logic are the wrong metalanguages to characterize such informational states.*

What is needed is more in the spirit of a functional account of informational content

[Birnbaum, 1991]. Such semantics are usually ugly. For in stating the role an informational state plays in a system's dispositions to behave, we characteristically need to mention myriad other states, since the contribution of a state is a function of other states as well.

Accordingly, not all informational states are best viewed as akin to English sentences. If we want to understand the full range of cognitive skills—especially those modular ones which are not directly hooked up to central inference—we will need to invoke some other language for describing information content. Frequently the best way to track a computation is not as a rational trajectory in a logical language.

Argument 2. The need for new languages to describe informational content has recently been re-iterated by certain connectionists who see in parallel distributing processing a different style of computation. Hewitt and Gasser have also emphasized a similar need for an alternative understanding of the computational processes occurring in distributed AI systems. It is old fashioned and parochial to hope for a logic-based denotational semantics for such systems.

The PDP concern can be stated as follows: In PDP, computation vectors of activation propagate through a partially connected network. According to Smolensky [Schank and Riesbeck, 1981] it is constructive to describe the behaviour of the system as a path in tensor space. The problem of interpretation is to characterize the significant events on this path. It would be pleasing if we could say "now the network is extracting the information that p, now the information that q", and so on, until the system delivers its answer. *Unfortunately, though, except for input and output vectors—whose interpretation we specifically set—the majority of vectors are not interpretable as carrying information which can be easily stated in English or logic. There need be no one-one mapping between significant events in the system's tensor space trajectory and its path in propositional space. Smolensky—whose argument this is—suggests that much of this intermediate processing is interpretable at the subconceptual level where the basic elements of meaning differ from those we have words for in English.*

One way of seeing the problem is to recognize that in a simple feed-forward network a given hidden unit can be correlated with a (possibly nested) disjunction of conjunctions of probabilities of input features. A vector, therefore, can be interpreted as a combination of these. The result is a compound that may make very little sense to us. For instance, it might correspond to a distribution over the entire feature set. Thus a single node might be tuned to respond to the weighted conjunction of features comprising the tip of my nose, my heel, plus the luminescence of my hands, or the weighted conjunction of. . . . Moreover, if we do not believe that the semantics of networks is correlational but rather functional we will prefer to interpret the meaning of a node to be its contribution (in conjunction with its superior nodes) to the capacity to classify.

In like manner, Hewitt and Gasser offer another argument for questioning whether we can track the information flowing through a complex system in propositional form. The question they ask is: How are we to understand the content of a message sent between two agents who are part of a much larger matrix of communicating agents? Superficially, each agent has its own limited perspective on the task. From agent-1's point of view, agent-2 is saying p, from agent-3's point of view, agent-2 is saying q. Is there a right answer? Is there a God's eye perspective that identifies the true content and gives the relativized perspective to each agent? If so, how is this relativized meaning to be determined? We will have to know not only whom the message is addressed to, but what the addressee is expecting, and what it can *do* with the message. Again, though, once we focus on the effects which messages have on a system we leave the simple

world of denotational semantics and opt for functional semantics. Just how we characterize *possible effects*, however, is very different than giving a translation of the message
in English. We will need a language for describing the behavioural dispositions of agents.

*Cognition as rational inference looks less universal once we leave the domain of
familiar sequential processing and consider massively parallel architectures.* (Kirsh,
1991, pp. 22–25; italics added)

The Fourth Assumption: The Separateness of Cognition from Learning

In the following section Kirsh (1991) compares the claim of logicism that
cognition is isolable from learning with the position of SOAR, PDP, and self-
modifying systems:

In a pure top-down approach, we assume it is possible to state what a system knows
without stating how it came to that knowledge. The two questions, competence and
acquisition, can be separated. Learning, on this view, is a switch that can be turned on
or off. It is a box that takes an early conceptualization and returns a more mature conceptualization. Thus learning and conceptualization are sufficiently distinct that the two
can be studied separately. Indeed, learning is often understood as the mechanism for
generating a trajectory of conceptualizations. This is clearly the belief of logic theorists
and developmental psychologists who maintain that what an agent knows at a given
stage of development is a theory, not fundamentally different in spirit than a scientific
theory, about the domain [Carey, 1985].

There are several problems with this view. First, it assumes we can characterize the instantaneous conceptualization of a system without having to study its various earlier conceptualizations. But what if we cannot *elicit* the system's conceptualization using the
standard techniques? To determine what a competent PDP system, for example, would
know about its environment of action, it is necessary to train it until it satisfies some adequacy metric. We cannot say in advance what the system will know if it is perfectly
competent because there are very many paths to competence, each of which potentially
culminates in a different solution. Moreover if the account of PDP offered above is correct it may be impossible to characterize the system's conceptualization in a logical language or in English. It is necessary to analyze its dispositions. But to do that one needs an
actual implementation displaying the competence. Hence the only way to know what a
PDP system will know if it is competent is to build one and study it. A purely top-down
stance, which assumes that learning is irrelevant, is bound to fail in the case of PDP.

The second argument against detaching knowledge and learning also focusses on the
in practice unpredictable nature of the learning trajectory. In SOAR it is frequently said
that chunking is more than mere speedup [Rosenbloom et al., 1991]. The results of
repeatedly chunking solutions to impasses has a nonlinear effect on performance. Once
we have nonlinear effects, however, we cannot predict the evolution of a system short
of running it. Thus in order to determine the steady state knowledge underpinning a skill
we need to run SOAR with its chunking module on.

A final reason we cannot study what a system knows without studying how it acquires
that knowledge is that a system may have special design features that let it acquire
knowledge. It is organized to self-modify. Hence we cannot predict what knowledge it

may contain unless we know how it integrates new information with old. There are many ways to self-modify.

For instance, according to Roger Schank, much of the knowledge a system contains is lodged in its indexing scheme [Schank and Riesbeck, 1981]. As systems grow in size they generally have to revise their indexing scheme. The results of this process of revision cannot be anticipated *a priori* unless we have a good idea of the earlier indexing schemes. The reason is that much of its knowledge is stored in cases. Case knowledge may be sensitive to the order the cases were encountered. Consequently, we can never determine the knowledge a competent system has unless we know something of the cases it was exposed to and the order they were met. History counts.

This emphasis on cases goes along with a view that much of reasoning involves noticing analogies to past experiences. A common corollary to this position is that concepts are not context-free intentions; they have a certain open texture, making it possible to flexibly extend their use and to apply them to new situations in creative ways. An agent which understands a concept should be able to recognize and generate analogical extensions of its concepts to new contexts.

Once we view concepts to be open textured, however, it becomes plausible to suppose that a concept's meaning is a function of history. It is easier to see an analogical extension of a word if it has already been extended in that direction before. But then, we can't say what an agent's concept of "container" is unless we know the variety of contexts it has seen the word in. If that is so, it is impossible to understand a creature's conceptualization in abstraction from its learning history. *Much of cognition cannot be studied independently of learning.* (Kirsh, 1991, pp. 25–27; italics added)

The Fifth Assumption: The Uniformity of Cognitive Architecture

The strong claim of Newell (1991) that the SOAR system unifies all of cognition by means of a small set of mechanisms within a uniform architecture is critically analyzed by Kirsh (1991) in the following account:

The final issue I will discuss is the claim made by Newell et al. that cognition is basically the product of running programs in a single architecture. According to Newell, too much of the research in AI and cognitive science aims at creating independent representational and control mechanisms for solving particular cognitive tasks. Each investigator has his or her preferred computational models which, clever as they may be, rarely meet a further constraint that they be integratable into a unified account of cognition. For Newell:

Psychology has arrived at the possibility of unified theories of cognition—theories that gain their power by positioning a single system of mechanisms that operate together to produce the full range of human cognition [Newell, 1991].

The idea that there might be a general theory of intelligence is not new. At an abstract level anyone who believes that domain knowledge plus inferential abilities are responsible for intelligent performance, at least in one sense, operates with a general theory of cognition. For, on that view, it is knowledge, ultimately, that is the critical element in cognition.

But Newell's claim is more concrete: not only is knowledge the basis for intelligence; knowledge, he argues further, will be encoded in a SOAR-like mechanism. This claim goes well beyond what most logicists would maintain. It is perfectly consistent with logicism that knowledge may be encoded, implemented or embedded in any of dozens of ways. A bare commitment to specification of cognitive skills at the knowledge level is hardly grounds for expecting a small set of ''underlying mechanisms, whose interactions and compositions provide the answers to all the questions we have—predictions, explanations, designs, controls'' [Newell, 1991] pertaining to the full range of cognitive performances. The SOAR project, however, is predicated on this very possibility. The goal of the group is to test the very strong claim that underpinning problem solving, decision making, routine action, memory, learning, skill, even perception and motor behaviour, there is a single architecture ''a single system [that] produces all aspects of behaviour . . . Even if the mind has parts, modules, components, or whatever, they mesh together . . .'' and work in accordance with a small set of principles.

It is not my intent to provide serious arguments for or against this position. I mention it largely because it is such a deep commitment of the SOAR research program and therefore an assumption that separates research orientations. The strongest support for it must surely be empirical, and it will become convincing only as the body of evidence builds up. There can be little doubt, though, that it is an assumption not universally shared.

Minsky, for instance, in *Society of Mind* [Minsky, 1986], has argued that intelligence is the product of hundreds, probably thousands of specialized computational mechanisms he terms agents. There is no homogeneous underlying architecture. In the society of mind theory, mental activity is the product of many agents of varying complexity interacting in hundreds of ways. The very purpose of the theory is to display the variety of mechanisms that are likely to be useful in a mind-like system, and to advocate the need for diversity. Evolution, Minsky emphasizes, is an opportunistic tinkerer likely to co-opt existing mechanisms in an *ad hoc* manner to create new functions meeting new needs. With such diversity and ad hoccery it would be surprising if most cognitive performances were the result of a few mechanisms comprising a principled architecture.

Brooks in a similar manner sets out to recreate intelligent capacities by building layer upon layer of mechanism, each with hooks into lower layers to suppress or bias input and output. Again, no non-empirical arguments may be offered to convince skeptics of the correctness of this view. The best that has been offered is that the brain seems to have diverse mechanisms of behaviour control, so it is plausible that systems with comparable functionality will too.

Again there is no quick way to justify the assumption of architecture homogeneity. More than any other foundational issue this is one for which non-empirical or philosophical arguments are misplaced. (Kirsh, 1991, pp. 28; italics added)

The Foundational Assumptions: Conclusions

Kirsh (1991) concludes his discussion of the pre-eminent foundational issues of artificial intelligence in the following terms:

I have presented five dimensions—five big issues—which theorists in AI, either tacitly or explicitly, take a stand on. Any selection of issues is bound to have a personal element to them. In my case I have focussed most deeply on the challenges of embodiment. How reliable can theories of cognition be if they assume that systems can be studied abstractly, without serious concern for the mechanisms that ground a system's conceptualization in perception and action? But other more traditional issues are of equal interest. How central is the role which knowledge plays in cognitive skills? Can most of cognition be seen as inference? What part does learning or psychological development play in the studying of reasoning and performance? Will a few mechanisms of control and representation suffice for general intelligence? *None of the arguments presented here even begin to be decisive. Nor were they meant to be. Their function is to encourage informed debate of the paramount issues informing our field.* (Kirsh, 1991, pp. 28–29; italics added)

PHILOSOPHICAL AND PSYCHOLOGICAL IMPLICATIONS OF A GENERAL AND VERSATILE COMPUTER INTELLIGENCE

It is useful to analyze the abstract assumptions of intelligence and intelligent systems in two categories: strategic cognition and automatic cognition.

Strategic Cognition

At the human level, strategic cognition has its clearest manifestation in lucid, deliberative, conscious thought directed toward a difficult intellectual problem. Knowledge, inference, and verbal, mathematical, or spatial language are required. At the system level, strategic cognition is similar except for the quality of consciousness. Applicatory here are Kirsh's first and third fundamental assumptions:

—*Pre-eminence of knowledge and conceptualization*: Intelligence that transcends insect-level intelligence requires declarative knowledge and some form of reasoning-like computation—call this *cognition*. Core AI is the study of the conceptualizations of the world presupposed and used by intelligent systems during cognition.

—*Kinematics of cognition are language-like*: It is possible to describe the trajectory of knowledge states or informational states created during cognition using a vocabulary very much like English or some regimented logico-mathematical version of English. (Kirsh, 1991, p. 4)

Automatic Cognition

At the human level, "automatic cognition" refers to unconscious and proceduralized mechanisms of language, thought, and memory. At the system level, automatic cognition is similar except for the quality of unconsciousness. Applicatory here are the neurally inspired concepts of roboticism.

A complete theory of intelligence and intelligent systems will need to account for both strategic cognition and automatic cognition. The attainment of such a theory represents one of the most formidable problems in all of science.

5

The Enhancement of Human Thinking

ARTIFICIAL INTELLIGENCE AND THE THRESHOLD OF KNOWLEDGE

The artificial intelligence objective of enhancing human thinking can be directed toward two domains of thinking: common sense reasoning and scientific reasoning. In the first part of this chapter, the enhancement of common sense reasoning from the perspective of artificial intelligence is considered in an account of and commentary on the long-range CYC research program. In the second part of the chapter, the enhancement of scientific thought concerned with the evaluation of competing scientific hypotheses is achieved in a connectionist architecture that is described in depth and followed by a succinct commentary.

In their article, "On the Thresholds of Knowledge," Lenat and Feigenbaum (1991) discuss their views on the centrality of knowledge in artificial intelligence systems and describe the comprehensive knowledge system CYC (letters derived from encyclopedia), a ten-year research project with an expected completion date of 1994 (Lenat and Feigenbaum, 1991).

Knowledge and Artificial Intelligence Research

Lenat and Feigenbaum (1991) summarize their approach to artificial intelligence in the following account:

We articulate the three major findings and hypotheses of AI to date:

(1) The Knowledge Principle: If a program is to perform a complex task well, it must know a great deal about the world in which it operates. In the absence of knowledge, all you have left is search and reasoning, and that isn't enough.

(2) The Breadth Hypothesis: To behave intelligently in unexpected situations, an agent must be capable of falling back on increasingly general knowledge and analogizing to specific but superficially far-flung knowledge. (This is an extension of the preceding principle.)

(3) AI as Empirical Inquiry: Premature mathematiztion, or focusing on toy problems, washes out details from reality that later turn out to be significant. Thus, we must test our ideas experimentally, *falsifiably*, on large problems. (Lenat and Feigenbaum, 1991, p. 185)

In the following section, Lenat and Feigenbaum (1991) assert that it is primarily knowledge that enables systems (presumably human as well as computer) to exhibit intelligence:

For over three decades, our field has pursued the dream of the computer that competently performs various difficult cognitive tasks. AI has tried many approaches to this goal and accumulated much empirical evidence. The evidence suggests the need for the computer to have and use domain-specific knowledge. We shall begin with our definition of intelligence:

> *Definition. Intelligence* is the power to rapidly find an adequate solution in what appears a priori (to observers) to be an immense search space.

So, in those same terms, we can summarize the empirical evidence: "Knowledge is Power" or, more cynically "Intelligence is in the eye of the (uninformed) beholder." The *knowledge as power* hypothesis has received so much confirmation that we now assert it as:

> *Knowledge Principle (KP)*. A system exhibits intelligent understanding and action at high level of competence primarily because of the *knowledge* that it can bring to bear: the concepts, facts, representations, methods, models, metaphors, and heuristics about its domain of endeavor.

The word *knowledge* in the KP is important. There is a tradeoff between knowledge and search; that is, often one can either memorize a lot of very detailed cases, or spend time applying very general rules. Neither strategy, carried to extremes, is optimal. On the one hand, *searching* is often costly, compared to the low cost of just not forgetting—of preserving the knowledge for future use. Our technological society would be impossible if everyone had to rediscover everything for themselves. On the other hand, even in a relatively narrow field, it's impractical if not impossible to have a pre-stored database of all the precise situations that one will run into. Some at least moderately general knowledge is needed, rules which can be applied in a variety of circumstances. Since *knowledge* includes control strategies and inference methods, one might ask what is *excluded* by the KP. The answer is that we exclude unbalanced programs: those which do not contain, and draw power from, a mixture of explicit and compiled knowledge, and we advocate programs in which the balance is tipped toward the explicit, declarative side . . .

Breadth Hypothesis (BH). Intelligent performance often requires the problem solver to fall back on increasingly general knowledge, and/or to analogize the specific knowledge from far-flung domains.

Are we, of all people, advocating the use of weak methods? Yes, but only in the presence of a breadth of knowledge far afield of the particular task at hand. We are adding to the KP here, not contradicting it. Much of the power still derives from a large body of task-specific expertise (cases and rules). We are adding to the KP a new speculation, namely that intelligent problem solvers cope with novel situations by analogizing and by drawing on "common sense". . . .

The natural tendency of any search program is to slow down (often combinatorially explosively) as additional assertions are added and the search space therefore grows. All our real and imagined intelligent systems must, at some level, be *searching* as they locate and apply general rules and as they locate and perform analogical (partial) matches. Is it inevitable, then, that programs must become less intelligent in their previously-competent areas, as their KB's grow? We believe not. The key to avoiding excess search is to have a little meta-knowledge to guide and constrain the search. Hence, the key to preserving effective intelligence of a growing program lies in judicious adding of meta-knowledge along with the addition of object-level knowledge. Some of the meta-knowledge is in the form of meta-rules, and some of it is encoded by the ontology of the KB; these are, respectively, the dynamic and static ways of effectively preserving whatever useful bundlings already existed in the KB. (Of course, meta-rules can and should be represented explicitly, declaratively, as well as having a procedural form. That way, meta-meta-knowledge can apply to *them*; and so on.) This is a prescription for one to gradually add and refine categories and predicates (types of slots) as one grows the KB. This is why we believe the KP works "in the large", why we can scale up a KB to immense size without succumbing to the combinatorial explosion. . . .

Empirical Inquiry Hypothesis (EH). The most profitable way to investigate AI is to embody our hypotheses into programs, and gather data by running the programs. The surprises usually suggest revisions that start the cycle over again. Progress depends on these experiments being able to *falsify* our hypotheses. Falsification is the most common and yet the most crucial of surprises. In particular, these programs must be capable of behavior not expected by the experimenter.

Difficult Problems Hypothesis. There are too many ways to solve simple problems. Raising the level and breadth of competence we demand of a system makes it *easier* to test—and raise—its intelligence.

The Knowledge Principle is a mandate for humanity to concretize the knowledge used in solving hard problems in various fields. This *might* lead to faster training based on explicit knowledge rather than apprenticeships. It has *already* led to thousands of profitable expert systems.

The Breadth Hypothesis is a mandate to spend the resources necessary to construct one immense knowledge base spanning human consensus reality, to serve as scaffolding for specific clusters of expert knowledge.

The Empirical Inquiry Hypothesis is a mandate to actually try to build such systems, rather than theorize about them and about intelligence. AI is a science when we use computers the way Tycho Brahe used the telescope, or Michaelson the interferometer—as a tool for looking at Nature, trying to test some hypothesis, and quite possibly getting rudely surprised by finding out that the hypothesis is false. There is quite a distinction between using a tool to gather data about the world, and using tools to, shall we say, merely fabricate ever more beautiful crystalline scale models of a geocentric universe. . . .

[The] various principles and hypotheses above combine to suggest a sweeping three-stage research program for the main enterprise of AI research:

(1) Slowly hand-code a large, broad knowledge base.

(2) Whenenough knowledge is present, it should be faster to acquire more from texts, databases, etc.

(3) To go beyond the frontier of human knowledge, the system will have to rely on learning by discovery, to expand its KB.

Some evidence is then presented that stages (1) and (2) may be accomplished by approximately this century; i.e., that artificial intelligence is within our grasp. Lenat's current work at MCC, on the CYC program, is a serious effort to carry out the first stage by the mid-1990's.

We are betting our professional lives—the few decades of useful research we have left in us—on KP, BH, and EH. That's a scary thought, but one has to place one's bets somewhere, in science. It's especially scary because:

(a) the hypotheses are not obvious to most AI researchers.

(b) they are unpalatable in many ways even to us, their advocates!

Why are they not obvious? Most AI research focuses on very small problems, attacking them with machinery (both hardware and search methods) that overpower them. The end result is a program that "succeeds" with very little knowledge, and so KP, BH, and EH *are irrelevant*. One is led to them only by tackling problems in difficult "real" areas, with the world able to surprise and falsify.

Why are our three hypotheses (KP, BH, EH) not particularly palatable? Because they are unaesthetic! And they entail person-centuries of hard knowledge-entry work. Until we are forced to them, Occam's Razor encourages us to try more elegant solutions, such as training a neutral net "from scratch"; or getting an infant-simulator and then "talking to it". Only as these fail do we turn, unhappily, to the "hand-craft a huge KB" tactic . . .

The biggest hurdle of all has already been put well behind us: the enormous local maximum of building and using *explicit-knowledge-free* systems. On the far side of that hill we found a much larger payoff, namely expert systems. We have learned how to build intelligent artifacts that perform well, using knowledge, on specialized tasks within narrowly defined domains. An industry has been formed to put this technological understanding to work, and widespread transfer of this technology has been achieved. Many fields are making that transition, from data processing to knowledge processing.

And yet we see expert systems technology, too, as just a local maximum. AI is finally beginning to move beyond that threshold. This paper presents what its authors glimpse on the far side of expert systems local-maximum hill; the promise of a large, broad KB serving as the nucleus of crystallization for programs which respond sensibly to novel situations because they can reason more by analogy than by perfect matching, and, ultimately, because, like us, they understand the meanings of their terms. (Lenat and Feigenbaum, 1991, pp. 185–189)

The Breadth Principle: Analogical Reasoning

Lenat and Feigenbaum (1991) summarize general uses of analogical reasoning in the following account:

Analogizing broadens the relevance of the entire knowledge base. It can be used to construct interesting and novel interpretations of situations and data; the retrieved knowledge that has not been stored the way that it is now needed; to guess values for attributes; to suggest methods that just might work; and as a device to help students learn and remember. It can provide access to powerful methods that might work in this case, but which might not otherwise be perceived as "relevant." E.g., Dirac analogized between quantum theory and group theory, and very gingerly brought the group theory results over into physics for the first time, with quite successful results.

Today, we suffer with laborious manual knowledge entry in building expert systems, carefully codifying knowledge and placing it in a data structure. Analogizing may be used in the future not only as an inference method inside a program, but also as an aid to adding new knowledge to it. (Lenat and Feigenbaum, 1991, p. 199)

CYC and Mapping Human Knowledge

According to Lenat and Feigenbaum (1991), it is possible to anticipate the general time frame and broad strategies required to construct a system that encompasses the realm of human knowledge:

AI must somehow get to that stage where—as called for by KP and BH—learning begins to accelerate due to the amount already known. Induction will not be an effective means to get to that stage, unfortunately; we shall have to hand-craft that large "seed" KB one piece at a time. In terms of the graph in [Figure 5.1], all the programs that have ever been written, including AM and EURISKO, lie so far toward the left edge of the x-axis that the learning rate is more or less zero. Several of the more successful recent additions to the suite of ML techniques can be interpreted as pushes in the direction of adding more knowledge from which to begin the learning.

The graph in [Figure 5.1] shows learning by induction (DISCOVERY) constantly accelerating: the more one knows, the faster one can discover still more. Once you speak fluently, learning by talking with other people (LANGUAGE) is more efficient than rediscovery, until you cross the frontier of what humanity already knows (the vertical line at $x = F$), at which point there is no one to tell you the next piece of knowledge. . . .

[Figure 5.1] illustrates two more things: learning by discovery is much *slower* than

Figure 5.1
The Rate at which One Can Learn New Knowledge (One can also integrate these three curves with respect to time, to see how the total amount known might grow over time.)

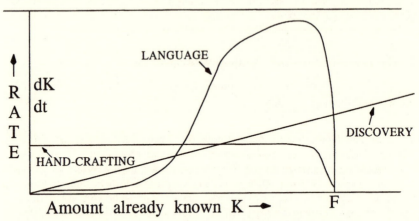

Source: Lenat and Feigenbaum (1991), p. 209. Reprinted with the permission of Elsevier Science Publishers.

other forms of learning—such as being told something in a natural language—but it is the chief method that extends the boundary F of human knowledge.

By contrast, the rate of hand-coding of knowledge is fairly constant, though it, too, drops to zero once we cross the boundary of what is already known by humanity. The hand-coding rate may slope down a bit, since the time to find related concepts will increase perhaps as the log of the size of the KB. Or, instead, the hand-coding rate may slope *up* a bit, since copy and edit is a powerful technique for knowledge entry, and, as the KB grows, there will be more chance that some very similar concept is already present.

This is an example of EH (the Empirical Inquiry Hypothesis . . .): Only by trying to hand-code the KB will we see which of those two counteracting factors outweighs the other, and by how much. Only by continued work on NL and ML will we determine whether or not there is a region, near where all three curves meet, where ML temporarily surpasses NL as a way to grow the KB. And only much further in the future, after our program crosses the frontier F will we find out if the discovery curve begins to slope up or down.

[Figure 5.1] suggests a sweeping three-stage research program for the coming three decades of AI research:

—Slowly hand-code a large knowledge base.

—When enough knowledge is present, it will be faster to acquire more through reading, assimilating databases, etc.

—To go beyond the frontier of human knowledge, the system will have to rely on learning by discovery, carrying out research and development projects to expand its KB.

Three decades? What are the scales on the axes of [Figure 5.1]? Why do we think it's not a three-*century* or three-*millennia* program? Even if the vague shapes of the curves are correct, and even if we are near the left edge, how far over to the right is that place where language understanding meets and then surpasses the hand-coding level? Might we need a trillion things in our knowledge base, in order to get analogy and generalization to pay off? The usefulness and timeliness of the Breadth Hypothesis rest on the following quantitative assumption:

> *Breadth is Within our Grasp.* A KB of about a million "frames" will provide a significant performance increase, due to generalization and analogy; this will consume about 2 person-centuries of time, about $50 million, and about 1 decade. Why such a "small size"? That's about all that people know! . . .

Two other ways for bounding the "bits" a human brain can store lead to much larger numbers: (1) counting neurons and synapses; but it's unclear how memories are stored in them; (2) counting pixels in our "mental images"; but controversy rages in cognitive psychology over whether mental imagery is just an illusion caused by the consistency and regularity in the world that lets us fill in missing pieces of memories—and of dynamic sensory experiences—with default values (see, e.g., Fodor & Pylyshyn, 1981). . . . (Also, though it's clearly an oversimplification, having a million entries means that there can be a trillion one-step inferences involving pairs of them. And it would surprise no one to discover that one-step inference is going on unconsciously in our minds constantly.)

Here again is a situation which one could apply to EH. Various theories give various estimates, and the way to settle the issue—and, perhaps, much more importantly, achieve the goal of having the KB we want—is to go off and try to build the large KB. Along the way, it will no doubt become clear how big it is growing and what the actual obstacles are that must be overcome. (Lenat and Feigenbaum, 1991, pp. 209–211)

In the process of building CYC, a number of surprising research results occur, as described in the following section:

Lenat started the CYC project in late 1984 for this very purpose. It is now halfway through its ten-year time frame, and, most surprisingly, it is still on schedule. A book describing the project and its philosophy has been published [Lenat and Guha, 1988], and the interested reader is referred there for details. Here, we shall just very briefly list a few of the surprises that actually trying to build this immense KB has engendered:

(1) The need for more formality, for a more principled representation language. In a typical expert system application, much of the meaning of an entry on a slot of a frame can be idiosyncratic to that particular application; but CYC, which might be used for any application, cannot afford such sloppiness. E.g., consider placing "IceCream" on the "likes" slot of the "Fred" frame. Does this mean that that's all he likes? Does he like all ice cream? In what sense does he like it? Has he

liked it from birth onward (and does it mean he'll like it until he dies), or is there some temporal sub-abstraction of Fred that likes it? etc.

(2) The search for a use-neutral control structure and use-neutral representation is not unlike the search for a single universal carpenter's tool. The pragmatic global *effect* of use-neutrality arises by having a large set of tools that complement each other (and sometimes overlap) and easily work together to get the most common jobs done. On very, very rare occasions, a new tool may have to get invented; use the existing ones to fabricate it then.

(3) In the case of control structure, CYC has by now amassed two dozen separate inference engines: inheritance, inverse slots, automatic classification, Horn clause rules, transfers through, etc. One lesson is that it is cost effective to write and fine-tune a separate truth (actually, justification) maintenance system (TMS) for each feature, rather than relying on any one general (but of necessity inefficient) TMS algorithm.

(4) In the case of representation, besides frames, we now have numerous other "tools". One of them is a powerful constraint language which is essentially predicate calculus. This is because much of the knowledge in the system is inherently constraint-like. Consider "The number of children that Joe and Sam have are equal." We could define a new slot sameNumberOfChildrenAs, and such tactics might well get us through any one application, but that's hardly a scalable solution. In general, though, we wanted, needed, and developed a general constraint language. The constraint language is superficially second-order; in almost all real uses, any quantification over predicates (slot names) can be mechanically reduced to first-order. Several dozen of the most common sorts of constraints (e.g., the domain and range of slots) have been "slotized"; i.e., special slots (in this case, makesSenseFor and entryIsA) have been created and optimized, but still the general language is there to fall back on when needed. From time to time, when numerous constraints of the same form have been entered, we "slotize" that form by defining a new slot. For instance, we could create sameNumberOfChildrenAs if there were really heavy use of that sort of constraint.

(5) There are almost ten times as many "frames" required as we had originally expected; luckily, our rate of knowledge entry is also that much faster, so we still hope to "finish" by 1994. In the search for eliminating ambiguity, the knowledge being entered must be more precise than we are used to being in everyday conversation. E.g., the meaning of "Japan" or "water" varies depending on the context of the conversation. Each separate meaning (e.g., political Japan of the 1890s) has its own frame, which is why there are more than we expected. But balancing that, it is relatively easy to build a knowledge entry tool which assists the user in copying and editing an entire cluster of related frames at once. So the two order-of-magnitude increases are not unrelated. By the way, "finishing in 1994" means approaching the crossover point [Figure 5.1], where it will be more cost effective to continue building CYC's KB by having it read online material, and ask questions about it, than to continue the sort of manual "brain-surgery" approach we are currently employing. (Lenat and Feigenbaum, 1991, pp. 211–212)

CYC and Expert Systems

Lenat and Feigenbaum (1991) address the problem of integrating hundreds of expert systems as an alternative strategy to that of CYC in attaining a single immense knowledge base.

The KP underlies the current explosion of work on expert systems (ESs). Still, there are additional things our position argues for, that are not yet realized in today's ESs. Knowledge space *in toto* is not a homogenous solid surface, but more like a set of self-supporting buttes, and one ought to be able to hop from one to its neighbors. But current ESs are too narrow, too independent, and too informal, as we discussed below.

One major power source for ESs, the reason they can be so readily constructed, is the synergistic additivity of many rules. Using a blackboard [Erman et al., 1980] or partitioned rule sets, it is possible to combine small packets of rules into mega-rules: knowledge sources for one large expert system.

The analogue at the next higher level would be to hook hundreds of large ESs together, and achieve even greater synergy. That dream repeatedly fails to materialize. Why? As we increase the domain of each "element" we are trying to couple together, the "semantic glue" we need gets to be larger and more sophisticated. The "gluing" or communicating is made all the more difficult by the unstated and often ambiguous semantics that typically exist in a single ES. We discussed, earlier, how the CYC project at MCC has been driven toward increased formality and precision as they have labored to build that large system. It seems to us that it will require the construction of such a system, as mandated by the Breadth Hypothesis, and built not haphazardly but with a clean and formalized semantics, before the true potential of ES technology will be realized.

Plateau-Hopping Requires Breadth

To harness the power of a large number of disparate expert systems will require something approaching full consensus reality—the millions of abstractions, models, facts, rules of thumb, representations, etc., that we all possess and that we assume everyone else does. Moreover, the ESs will need to be coded in a clean, formal representation, and integrated into a global ontology of knowledge. The INTERNIST program is carefully engineered to do a good job of diagnosing diseases from symptoms. But consider coupling it to a machine learning program, which tries to speculate on new disease mechanisms for epidemiology. The knowledge in INTERNIST isn't stored in "the right way", and much of the needed mechanism knowledge has *already* been compiled away, condensed into numeric correlations. Clancey encountered similar difficulties when he tried to adapt MYCIN's diagnostic KB to *teach* medical students [Clancey, 1979].

As we try to combine ESs from various tasks, even somewhat related tasks, their particular simplifications and idiosyncrasies prevent synergy. The simplifying was done in the interests of highly efficient and competent problem solving; breadth was not one of the engineering goals.

This naturally results in each ES being a separate, simplified, knowledge universe. Sometimes the ES's precipitous fall into incompetent behavior is obvious, but sometimes its explanations remain dangerously plausible. Meta-rules about the system's area of competence can guard against this accidental misuse, but that is just a patch. A true solution would be to provide a broad KB so that (1) the plateau sloped off gently on all sides, and (2) we could hop from one ES's plateau or butte to another.

> *The Local Consistency Hypothesis.* There is no need—and probably not even any possibility—of achieving a *global* consistent unification of several expert systems' KBs (or, equivalently, for one very large KB). Large systems need *local consistency*.
> *The Coherence Hypothesis.* Moreover, whenever two large internally consistent chunks C_1, C_2 are similar, their heuristics and analogies should *cohere*; e.g., if the "going up" metaphor usually means "getting better" for C_1, then it should again mean "getting better" for C_2, or else it should not apply at all there.

As regards local consistency, consider how physics advanced for many decades with inconsistent particle and wave models for light. Local consistency is what permits each knowledge-space butte to be independent of the others; as with large office buildings, independent supports should make it easier for the whole structure to weather tremors such as local anomalies. In a locally consistent system, inferring an inconsistency is only slightly more serious than the usual sort of "dead-end" a searcher runs into; the system should be able to back up a bit and continue on. Intelligent behavior derives not from the razor's edge of absolute true versus absolute false—from perfect matching—but rather is suggested by plausibility heuristics and supported by empirical evidence.

Coherence is what keeps one from getting disoriented in stepping from one KB butte to its neighbor. Having the metaphors line up coherently can make the hops so small that one is unaware they have hopped at all: "Her academic career, her mood, and her prospects were all going up." See [Lakoff and Johnson, 1980] for many more examples, and a more detailed discussion of this phenomenon. Coherence applies at the conceptual level, not just at the word level. It is not so much the *words* "going up" as the concept, the *script* of moving upwards, that applies coherently in so many situations. (Lenat and Feigenbaum, 1991, pp. 215–218; italics added)

CYC: Overcoming Limitations

In the following section, Lenat and Feigenbaum (1991) discuss their solutions to both "in principle" limitations and to problems encountered during the construction of CYC.

Problem 1. Possible "in-principle" limitations. There are several extremes that one can point to where the Knowledge Principle and Breadth Hypothesis might be inapplicable or even harmful: perceptual and motor tasks; certain tasks which must be performed in small pieces of real time; tasks that involve things we don't yet know how to represent well (the word "yet" is very important here); tasks for which an adequate algorithm exists; tasks so poorly understood that no one can do it well yet; and (until our proposed large KB becomes reality) tasks involving large amounts of common sense.

Just as we believe that language faculties will require a large consensual reality KB, we expect it to be invaluable in most of the image understanding process (beyond retina-level edge detection and similar operations).

Our response—in principle and in CYC—is to describe perception, emotion, motion, etc., down to some level of detail that enables the system to understand humans doing those things, and/or to be able to reason simply about them. As discussed under Problem 2, below, we let a large body of examples dictate what sorts of knowledge, and to what depth, are required.

A similar answer applies to all the items which we don't yet know very clearly how to represent. In building CYC, e.g., a large amount of effort in the first five years was spent on capturing an adequate body of knowledge (including representations and problem-solving strategies) for time, space, belief, substances, and so on. We did not set out to do this, the effort was driven completely empirically, completely by need, as we examined snippets of encyclopedia and newspaper articles and had to develop machinery to represent them and answer questions about them. Our response is a tactical hypothesis, not a strategic one; we would find it interesting if it is falsified, but the effect would be negligible on our overall research strategy.

Tasks which can be done without knowledge, or which require some that no one yet possesses, should be shied away from. One does not use a hammer to type with. . . .

This research opportunity is finally being pursued; but until CYC or a similar project succeeds, the knowledge-based approach must shy away from tasks that involve a great deal of wide-ranging common sense or analogy.

Problem 2. How exactly do we get the knowledge? Knowledge must be extracted from people, from databases, from the intelligent systems' KBs themselves (e.g., thinking up new analogies), and from Nature directly. Each source of knowledge requires its own special extraction methods.

In the case of the CYC project, the goal is to capture the full breadth of human knowledge. To drive the acquisition task, Lenat and his team examine pieces of text (chosen from encyclopediae, newspapers, advertisements, and so on), sentence by sentence. They aren't just entering the facts as stated, but—much more importantly—are encoding what the writer of that sentence already knew about the world. These are the facts and heuristics and simplified models of the world which one would need in order to understand the sentence, things which should be insulting or confusing for the writer to have actually stated explicitly (e.g., if coke is commercially consumed to turn ore into metal, then coke and ore must both be worth less than metal). They also generalize each of these as much as possible (e.g., the products of commercial processes are more valuable than their inputs). Another useful place they focus is the inter-sentential gap; in a historical article, what actions should the reader infer have happened between each sentence and the next one? Yet another focus: what questions should anyone be able to answer having just read that article? These foci drive the extraction process. Eventually, CYC itself began helping to add knowledge, by proposing analogues, extending existing analogies, and noticing gaps in nearly symmetric structures. . . .

Problem 3. How do we adequately represent it? Human experts choose or devise representations that enable the significant features of the problem to remain distinguished, for the relevant connections to be quickly found, etc. Thus, one can reduce this to a special case of Problem 2, and try to elicit appropriate representations from human experts. CYC takes a pragmatic approach: when something proves awkward to represent, add new kinds of slots to make it compactly representable. In extreme cases, add a whole new representation language to the toolkit. Besides frames and "rules" and our formal constraint language (described above), we use stored images and neural nets as representation schemes. Images are useful for users to point at; e.g., to say something about the strike plate of a door lock—if you don't happen to know what it's called, but you could pick it out instantly given a photo of a door lock. Statistical space partitioning (neural nets) may be useful for certain kinds of user modeling (e.g., gesture level), and the CYC group is currently training one on examples of good analogizing, so as to suggest promising "hunches" of new analogies to investigate, an activity which CYC will then do symbolically.

The quality of the solutions to many of these "Problems", including this one, depend on the quality of our system's emerging ontology. What category boundaries are drawn; what individuals get explicitly represented; what is the vocabulary of predicates (slots) with which to describe and interrelate them, etc.? Much of the 1984–89 work on CYC has been to get an adequate global ontology; i.e., has been worrying about ways to represent knowledge; most of the 1990–94 work will be actually representing knowledge, entering it into CYC. That is why we have "only" a million entries of CYC's KB today, but expect dozens of times that many in 1994. (Lenat and Feigenbaum, 1991, pp. 218–220)

CYC: Guiding Principles

Lenat and Feigenbaum (1991) summarize the basic principles underlying the CYC research project in the in the following account:

Our position includes the statements:

—One must include *domain-specific* knowledge to solve difficult problems effectively.

—One must also include both *very general* knowledge (to fall back on) and very *wide-ranging* knowledge (to analogize to) to cope with novel situations.

—We already have plenty of theories about mechanisms of intelligence; we need to proceed empirically: go off and build large testbeds for performing, analogizing, ML, NL, . . .

—Despite the progress in learning, language understanding, and other areas of AI, *hand-crafting* is still the fastest way to get the knowledge into the program for at least the next several years.

—With a large KB of facts, heuristics, and methods, the fastest way will, after some years, tip toward NL (reading online textual material), and then eventually toward ML (learning by discovery).

—The hand-crafting and language-based learning phases may each take about one decade, partially overlapping (ending in 1994 and 2001, respectively, although the second stage never quite "ends"), culminating in a system with human-level breadth and depth of knowledge.

Each of those statements is more strongly believed than the one following it. There is overwhelming evidence for the KP and EH. There is strong evidence in favor of the BH. There is a moderate basis for our three-stage program. And there is suggestive evidence that it may be possible to carry out the programs this century. (Lenat and Feigenbaum, 1991, pp. 223–224)

CYC: Social Implications

Lenat and Feigenbaum (1991) discuss the social implications of CYC and artificial intelligence, more generally, in the following section:

The impact of systems mandated by the KP and BH cannot be overestimated. Public education, e.g., is predicated on the *un*availability of an intelligent, competent tutor for each individual for each hour of their life. AI will change that. Our present entertainment industry is built largely on passive viewing; AI will turn "viewers" into "doers". What will happen to society as the cost of wisdom declines, and society routinely applies the best of what it knows? Will a *knowledge utility* arise, like an electric utility, and how might it (and other AI infrastructures) effect what will be economically affordable for personal use?

When we give talks on expert systems, on commonsense reasoning, or on AI in general, we are often asked about the ethical issues involved, the *mental* "environmental impact" it will have, so to speak, as well as the direct ways it will alter everyday life. We believe that this technology is the analogue of language. We cannot hold AI back any more than primitive man could have suppressed the spread of speaking. It is too powerful a technology for that. Language marks the start of what we think of as civilization; we look back on pre-linguistic cultures as uncivilized, as comprised of intelligent apes but not really human beings yet. Can we even imagine what it was like when people couldn't talk to each other? Minsky recently quipped that a century from now people might look back on us and wonder "Can you imagine when they used to have libraries where the books didn't talk to each other?" Our distant descendants may look back on the synergistic man-machine systems that emerge from AI, as the natural dividing line between "real human beings" and "animals". We stand, at the end of the 1980s, at the interstice between the first era of intelligent systems (competent, thanks to the KP, but quite brittle and incombinable) and the second era, the era in which the Breadth Hypothesis will finally come into play.

Man-Machine Synergy Prediction. In that "second era" of knowledge systems, the "system" will be reconceptualized as a kind of colleagular relationship between intelligent computer agents and intelligent people. Each will perform the tasks that he/she/it does best, and the intelligence of the system will be an emergent of the collaboration.

The interaction may be sufficiently seamless and natural that it will hardly matter to anyone which skills, which knowledge, and which ideas resided where (in the head of the person or the knowledge structures of the computer). It would be inaccurate to identify Intelligence, then, as being "in the program". From such man-machine systems will emerge intelligence and competence surpassing the unaided human's. Beyond that threshold, in turn, lie wonders which we (as unaided humans) literally cannot today imagine. (Lenat and Feigenbaum, 1991, pp. 224–225; italics added)

PHILOSOPHICAL AND PSYCHOLOGICAL IMPLICATIONS OF THE CYC PROJECT

The greatest of challenges for the CYC project is not the efficient organization of immense amounts of knowledge. A truly advanced intelligence must include a deep self-heightened comprehension of its own electronic information.

SHRDLU, ELIZA, PARRY, and other automata rely for any sense they make on the human users who project their full understanding and allowance onto an ignorant limited artifice that uses words but does not understand what the words mean, a situation analogous to that of the compact disc player that cannot understand what it is that it is performing that we recognize and appreciate as the violin trio.

Regarding SHRDLU (Winograd, 1972); ELIZA (Weizenbaum, 1965); PARRY (Colby, Weber, and Hilif, 1971); MYCIN (Shortliffe, 1976); MACSYMA (Norman, 1975; Zippel, 1976); DENDRAL (Lindsey et al., 1980); and so on none of these "artificial intelligences" know what they are talking about. They use words by parroting them or as children of six or seven might be taught to say $E = MC^2$ or indeed as college students can repeat a formula in mathematics or physics but not be able to put it into their own words to show that they know what they are talking about, what the structures of the mathematical symbols mean.

In their "intelligent" interactions with human beings, SHRDLU does not know what blocks are, ELIZA does not know what psychotherapy clients are, PARRY does not know what psychiatrists are, MACSYMA does not know mathematicians, MYCIN fails to know physicians, and DENDRAL is ignorant of chemists.

What happens is that humans project human knowledge on to the machines as they project advanced knowledge on to children who recite $E = MC^2$ or "vanity of vanities, all is vanity." We give to children, through a more advanced education, increasing knowledge of what it is that they are talking about, and, gradually, their understanding deepens and widens so that they can use mathematical symbols and literary phrases with the specific nuance required in given contexts.

Even if we so educate and develop our machines' artificial intelligence, there would be no point to doing so because it is, indeed, their automatic functions that we have designed them for—to perform symbolic operations for us, to perform services for us, to save us effort, to enable us to avoid repetitive tasks, and to protect us from mechanical errors. Human designers provide to machines only the minimum or necessary conditions to enable them to perform the skills of being mechanical intellectual servants; intellectual in the sense of performing mechanically some intellectual tasks rather than mechanically performing some physical task such as a plowing machine.

However, we do not give to machines, in addition to the necessary conditions, the sufficient conditions that involve knowledge of what it is that the machines are doing and judgments as to when that additional set of knowledge involved in the sufficient conditions renders the products of the machines valid.

And yet, paradoxically and poignantly, the automatic functions that computers achieve for us may result, in case of the most intellectual disciplines—mathematics—, in a desperate or laughable situation in which computers achieve mathematical proofs for us and cavalierly assert that we are incapable of comprehending their proofs.

Ronald L. Graham of AT&T Bell Laboratories suggests that the trend away from short, clear, conventional proofs that are beyond reasonable doubt may be inevitable. "The things you can prove may be just tiny islands, exceptions, compared to the vast sea of results that cannot be proved by human thought alone," he explains. Mathematicians become increasingly dependent on experiments, probabilistic proofs and other guides. "You may not be able to provide proofs in a classical sense," Graham says.

Of course, mathematics may yield fewer aesthetic satisfactions as investigators become more dependent on computers. "It would be very discouraging," Graham remarks, "if somewhere down the line you could ask a computer if the Riemann hypothesis is correct and it said, 'Yes, it is true, but you won't be able to understand the proof.' "

Traditionalists no doubt shudder at the thought. (Horgan, 1993, p. 103)

EXPLANATORY COHERENCE AND THE ECHO SYSTEM

The Theory of Explanatory Coherence: Overview

Thagard (1989) has developed an important theory of intelligent explanatory reasoning. The theory of explanatory coherence has been implemented in the ECHO system. Thagard (1989) presents a summary of his theory and his research program in the account.

This target article presents a new computational theory of explanatory coherence that applies to the acceptance and rejection of scientific hypotheses as well as to reasoning in everyday life. The theory consists of seven principles that establish relations of local coherence between a hypothesis and other propositions. A hypothesis coheres with propositions that it explains, or that explain it, or that participate with it in explaining other propositions, or that offer analogous explanations. Propositions are incoherent with each other if they are contradictory. Propositions that describe the results of observation have a degree of acceptability on their own. An explanatory hypothesis is accepted if it coheres better overall than its competitors. The power of the seven principles is shown by their implementation in a connectionist program called ECHO, which treats hypothesis evaluation as a constraint satisfaction problem. Inputs about the explanatory relations are used to create a network of units representing propositions, while coherence and incoherence relations are encoded by excitatory and inhibitory links. *ECHO provides an algorithm for smoothly integrating theory evaluation based on considerations of explanatory breadth, simplicity, and analogy. It has been applied to such important scientific cases as Lavoisier's argument for oxygen against the phlogiston theory and Darwin's argument for evolution against creationism, and also to cases of legal reasoning.* The theory of explanatory coherence has implications for artificial intelligence, psychology, and philosophy. (Thagard, 1989, p. 435; italics added)

The Theory of Explanatory Coherence: Principles

Thagard (1989) states the basic principles of the theory of explanatory coherence in the following terms:

I now propose seven principles that establish relations of explanatory coherence and make possible an assessment of the global coherence of an explanatory system S. S consists of propositions P, Q, $P_1 \ldots P_N$. Local coherence is a relation between two propositions. I coin the term "incohere" to mean more than just that two propositions do not cohere: To incohere is to *resist* holding together. The principles are as follows:

Principle 1. Symmetry

(a) If P and Q cohere, then Q and P cohere.
(b) If P and Q incohere, then Q and P incohere.

Principle 2. Explanation

If $P_1 \ldots P_N$ explain Q, then:
(a) For each P_X in $P_1 \ldots P_N$, P and Q cohere.
(b) For each P_X and P_Y in $P_1 \ldots P_N$, P_X and P_Y cohere.
(c) In (a) and (b), the degree of coherence is inversely proportional to the number of propositions $P_1 \ldots P_N$.

Principle 3. Analogy

(a) If P_1 explains Q_1, P_2 explains Q_2, P_1 is analogous to P_2, and Q_1 is analogous to Q_2, then P_1 and P_2 cohere, and Q_1 and Q_2 cohere.
(b) If P_1 explains Q_1, P_2 explains Q_2, Q_1 is analogous to Q_2, but P_1 is disanalogous to P_2, then P_1 and P_2 incohere.

Principle 4. Data Priority

Propositions that describe the results of observation have a degree of acceptability on their own.

Principle 5. Contradiction

If P contradicts Q, then P and Q incohere.

Principle 6. Acceptability

(a) The acceptability of a proposition P in a system S depends on its coherence with the proposition in S.
(b) If many results of relevant experimental observations are unexplained, then the acceptability of a proposition P that explains only a few of them is reduced.

Principle 7. System Coherence

The global explanatory coherence of a system S of propositions is a function of the pairwise local coherence of those propositions. (Thagard, 1989, pp. 436–437)

Thagard (1989) discusses the above seven principles of explanatory coherence theory in the following account:

Principle 1, Symmetry, asserts that pairwise coherence and incoherence are symmetric relations, in keeping with the everyday sense of coherence as holding together. The coherence of two propositions is thus very different from the nonsymmetric relations of entailment and conditional probability. Typically, P entails Q without Q entailing P, and the conditional probability of P given Q is different from the probability of Q given P. But if P and Q hold together, so do Q and P. The use of symmetrical relation has advantages that will become clearer in the discussion of the connectionist implementation below.

Principle 2, Explanation, is by far the most important for assessing explanatory coherence, because it establishes most of the coherence relations. Part (a) is the most obvious: If a hypothesis P is part of the explanation of a piece of evidence Q, then P and Q cohere. Moreover, if a hypothesis P_1 is explained by another hypothesis P_2, then P_1 and P_2 cohere. Part (a) presupposes that explanation is a more restrictive relation than deductive implication, because otherwise we could prove that any two propositions cohere; unless we use relevance logic (Anderson & Belnap, 1975), P_1 and the contradiction P_1 & not-P_1 imply any Q, so it would follow that P_1 coheres with Q. *It follows from Principle 2 (a), in conjunction with Principle 6, that the more a hypothesis explains, the more coherent and hence acceptable it is. Thus, this principle subsumes the criterion of explanatory breadth (which Whewell, 1967, called "consilience") that I have elsewhere claimed to be the most important for selecting the best explanation* (Thagard, 1978, 1988a).

Whereas part (a) of Principle 2 says that what explains coheres with what is explained, part (b) states that 2 propositions cohere if together they provide an explanation. Behind part (b) is the Duhem-Quine idea that the evaluation of a hypothesis depends partly on the other hypotheses with which it furnishes explanations (Duhem, 1954; Quine, 1961; ...). I call two hypotheses that are used together in an explanation "cohypotheses." Again I assume that explanation is more restrictive than implication; otherwise it would follow that any proposition that explained something was coherent with every other proposition, because if P_1 implies Q, then so does P_2 & P_N. But any scientist who maintained at a conference that the theory of general relativity and today's baseball scores together explain the motion of planets would be laughed off the podium. Principle 2 is intended to apply to explanations and hypotheses actually proposed by scientists.

Part (c) of Principle 2 embodies the claim that if numerous propositions are needed to furnish explanation, then the coherence of the explaining propositions with each other and with what is explained is thereby diminished. Scientists tend to be skeptical of hypotheses that require myriad *ad hoc* assumptions in their explanations. There is nothing wrong in principle in having explanations that draw on many assumptions, but we should prefer theories that generate explanations using a unified core of hypotheses. I have elsewhere contended that the notion of *simplicity* most appropriate for scientific theory choice is a comparative one preferring theories that make fewer special assumptions (Thagard, 1978, 1988a). Principles 2 (b) and 2 (c) together subsume this criterion. I shall not attempt further to characterize "degree of coherence" here, but the connectionist algorithm described below provides a natural interpretation. Many other notions of simplicity have been proposed (e.g., Foster & Martin, 1966; Harman et al., 1988), but none is so directly relevant to considerations of explanatory coherence as the one embodied in Principle 2.

The third criterion for the best explanation in my earlier account was analogy, and this is subsumed in Principle 3. There is controversy about whether analogy is of more heuristic use, but scientists such as Darwin have used analogies to defend their theories; his argument for evolution by natural selection is analyzed below. Principle 3 (a) does not say simply that any two analogous propositions cohere. There must be an explanatory analogy, with two analogous propositions occurring in explanations of two other propositions that are analogous to each other. Recent computational models of analogical mapping and retrieval show how such correspondences can be noticed (Thagard, et al., 1989). Principle 3 (b) says that when similar phenomena are explained by dissimilar hypotheses, the hypotheses incohere. Although the use of such disanalogies is not as common as the use of analogies, it was important in the reasoning that led Einstein (1952) to the special theory of relativity: He was bothered by asymmetries in the way Maxwell's electrodynamics treated the case of (1) a magnet in motion and a conductor at rest quite differently from the case of (2) a magnet at rest and a conductor in motion.

Principle 4, Data Priority, stands much in need of elucidation and defense. In saying that a proposition describing the results of observation has a degree of acceptability on its own, I am not suggesting that it is indubitable, but only that it can stand on its own more successfully than can a hypothesis whose sole justification is what it explains. A proposition Q may have some independent acceptability and still end up not accepted, if it is only coherent with propositions that are themselves not acceptable.

From the point of view of explanatory coherence alone, we should not take propositions based on observation as independently acceptable without any explanatory relations to other propositions. As Bonjour (1985) argues, the coherence of such propositions is of a nonexplanatory kind, based on background knowledge that observations of certain sorts are very likely to be true. From past experience, we know that our observations are very likely to be true, so we should believe them unless there is substantial reason not to. Similarly, at a very different level, we have some confidence in the reliability of descriptions of experimental results in carefully refereed scientific journals. . . .

Principle 5, Contradiction, is straightforward. By "contradictory" here I mean not just syntactic contradictions like P & not-P, but also semantic contradictions such as "This ball is black all over" and "This ball is white all over." In scientific cases, contradiction becomes important when incompatible hypotheses compete to explain the same evidence. Not all competing hypotheses incohere, however, because many phenomena have multiple causes. For example, explanations of why someone has certain medical symptoms may involve hypotheses that the patient has various diseases, and it is possible that more than one disease is present. Competing hypotheses incohere if they are contradictory or if they are framed as offering *the* most likely cause of a phenomenon. In the latter case, we get a kind of pragmatic contradictoriness: Two hypotheses may not be syntactically or semantically contradictory, yet scientists will view them as contradictory because of background beliefs suggesting that only one of the hypotheses is acceptable. For example, in the debate over dinosaur extinction (Thagard, 1988b), scientists generally treat as contradictory the following hypotheses:

(1) Dinosaurs became extinct because of a meteorite collision.

(2) Dinosaurs became extinct because the sea level fell.

Logically, (1) and (2) could both be true, but scientists treat them as conflicting explanations, possibly because there are no explanatory relations between them and their conjunction is unlikely.

The relation "cohere" is not transitive. If P_1 and P_2 together explain Q, while P_1 and P_3 together explain not-Q, then P_1 coheres with both Q and not-Q, which incohere. Such cases do occur in science. Let P_1 be the gas law that volume is proportional to temperature, P_2 a proposition describing the drop in temperature of a particular sample of gas, P_3 a proposition describing the rise in temperature of the sample, and Q a proposition about increases in the sample's volume. Then P_1 and P_2 together explain a decrease in the volume, while P_1 and P_3 explain the increase.

Principle 6, Acceptability, proposes in part (a) that we can make sense of the overall coherence of a proposition in an explanatory system just from the pairwise coherence relations established by Principles 1–5. If we have a hypothesis P that coheres with evidence Q by virtue of explaining it, but incoheres with another contradictory hypothesis, should we accept P? To decide, we cannot merely count the number of propositions with which P coheres and incoheres, because of the acceptability of P depends in part on the acceptability of those propositions themselves. We need a dynamic and parallel method of deriving general coherence from particular coherence relations; such a method is provided by the connectionist program described below.

Principle 6 (b), reducing the acceptability of a hypothesis when much of the relevant evidence is unexplained by any hypothesis, is intended to handle cases where the best available hypothesis is still not very good, in that it accounts for only a fraction of the available evidence. Consider, for example, a theory in economics that could explain the stock market crashes of 1929 and 1987 but that had nothing to say about myriad other similar economic events. Even if the theory gave the best available account of the two crashes, we would not be willing to elevate it to an accepted part of general economic theory. What does "relevant" mean here? [See BBS multiple book review of Sperber and Wilson's *Relevance*, 1987.] As a first approximation, we can say that a piece of evidence is *directly* relevant to a hypothesis if the evidence is explained by it or by one of its competitors. We can then add that a piece of evidence is relevant if it is directly relevant or if it is similar to evidence that is relevant, where similarity is a matter of dealing with phenomena of the same kind. Thus, a theory of the business cycle that applies to the stock market crashes of 1929 and 1987 should also have something to say about nineteenth-century crashes and major business downturns in the twentieth century.

The final principle, System Coherence, proposes that we can have some global measure of the coherence of a whole system of propositions. Principles 1–5 imply that, other things being equal, a system S will tend to have more global coherence than another if,

(1) S has more data in it;

(2) S has more internal explanatory links between propositions that cohere because of explanations and analogies, and;

(3) S succeeds in separating coherent subsystems of propositions from conflicting subsystems.

The connectionist algorithm described below comes with a natural measure of global system coherence. It also indicates how different priorities can be given to the different principles. (Thagard, 1989, pp. 437–438; italics added)

ECHO: Input Formulas

The principles of explanatory coherence are represented in the connectionist program ECHO. In the following section, Thagard (1989) describes the input formulas to ECHO:

Let us now look at ECHO, a computer program written in Common LISP that is a straightforward application of connectionist algorithms to the problem of explanatory coherence. In ECHO, propositions representing hypotheses and results of observations are represented by units. Whenever Principles 1–5 state that two propositions cohere, an excitatory link between them is established. If two propositions incohere, an inhibitory link between them is established. In ECHO, these links are symmetric, as Principle 1 suggests: The weight from unit 1 to unit 2 is the same as the weight from unit 2 to unit 1. Principle 2 (c) says that the larger the number of propositions used in an explanation, the smaller the degree of coherence between each pair of propositions. ECHO therefore counts the number of propositions that do the explaining and proportionately lowers the weight of the excitatory links between units representing coherent propositions. . . .

The following are some examples of the LISP formulas that constitute ECHO's inputs (I omit LISP quote symbols; see [Tables 5.1–5.4] for actual input):

1. (EXPLAIN (H1 H2) E1)
2. (EXPLAIN (H1 H2 H3) E2)
3. (ANALOGOUS (H5 H6) (E5 E6))
4. (DATA (E1 E2 E5 E6))
5. (CONTRADICT H1 H4)

Formula 1 says that hypotheses H1 and H2 together explain evidence E1. As suggested by the second principle of explanatory coherence proposed above, formula 1 sets up three excitatory links, between units representing H1 and E1, H2 and E1, and H1 and H2. Formula 2 sets up six such links, between each of the hypotheses and the evidence, and between each pair of hypotheses, but the weight on the links will be less than those established by formula 1, because there are more cohypotheses. In accord with Principle 3 (a), Analogy, formula 3 produces excitatory links between H5 and H6, and between E5 and E6, if previous input has established that H5 explains E5 and H6 explains E6. Formula 4 is used to apply Principle 4, Data Priority, setting up explanation-independent excitatory links to each data unit from a special evidence unit. Finally, formula 5 sets up an inhibitory link between contradictory hypotheses H1 and H4, as prescribed by Principle 5. A full specification of ECHO's inputs and algorithms is provided in the Appendix. (Thagard, 1989, pp. 439–440)

ECHO: General Characteristics

In the following section Thagard (1989) summarizes the chief characteristics and capabilities of ECHO.

Program runs show that the networks thus established have numerous desirable properties. *Other things being equal, activation accrues to units corresponding by hypotheses that explain more, provide simpler explanations, and are analogous to other explanatory hypotheses.* The considerations of explanatory breadth, simplicity, and analogy are smoothly integrated. The networks are holistic, in that the activation of every unit can potentially have an effect on every other unit linked to it by a path, however lengthy. Nevertheless, the activation of a unit is directly affected by only those units to which it is linked. Although complexes of coherent propositions are evaluated together, different hypotheses in a complex can finish with different activations, depending on their particular coherence relations. The symmetry of excitatory links means that the active units tend to bring up the activation of units with which they are linked, whereas units whose activation sinks below O tend to bring down the activation of units to which they are linked. Data units are given priority, but can nevertheless be deactivated if they are linked to units that become deactivated. So long as excitation is not set too high . . . , the networks set up by ECHO are stable: In most of them, all units reach asymptotic activation levels after fewer than 100 cycles of updating. The most complex network implemented so far, comparing the explanatory power of Copernicus's heliocentric theory with Ptolemy's geocentric one, requires about 210 cycles before its more than 150 units have all settled. (Thagard, 1989, p. 440; italics added)

ECHO: Applications to Scientific Explanatory Reasoning

ECHO has been applied to the comparative evaluation of competing scientific explanations as described by Thagard (1989) in the following section:

To show the historical application of the theory of explanatory coherence, I shall discuss two important cases of arguments concerning the best explanation: Lavoisier's argument for his oxygen theory against the phlogiston theory, and Darwin's argument for evolution by natural selection. ECHO has been applied to the following:

Contemporary debates about why the dinosaurs became extinct (Thagard, 1988b);

Arguments by Wegener and his critics for and against continental drift (Thagard & Nowak 1988);

Psychological experiments on how beginning students learn physics (Ranney & Thagard 1988) and;

Copernicus's case against Ptolemaic astronomy (Nowak & Thagard, forthcoming). (Thagard, 1989, p. 444)

ECHO Applied to the Scientific Explanatory Reasoning of Lavoisier

In the following section Thagard (1989) presents an interesting account of how the competing phlogiston and oxygen theories were evaluated by ECHO:

In the middle of the eighteenth century, the dominant theory in chemistry was the phlogiston theory of Stahl, which provided explanations of important phenomena of combustion, respiration, and calcination (what we would call oxidation). According to

Table 5.1
Input Propositions for Lavoisier (1862) Example

Evidence

(proposition 'E1	"In combustion, heat and light are given off.")
(proposition 'E2	"Inflammability is transmittable from one body to another.")
(proposition 'E3	"Combustion only occurs in the presence of pure air.")
(proposition 'E4	"Increase in weight of a burned body is exactly equal to the weight of the air absorbed.")
(proposition 'E5	"Metals undergo calcination.")
(proposition 'E6	"In calcination, bodies increase weight.")
(proposition 'E7	"In calcination, volume of air diminishes.")
(proposition 'E8	"In reduction, effervescence appears.")

Oxygen Hypotheses

(proposition 'OH1	"Pure air contains oxygen principle.")
(proposition 'OH2	"Pure air contains matter of fire and heat.")
(proposition 'OH3	"In combustion, oxygen from the air combines with the burning body.")
(proposition 'OH4	"Oxygen has weight.")
(proposition 'OH5	"In calcination, metals add oxygen to become calxes.")
(proposition 'OH6	"In reduction, oxygen is given off.")

Phlogiston Hypotheses

(proposition 'PH1	"Combustible bodies contain phlogiston.")
(proposition 'PH2	"Combustible bodies contain matter of heat.")
(proposition 'PH3	"In combustion, phlogiston is given off.")
(proposition 'PH4	"Phlogiston can pass from one body to another.")
(proposition 'PH5	"Metals contain phlogiston.")
(proposition 'PH6	"In combustion, phlogiston is given off.")

Source: Thagard (1989), p. 444. Reprinted with the permission of Cambridge University Press.

the phlogiston theory, combustion takes place when phlogiston in burning bodies is given off. In the 1770's, Lavoisier developed the alternative theory that combustion takes place when burning bodies combine with oxygen from the air (for an outline of the conceptual development of his theory, see Thagard, in press b). More than ten years after he first suspected the inadequacy of the phlogiston theory, Lavoisier mounted a full-blown attack on it in a paper called "Reflexions sur le Phlogistique" (Lavoisier, 1862).

[Tables 5.1 and 5.2] present the input given to ECHO to represent Lavoisier's argument in his 1783 polemic against phlogiston. [Table 5.1] shows the 8 propositions used to represent the evidence to be explained and the 12 used to represent the competing theories. The evidence concerns different properties of combustion and calcination, while there are two sets of hypotheses representing the oxygen and phlogiston theories, respectively. . . .

Table 5.2
Input Explanations and Contradictions in Lavoisier (1862) Example

---

Oxygen Explanations
    (explain '(OH1 OH2 OH3) 'E1)
    (explain '(OH1 OH3) 'E3)
    (explain '(OH1 OH3 OH4) 'E4)
    (explain '(OH1 OH5) 'E5)
    (explain '(OH1 OH4 OH5) 'E6)
    (explain '(OH1 OH5) 'E7)
    (explain '(OH1 OH6) 'E8)

Phlogiston Explanations
    (explain '(PH1 PH2 PH3) 'E1)
    (explain '(PH1 PH3 PH4) 'E2)
    (explain '(PH5 PH6) 'E5)

Contradictions
    (contradict 'PH3 'OH3)
    (contradict 'PH6 'OH5)

Data
    (data '(E1 E2 E3 E4 E5 E6 E7 E8))

Source: Thagard (1989), p. 445. Reprinted with the permission of Cambridge University Press.

[Table 5.2] shows the part of the input that sets up the network used to make a judgement of explanatory coherence. The "explain" statements are based directly on Lavoisier's assertions about what is explained by the phlogiston theory and the oxygen theory. The "contradict" statements reflect my judgement of which of the oxygen hypotheses conflict directly with which of the phlogiston theories. . . . When ECHO runs this network, starting with all hypotheses at activation .01, it quickly favors the oxygen hypotheses, giving them activations greater than 0. In contrast, all of the phlogiston hypotheses become deactivated.

Lavoisier's argument represents a relatively simple application of ECHO, showing two sets of hypotheses competing to explain the evidence. But more complex explanatory relations can also be important. Sometimes a hypothesis that explains the evidence is itself explained by another hypothesis. Depending on the warrant for the higher-level hypothesis, this extra explanatory layer can increase acceptability: A hypothesis gains from being explained as well as by explaining the evidence. The Lavoisier example does not exhibit this kind of coherence, because neither Lavoisier or the phlogiston theorists attempted to explain their hypotheses using higher-level hypotheses; nor does the example display the role that analogy can play in explanatory coherence. (Thagard, 1989, pp. 445–446)

ECHO Applied to the Scientific Explanatory Reasoning of Darwin

The power of ECHO to evaluate competing scientific arguments is demonstrated in the following comparison of evolutionary and creationist theories:

Both these aspects—coherence based on being explained and on analogy—were important in Darwin's argument for his theory of evolution by natural selection (Darwin 1962). His two most important hypotheses were:

DH2—Organic beings undergo natural selection.

DH3—Species of organic beings have evolved.

These hypotheses together enabled him to explain a host of facts, from the geographical distribution of similar species to existence of vestigial organs. Darwin's argument was explicitly comparative: There are numerous places in the *Origin* where he points to phenomena that his theory explains but that are inexplicable on the generally accepted rival hypothesis that species were separately created by God.

Darwin's two main hypotheses were not simply cohypotheses, however, for he also used DH2 to explain DH3! That is, natural selection explains why species evolve: If populations of animals vary, and natural selection picks out those with features well adapted to particular environments, then new species will arise. Moreover, he offers a Malthusian explanation for why natural selection occurs as the result of the geometrical rate of population growth contrasted with the arithmetical rate of increase in land and food. Thus Malthusian principles explain why evolution occurs, and natural selection and evolution together explain a host of facts better than the competing creation hypothesis does.

The full picture is even more complicated than this, for Darwin frequently cites the analogy between artificial and natural selection as evidence for his theory. He contends that just as farmers are able to develop new breeds of domesticated animals, so natural selection has produced new species. He uses this analogy not simply to defend natural selection, but also to help in the explanations of the evidence: Particular explanations using natural selection incorporate the analogy with artificial selection. Finally, to complete the picture of explanatory coherence that the Darwin example offers, we must consider the alternative theological explanations that were accepted by even the best scientists until Darwin proposed his theory.

Analysis of *On the origin of species* suggests the 15 evidence statements shown in [Table 5.3]. Statements E1–E4 occur in Darwin's discussion of objections to his theory; the others are from the later chapters where he argues for his theory. [Table 5.3] also shows Darwin's main hypotheses. DH2 and DH3 are the core of the theory of evolution by natural selection, providing explanations of its main evidence, E5–E15. DH4–DH6 are auxiliary hypotheses that Darwin uses in resisting objections based on E1–E3. He considers the objections concerning the absence of transitional forms to be particularly serious, but explains it away by saying the geological record is so imperfect that we should not expect to find fossil evidence of the many intermediate species his theory requires.... The creationist opposition frequently mentioned by

Table 5.3
Explanations and Contradictions for Darwin (1962) Example

Darwin's Evidence

(proposition 'E1	"The fossil record contains few transitional forms.")
(proposition 'E2	"Animals have complex organs.")
(proposition 'E3	"Animals have instincts.")
(proposition 'E4	"Species when crossed become sterile.")
(proposition 'E5	"Species become extinct.")
(proposition 'E6	"Once extinct, species do not reappear.")
(proposition 'E7	"Forms of life change almost simultaneously around the world.")
(proposition 'E8	"Extinct species are similar to each other and to living forms.")
(proposition 'E9	"Barriers separate similar species.")
(proposition 'E10	"Related species are concentrated in the same areas.")
(proposition 'E11	"Oceanic islands have few inhabitants, often of peculiar species.")
(proposition 'E12	"Species show systematic affinities.")
(proposition 'E13	"Different species share similar morphology.")
(proposition 'E14	"The embryos of different species are similar.")
(proposition 'E15	"Animals have rudimentary and atrophied organs.")

Darwin's Main Hypotheses

(proposition 'DH1	"Organic beings are in a struggle for existence.")
(proposition 'DH2	"Organic beings undergo natural selection.")
(proposition 'DH3	"Species of organic beings have evolved.")

Darwin's Auxiliary Hypotheses

(proposition 'DH4	"The geological record is very imperfect.")
(proposition 'DH5	"There are transitional forms of complex organs.")
(proposition 'DH6	"Mental qualities vary and are inherited.")

Darwin's Facts

(proposition 'DF1	"Domestic animals undergo variation.")
(proposition 'DF2	"Breeders select desired features of animals.")
(proposition 'DF3	"Domestic varieties are developed.")
(proposition 'DF4	"Organic beings in nature undergo variation.")
(proposition 'DF5	"Organic beings increase in population at a high rate.")
(proposition 'DF6	"The sustenance available to organic beings does not increase at a high rate.")
(proposition 'DF7	"Embryos of different domestic varieties are similar.")

Creationist Hypothesis

(proposition 'CH1	"Species were separately created by God.")

Source: Thagard (1989), p. 448. Reprinted with the permission of Cambridge University Press.

Darwin is represented by the single hypothesis that species were separately created by God.

[Table 5.4] shows the explanation and contradiction statements that ECHO uses to set up its network,.... [There is a] hierarchy of explanations, with the high rate of population increase explaining the struggle for existence, which explains natural selec-

Table 5.4

Input Explanations and Contradictions in Darwin (1962) Example

---

Darwin's Explanations

    (a) of natural selection and evolution
    (explain '(DF5 DF6) 'DH1)
    (explain '(DH1 DF4) 'DH2)
    (explain '(DH2) 'DH3)
    (b) of potential counterevidence
    (explain '(DH2 DH3 DH4) 'E1)
    (explain '(DH2 DH3 DH5) 'E2)
    (explain '(DH2 DH3 DH6) 'E3)
    (c) of diverse evidence
    (explain '(DH2) 'E5)
    (explain '(DH2 DH3) 'E6)
    (explain '(DH2 DH3) 'E7)
    (explain '(DH2 DH3) 'E8)
    (explain '(DH2 DH3) 'E9)
    (explain '(DH2 DH3) 'E10)
    (explain '(DH2 DH3) 'E11)
    (explain '(DH2 DH3) 'E12)
    (explain '(DH2 DH3) 'E13)
    (explain '(DH2 DH3) 'E14)
    (explain '(DH2 DH3) 'E15)
Darwin's Analogies
    (explain '(DF2) 'DF3)
    (explain '(DF2) 'DF7)
    (analogous '(DF2 DH2) '(DF3 DH3))
    (analogous '(DF2 DH2) '(DF7 E14))
Creationist Explanations
    (explain '(CH1) 'E1)
    (explain '(CH1) 'E2)
    (explain '(CH1) 'E3)
    (explain '(CH1) 'E4)
Contradiction
    (contradict 'CH1 'DH3)
Data
    (data '(E1 E2 E3 E4 E5 E6 E7 E8 E9 E10 E11 E12 E13 E14 E15))
    (data '(DF1 DF2 DF3 DF4 DF5 DF6 DF7))

Source: Thagard (1989), p. 449. Reprinted with the permission of Cambridge University Press.

tion, which explains evolution. Natural selection and evolution together explain many pieces of evidence. The final component of Darwin's argument is the analogy between natural and artificial selection. . . . Just as breeders' actions explain the development of domestic varieties, so natural selection explains the evolution of species. At another level, Darwin sees an embryological analogy. The embryos of different domestic varieties are quite similar to each other, which is explained by the fact that breeders do not select for properties of embryos. Similarly, nature does not select for most properties of embryos, which explains the similarities between embryos of different species.

Darwin's discussion of objections suggests that he thought creationism could naturally explain the absence of transitional forms and the existence of complex organs and instincts. Darwin's argument was challenged in many ways, but based on his own view of the relevant explanatory relations, at least, the theory of evolution by natural selection is far more coherent than the creation hypothesis. Creationists, of course, would marshal different arguments. . . . Running ECHO to adjust the network to maximize harmony produces the expected result: Darwin's hypotheses are all activated, whereas the creation hypothesis is deactivated. In particular, the hypothesis DH3—that species evolved—reaches an asymptote at .921, while the creation hypothesis, CH1, declines to $-.491$. DH3 accrues activation in three ways. It gains activation from above, from being explained by natural selection, which is derived from the struggle for existence, and from below, by virtue of the many pieces of evidence that it helps to explain. In addition, it receives activation by virtue of the sideways, analogy-based links with explanations using artificial selection. . . .

The Lavoisier and Darwin examples show that ECHO can handle very complex examples of actual scientific reasoning. One might object that in basing ECHO analyses on written texts, I have been modeling the rhetoric of the scientists, not their cognitive processes. Presumably, however, there is some correlation between what we write and what we think. ECHO could be equally well applied to explanatory relations that were asserted in the heat of verbal debate among scientists. Ranney and Thagard (1988) describe ECHO's simulation of naive subjects learning physics, where the inputs to ECHO were based on verbal protocols. (Thagard, 1989, pp. 446–449)

ECHO as a Psychological Model of Belief Change

The psychological validity of ECHO as a model of belief change has been experimentally investigated by Ranney and Thagard (1988). A brief summary of this research is given in the following section:

Ranney and Thagard (1988) describe the use of ECHO to model the inferences made by naive subjects learning elementary physics by using feedback provided on a computer display (Ranney 1987). Subjects were asked to predict the motion of several projectiles and then explain these predictions. Analysis of verbal protocol data indicate that subjects sometimes underwent dramatic belief revisions while offering predictions or receiving empirical feedback. ECHO was applied to two particularly interesting cases of belief revision with propositions and explanatory relations based on the verbal protocols. The simulations captured well the dynamics of belief change as new evidence was added to shift the explanatory coherence of the set of propositions. (Thagard, 1989, p. 461)

The Theory of Explanatory Coherence: Scope and Power

Thagard (1989) provides the following summary account of the major strengths of the theory of explanatory coherence and the ECHO system:

I conclude with a brief summary of the chief accomplishments of the theory of explanatory coherence offered here.

First, it fits directly with the actual arguments of scientists such as Lavoisier and Darwin who explicitly discuss what competing theories explain. There is no need to postulate probabilities or contrive deductive relations. The theory and ECHO have engendered a far more detailed analysis of these arguments than is typically given by proponents of other accounts. Using the same principles, it applies to important cases of legal reasoning as well.

Second, unlike most accounts of theory evaluation, this view based on explanatory coherence is inherently comparative. If two hypotheses contradict each other, they incohere, so the subsystems of propositions to which they belong will compete with each other. As ECHO shows, successful subsystems of hypotheses and evidence can emerge gracefully from local judgements of explanatory coherence.

Third, the theory of explanatory coherence permits a smooth integration of diverse criteria such as explanatory breadth, simplicity, and analogy. *ECHO's connectionist algorithm shows the computability of coherence relations. The success of the program is best attributed to the usefulness of the connectionist architectures for achieving parallel constraint satisfaction, and to the fact that the problem inherent in inference to the best explanation is the need to satisfy multiple constraints simultaneously.* Not all computational problems are best approached this way, but parallel constraint satisfaction has proven to be very powerful for other problems as well—for example, analogical mapping (Holyoak and Thagard, 1989).

Finally, my theory surmounts the problem of holism. The principles of explanatory coherence establish pairwise relations of coherence between propositions in an explanatory system. Thanks to ECHO, we know that there is an efficient algorithm for adjusting a system of propositions to turn coherence relations into judgements of acceptability. The algorithm allows every proposition to influence every other one, because there is typically a path of links between any two units, but the influences are set up systematically to reflect explanatory relations. Theory assessment is done as a whole, but a theory does not have to be rejected or accepted as a whole. Those hypotheses that participate in many explanations will be much more coherent with the evidence, and with each other, and will therefore be harder to reject. More peripheral hypotheses may be deactivated even if the rest of the theory they are linked to wins. We thus get a holistic account of inference that can nevertheless differentiate between strong and weak hypotheses. Although our hypotheses face evidence only as a corporate body, evidence and relations of explanatory coherence suffice to separate good hypotheses from bad. (Thagard, 1989, p. 465; italics added)

Commentary

There are two primary ways in which to establish the significance of the theory of explanatory coherence and the ECHO system. The first regards the adequacy of ECHO as a model of human explanatory reasoning. The second regards its adequacy as a computational approach to explanatory reasoning.

ECHO as a Model of Human Explanatory Reasoning

Human explanatory reasoning involves both conscience, symbolic, intentional, and serial processing and unconscious, implicit, emergent, and parallel processing periods. ECHO cannot serve as a model of the former set of characteristics, but as a connectionist architecture it may serve as an approximation to the latter set of characteristics.

ECHO as a Computational Approach to Explanatory Reasoning

ECHO appears to be an important computational approach to establishing the coherence of hypotheses and evidence. ECHO accomplishes its integrated function by means of an algorithm that meets the requirements of parallel constraint satisfaction.

ECHO is a computational mechanism that embodies the basic principles of the theory of explanatory coherence. ECHO and its underlying theory can be evaluated against the criterion of generality of application. Table 5.5 demonstrates generality across the domains of scientific and everyday explanatory reasoning.

Table 5.5
The Generality of Intelligent Explanatory Reasoning: Applications of ECHO

Application of ECHO	Reference
Evaluation of the oxygen theory versus the phlogiston theory (Lavoisier)	Thagard (1989)
Evaluation of evolutionary theory versus creationist theory (Darwin)	Thagard (1989)
Evaluation of theories concerning extinction of the dinosaurs	Thagard (1988b)
Evaluation of theories concerning continental drift	Thagard & Nowak (1988; in press)
Application of problem solving in physics	Ranney & Thagard (1988)
Evaluation of Copernican astronomy versus Ptolemian astronomy	Nowak & Thagard (forthcoming)
Evaluation of legal reasoning	Thagard (1989)
Evaluation of text comprehension	Schank & Ranney (1991)
Evaluation of belief revision in naive physics	Schank & Ranney (1992)
Evaluation of adversarial argumentation	Thagard (1993)
Perception of social relationships	Miller & Read (1991); Read & Marcus-Newell (1991)
Evaluation of debate between Newton and DeCarr	Nowak (in press-b)

6

The Surpassing of Human Intelligence

ARTIFICIAL INTELLIGENCE AND THE PROCESSES OF SCIENTIFIC DISCOVERY

The General Logic of Computational Theories of Scientific Discovery

The general logic of computational theories of scientific discovery includes the assumption that the creative processes of scientific discovery are knowable and definable, the assumption that they represent subsets of general strategies of problem solving, the assumption that they can be modeled by the standard heuristics of problem-solving computational systems, and the assumption that scientific discovery systems cannot only replicate discovery processes and products but also make independent and original discoveries. Each of these assumptions is now briefly discussed.

The assumption that creative and discovery processes are not unknowable or undefinable is in conflict with the prevalent and ancient belief that human creativity is mysterious and beyond the ken of science. Creativity, whether artistic, literary, musical, philosophical, mathematical, or scientific, was a gift from capricious muses; a special blessing from God; the crystallization of unconscious dynamics in a neurotic personality; an inexplicable and sudden inspiration (*sic*, spirit); or the intuitive insight that illumines, as if by magic, the nature of the solution to a puzzle, problem, or paradox.

The assumption that the inductive and deductive logics of scientific discovery can be mapped as sets of mechanistic problem-solving heuristics may be unacceptable, as it appears to deny or foreshorten the significance of the human

Table 6.1
Equations Discovered by BACON.3

Ideal gas law	$pV/nT = K_1$
Kepler's third law	$d^3[(a - k_2)/t]^2 = k_3$
Coulomb's law	$Fd^2/q_1q_2 = k_4$
Galileo's laws	$dP^2/Lt^2 = k_5$
Ohm's law	$D^2T/(LI + k_6D^2I) = k_7$

Source: Langley (1981), p. 172. Reprinted with the permission of the Ablex Publishing
   Corporation.

qualities of curiosity about a problem, interest in a phenomenon, disappointment in an experimental outcome, surprise in the face of an unexpected scientific result, frustration over failure, and elation in response to minor successes that give encouragement to the continuation of a difficult and challenging scientific enterprise. The assumption that a mechanism is necessary and sufficient appears to be unacceptable because it denies exclusivity of intellect to humans and denies the necessity of nonintellective processes.

The assumption that computer programs can replicate scientific and mathematical discoveries has received some justification. Lenat's Automatic Mathematician (AM) program (Davis and Lenat, 1980) discovered the fundamental theorem of arithmetic and the concept of prime numbers. Langley's BACON.3 program (Langley et al., 1987) rediscovered Kepler's law of planetary motion, Galileo's laws of acceleration, Ohm's laws of electricity, and the ideal gas law. Table 6.1 presents equations for the physical laws discovered by BACON.3.

The assumption that computer programs can make independent and original scientific discoveries has received some support. The Meta-DENDRAL program (Buchanan and Feigenbaum, 1978) has made discoveries in chemistry that were considered sufficiently significant to be published in a prestigious scientific journal.

These programs demonstrate the power of mechanistic problem solving. However, they were not designed to illumine or precisely model the nature of the scientist's creative process. For example, BACON.3 rediscovered Kepler's laws of the solar system by applying general heuristics for relating variables to data presented to it; but unlike Johannes Kepler, BACON.3 did not construct and reconstruct hypotheses, explanations, and theories. Similarly, BACON.3 was provided with data from which it constructed the equations for Coulomb's laws; but unlike Charles Coulomb, it did not conduct the complex experimentation and theorizing that culminated in the collected data.

In order to advance the computational theory of scientific discovery, it is necessary to develop programs that can model the scientist's experimental concepts and procedures. The KEKADA program (Kulkarni and Simon, 1988) was developed to model the creative processes of Hans Krebs, who made important discoveries in biochemistry.

Krebs's Discovery of the Ornithine Effect

In 1932, by means of systematic experimentation, Hans Krebs discovered the metabolic cycle and biochemical events involved in the liver's synthesis of urea. The discovery was highly significant in its own right, and as a model of biochemical metabolic theory it has been characterized by J. S. Fruton as a ''new stage in the development of biochemical thought'' (1972, p. 95). A highly detailed reconstruction of the experimental and conceptual steps by which Krebs made his discovery was achieved by F. L. Holmes (1980) on the basis of interviews with Krebs and the examination of Krebs's meticulous laboratory logs of his ongoing experiments. Holmes's description of the processes of Krebs's scientific discovery was used by D. Kulkarni and H. A. Simon (1988) to develop KEKADA, a program that would duplicate those processes and contribute to a computational theory of scientific discovery.

Before discussing KEKADA and the quality of its simulation of the processes by which Krebs made his discoveries, a brief summary of Holmes's (1980) account of those discoveries is in order.

The problem that Krebs attacked, to discover how urea was synthesized in living mammals from the decomposition products of proteins, had been investigated extensively for many years with very limited success. The methods used in Krebs's discovery, and the general nature of the catalytic process discovered, served as prototypes for much subsequent research and theory on metabolic phenomena (Holmes, 1980).

Course of Krebs's Research

The account of Krebs's research can be divided conveniently into three major segments: the first from July 26, 1931, to November 15, 1931, when the effects of ornithine were first noticed; the second from November 15, 1931, until about January 14, 1932, when evidence indicated that the effect was quite specific to ornithine; the third from January 14 to April 13, 1932, when Krebs was sufficiently convinced that he had discovered the synthesis mechanism that he wrote and submitted a paper for publication. Thus the critical phenomenon that led to the solution of the problem was detected after about three and a half months of work, while interpreting the new phenomenon and testing the theory required another five months.

1. *The Ornithine Effect.* Krebs began with the idea of using the tissue-slice method, a technique he had acquired in Otto Warburg's laboratory, to study urea synthesis. He tested the efficacy of various amino acids in producing urea, with generally negative results. When he carried out the experiment with ornithine (one of the less common amino acids) and ammonia, unexpectedly large amounts of urea were produced. He then focused on the ornithine effect.

2. *Determination of scope.* Krebs next followed a standard strategy: If a given compound exerts a particular action, check whether derivatives of that compound have a similar action. Thus, he carried out tests on some ornithine derivatives and substances similar to ornithine; but none of these substances had effects comparable to ornithine.

3. *Discovery of reaction path.* New apparatus that he obtained at this time enabled him to determine that the nitrogen in the urea produced was comparable in quantity to the nitrogen in the ammonia consumed. He concluded that the ammonia, not the amino acids, was the source of the nitrogen. Krebs now sought to elucidate the mechanisms of the ornithine effect. It occurred to him that the (known) arginine reaction, by which arginine is converted to ornithine and urea, might be related to the ornithine effect. Concluding from the quantitative data that the ornithine could be a catalyst, he inferred that ornithine with ammonia produces arginine, which in turn produces urea and ornithine. Later experiments indicated that citrulline was an intermediate substance between ornithine and arginine.

We must now spell out the details of Krebs's experiments and reasoning somewhat more fully, still following closely the account of Holmes.

The Ornithine Effect. When Krebs got freedom to initiate a major research enterprise of his own, in 1931, he decided to begin experiments of the sort he had conceived. Urea synthesis was an obvious choice of a metabolic reaction that had received a great deal of attention. At the onset, he had no specific hypotheses about the reaction mechanism, but a number of more general questions: Is ammonia an obligatory intermediate; and how do rates of urea formation from various amino acids compare? These were not new questions, but Krebs thought that the tissue-slice method would give him greater flexibility and more quantitative precision in seeking answers than did the methods used previously.

Krebs carried out his first experiment with alanine. The amount of urea produced in this experiment was much less than estimated according to the assumed equation of complete oxidation. Next, he compared rates of urea formation from glycine, from alanine, and from ammonium chloride, in each case with glucose present in the medium. He found very little urea formation from glycine or alanine, but substantial amounts from ammonium chloride. He also noted that the rate of formation of urea from alanine declined in the presence of glucose. Therefore, Krebs concluded that the glucose inhibited the formation of ammonia from the amino acid. He apparently spent about four weeks characterizing the formation of urea from ammonia: checking the quantitative relations and the necessity of aerobic conditions, and testing the effects of changes in the pH. He verified that the reactions proceeded only in liver tissue. All of this work was essentially a verification of known results.

From this point on, the work was carried on with the assistance of a new medical student, Henseleit. Krebs now turned back to determining the initial source of the urea nitrogen, which he presumed to be the amino acids. Testing alanine, phenylalanine, glycine, cysteine, and cystine, he found they all produced urea at lower rates than did ammonium chloride. He also included other substances that might contribute amino groups that would be oxidized to ammonia, with the same result. Similar negative results were obtained in comparisons of ammonium chloride alone and in combination with amino acids; none of the combinations yielded urea at a higher rate than ammonium chloride alone.

During the first two weeks in November, the investigators turned to a new line of inquiry: the influence of glucose, fructose, lactate, and citrate, all substances involved as intermediates in carbohydrate metabolism. They had no specific hypotheses, but were exploring in this direction because a difference had been found in urea production in liver slices from well-fed and starved rats.

On November 15, Henseleit was continuing these experiments, but also ran a test with the amino acid, ornithine, and with a combination of ornithine and ammonium chloride. The combination produced urea at an unexpectedly high rate, and Krebs immediately turned his attention to the ornithine effect. The laboratory logs (and Krebs's later recollections, as well) do not provide conclusive information as to why the ornithine experiment, which represented a departure from the current activity, was run at that particular time. Krebs in his recollections insisted that he took ornithine just because it was available. But Holmes speculates that he chose ornithine because the metabolic rate of ornithine was an unsolved problem. It is possible to speculate further about the reasons for the experiment, but we will leave the question unanswered here. . . .

Determination of Scope. In investigating the ornithine effect, Krebs employed ''a standard biochemical strategy: if a given compound exerts some particular action, check whether derivatives of that compound have similar actions.'' None of the substances tested had effects similar to the ornithine effect, and Krebs became more and more convinced that the effect was quite specific to ornithine, although he had no clear hypothesis of a mechanism to account for it. This phase of the inquiry extended from the middle of November to the middle of January, 1932. . . .

Discovery of Reaction Path. On January 14, Krebs and Henseleit used, for the first time, new apparatus that permitted accurate comparison of the amounts of ammonia consumed with the amounts of urea formed. Although some of the results were ambiguous, it was fairly clear by January 23 that the ammonia was the precursor of all of the nitrogen in the urea.

Now some function had to be found for the ornithine, and Krebs gradually arrived at the conclusion that it served as a catalyst. While this conclusion might seem obvious to us, it was much less obvious in 1932, when the study of catalytic reactions was relatively new.

A known reaction existed, the conversion of arginine to urea and ornithine, that could serve as the second stage of the cycle. Krebs had, in fact, studied this reaction in an experiment performed the previous October. At some point, it occurred to him that this reaction might enter into the picture. The fact that arginase is abundant in the livers of animals that excrete urea seemed significant. While Krebs was trying to conceive of a specific reaction path for the catalytic action of ornithine, he continued to direct Henseleit

Figure 6.1
The Ornithine Cycle

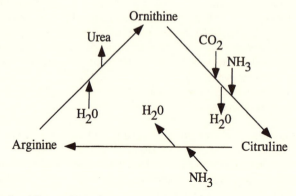

Source: Kulkarni and Simon (1988), p. 144. Reprinted with the permission of the Ablex Publishing Corporation.

in experiments to elucidate further the ornithine effect, and also its interaction with arginine. During March, they also performed experiments to show specifically that the ornithine effect could be obtained with very small amounts of ornithine (in relation to the amounts of urea produced), and must therefore be catalytic. A very successful experiment of this kind was performed on April 13, in which 24.5 molecules of urea were formed for each molecule of ornithine that was present.

Gradually, Krebs inferred a specific reaction path consistent with all of the known facts. On chemical grounds, it was evident that the conversion of ornithine to arginine could not proceed in a single step, and the theory was improved when Krebs found in the literature a 1930 paper reporting a substance, citrulline, that had the properties of a satisfactory intermediate between ornithine and arginine. Even before he obtained some citrulline, with which he could test his hypothesis, he felt sufficiently confident of his theory (sans the citrulline intermediate) to publish it. On April 25, five days before the paper appeared, he performed a test with citrulline, and by the middle of May, on the basis of further experiments, Krebs sent off a second paper describing the elaborated theory. The ornithine cycle as it was understood and depicted in 1932 is shown in Figure 6.1. Other researchers have since further elaborated the steps in the cycle, and the ornithine cycle as we understand today is somewhat more complex. (Kulkarni and Simon, 1988, pp. 143–147)

General Characteristics of the KEKADA Program

Intended to simulate Krebs's processes of discovery, as described by Holmes (1980), KEKADA's discovery processes followed the conceptual structure of general problem solving as developed by Simon and Lea (1974):

The overall organization of KEKADA is based on the two-space model of learning proposed by Simon and Lea (1974) shown in [Figure 6.2]. The system searches in an

Figure 6.2
The Two-Space Model of Learning

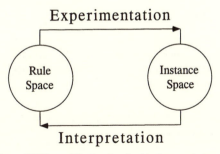

Experimentation

Rule
Space

Instance
Space

Interpretation

Source: Kulkarni and Simon (1988), p. 150. Reprinted with the permission of the Ablex Publishing
Corporation.

instance space and a role space. The possible experiments and experimental outcomes
define the instance space, which is searched by performing experiments. The hypotheses
and other higher-level descriptions, coupled with the confidences assigned to these, define
the rule space. On the basis of the current state of the rule space (what hypotheses are
held, with what confidence), the system chooses an experiment to carry out. The outcome
of the experiment modifies the hypotheses and confidences. . . .

Operators to carry out the search in the instant space. The heuristic operators used
to search the operator space fall into two categories:

1. *Experiment-proposers*, which propose experiments based on the existing hypotheses.

2. *Experimenters*, which carry out the experiments.

Operators to carry out the search in the rule space. The heuristic operators used to
search the rule space fall into the following categories:

1. *Hypothesis or strategy proposers*: When the system has decided to focus on a
   particular problem, these decide which hypothesis or hypotheses to focus on or
   which strategy to adopt for the work on the problem.

2. *Problem-generators*, which propose new problems or subproblems on which the
   system can focus attention.

3. *Problem-choosers*, which choose which task the system should work on next.

4. *Expectation-setters*, which set expectations for the experiments to be carried out.

5. *Hypothesis-generators*, which generate new hypotheses about unknown mechanisms or phenomena.

6. *Hypotheses-modifiers*, which modify the hypotheses on the basis of new evidence.

7. *Confidence-modifiers*, which modify confidences about hypotheses on the basis of
   the interpretations of experiments. (Kulkarni and Simon, 1988, pp. 149–150)

KEKADA possesses decision-maker heuristics that determine which of the operator heuristics are applicable at a given point in the discovery process:

Heuristics to make choices: In KEKADA, only certain alternatives are applicable at any stage. If more than one alternative is applicable, heuristics called *decision-makers*, are used to choose between the operators. *Decision-makers* determine, for example, which of the various problems proposed by problem-proposer heuristics will be worked on. (Kulkarni and Simon, 1988, p. 150)

As KEKADA searches its problem spaces and seeks to make its discoveries, its heuristics interact appropriately:

Interaction of Heuristics. We now can describe in more detail how the heuristics in various categories interact as the system works on a problem. If the system has not decided on which task to work (or in situations where new tasks have been added to the agenda), problem-choosers will decide which problem the system should start working on. Hypothesis-generators create hypotheses when faced with a new problem. Thus, at any given stage a certain number of hypotheses with varying confidences are present in working memory.

When working on a given task, the *hypothesis or strategy-proposers* will choose a strategy to work on. Then the experiment-proposers will propose the experiments to be carried out. Both of these types of heuristics may need the decision-makers. Then expectation-setters set expectations and experimenters carry out experiments. The results of the experiments are interpreted by the hypothesis-modifiers and the confidence-modifiers. When applicable, problem-generators may add new problems to the agenda and preempt the system to focus on a different problem. (Kulkarni and Simon, 1988, pp. 150–151)

A computer program like KEKADA, which attempts to simulate the discovery processes of the human scientist, must be alert to unexpected turns and results in the course of experimentation. KEKADA has mechanisms that simulate the cognitive (if not the affective) aspects of surprise that are present in the discovery process:

The ability to react to surprise, and to attempt to explain the puzzling phenomena, plays an important role in many discoveries. KEKADA has an ability to notice a phenomenon as "surprising." Before any experiment is carried out, expectations are formed by expectation-setters and are associated with the experiment. These expectations consist of expected output substances of the reaction, and expected lower and upper bounds on the quantities or the rates of their outputs. If the results of the experiments violates these bounds, this is noted as a surprise. We give in [Figure 6.3] a slightly simplified version of the OPS5 code (see Brownston, Farrell, Kant, and Martin, 1985) which implements the PG1 heuristics: if the outcome of an experiment violates the expectations for it, then make the study of this puzzling phenomenon a task and add it to the agenda. The bold lines beginning with a semicolon (;) are comments about the OPS5 code. (Kulkarni and Simon, 1988, p. 151)

Figure 6.3
OPS5 Code for the Surprise-Detector Heuristic

```
;Name of the rule
(p note-surprise

;LEFT HAND SIDE (Condition of the rule)
;if this rule is of type problem-generator
(context ^name problem-generator)
;if given experiment with inputs <i1>, <i2>, and<i3>is found to
; to have output <o> and the rate-of-output <r-o>
(experiment ^status just-done ^input1<i1> ^input2<i2> ^input3<i3>
            ^expected-output <e-o>
            ^expected-lower-bound <lb> ^expected-upper-bound <ub>
            ^output <o> ^rate-of-output <r-o>)
;and if expectations set with the experiment are: output <e-o>
; upper-bound on the output-rate <ub>, and
; lower-bound on the output-rate <lb>
; and if the results of the experiment violate these expectations
-(experiment ^status just-done ^input1<i1> ^input2<i2> ^input3<i3>
            ^expected-output <e-o>
            ^expected-lower-bound <lb> ^expected-upper-bound <ub>
            ^output <e-o> ^rate-of-output {>=<lb> <=<ub>})


;THEN
->


;RIGHT HAND SIDE (Action taken if the condition is met)
;Note this as a surprise and add to the agenda, with associated
;information on actual and expected outputs.
(bind<newid>)
(make agenda ^task-name<newid>)
(make surprise ^name<newid> ^input1<i1> ^input2<i2> ^input3<i3>
            ^expected-output <e-o>
            ^expected-lower-bound <lb> ^expected-upper-bound <ub>
            ^output <o> ^rate-of-output <r-o>)
```

Source: Kulkarni and Simon (1988), p. 153. Reprinted with the permission of the Ablex Publishing Corporation.

KEKADA must not only be able to recognize surprises and puzzling events occurring in the experimental process, but it must also be able to advance hypotheses that guide the continuation of exploration:

Hypothesis-Generators

[HG1]   If a surprising outcome occurs involving A as one of the reactants, then hypothesize that there is a class of substances containing A (or its derivatives) that will produce the same outcome.

[HG2]   If there is a surprisingly low output of substance A under some experimental conditions but not others, and if it is possible that another substance S is present in the latter conditions but not in the former, hypothesize that the absence of S is causing the low output.

[HG3]   If a reaction has subprocesses and the outcome of the reaction is surprising, hypothesize that the surprising result depends on one of the subprocesses (divide and conquer strategy).

[HG4]   If a reaction produces some output, create hypotheses asserting which reactant donates which group to the output substance and that a reactant may be a catalyst.

[HG5]   If a one-step stereochemical transformation from inputs to outputs of a reaction is not possible, then create the hypothesis that an intermediate exists. Otherwise create a hypothesis that there is a one-step stereochemical reaction.

[HG6]   If the goal is to study a puzzling phenomenon and if the given reaction and the surprising phenomenon contain two common substances, then create a hypothesis that they may be related.

[HG7]   If the output from A and from B is different from the sum of the outputs from A and B, then create a hypothesis that there is mixed action from A and B, otherwise create the hypothesis that the effect is additive.

[HG8]   Properties of a class are true for a member. (Kulkarni and Simon, 1988, pp. 156–157)

Krebs began his work with a certain technical knowledge. During the course of his work, he acquired additional knowledge from scientific journals and from professional colleagues. All this knowledge influenced the choice and course of his experimentation. In order to simulate the onset and course of Krebs's experiments and discoveries, KEKADA was provided with the same knowledge:

Background Knowledge. The background knowledge takes two forms. Some of it is contained in domain-specific heuristics embedded in KEKADA, that are described in previous subsections. Other knowledge is created using "make" statements before KEKADA is run. "Make" statements create initial working memory elements of various kinds. These working memory elements constitute the system's initial knowledge. Prior knowledge falls in 3 categories: knowledge about substances, knowledge about processes, and knowledge about previous experiments.

1. Knowledge about substances including the amino acids, glucose, and so forth, includes their chemical formula, cost, availability, and the class to which they belong. KEKADA also knows the typical low, medium, and high quantity of a substance to be used in the experiments. Besides KEKADA knows the partial order relation stating which of the two substances is more similar to a given substance.

2. KEKADA also has knowledge about chemical reactions. This includes the inputs, outputs, the class to which the reaction belongs and some supplementary facts. When the exact place or condition under which the process takes place is not known, supplementary facts may give various possible places or conditions where the process might be taking place. Also associated with each supplementary fact is the confidence that the process does take place at this place. The knowledge

also includes various possibilities previously considered likely regarding where the process takes place.

3. Before Krebs undertook the research program that lead to the ornithine cycle discovery, he had read about the experiments others had carried out on urea synthesis. It is assumed that his initial expectations about the outcomes were set either by the previous experiments or by some previously known theory. Therefore, the summary of these previous experiments is made available to KEKADA. KEKADA uses this knowledge only to set the expectations for the initial experiments.

Acquiring Knowledge through Literature and from Colleagues. Apart from the results of his own experiments, Krebs's research was also influenced by such factors as the availability of a new instrument and the research results published by other scientists. Correspondingly, OPS5 allows the creation of new working memory elements at intermediate stages in the progress of KEKADA to allow such factors to enter. (Kulkarni and Simon, 1988, pp. 159–160)

KEKADA's Simulation of Krebs's Discoveries

In this section, an extended example of KEKADA's discovery processes and a comparison of Krebs's discovery processes are presented. The example of KEKADA's discovery processes takes the form of a log of its performance:

Simulation of the Discovery of the Ornithine Cycle

We present here the log of a particular run of KEKADA described in terms of the numbered heuristics we have described. An asterisk (*) denotes repeated application of a set of heuristics. Seq$i$ names the sequence of firings of heuristics that is enclosed in the following pair of dashed lines. [Explanation of the abbreviations for heuristics is given in Table 6.2.]

Heuristics Results

PCO	Considers various alternative tasks on the agenda. Considers as possible candidates urea synthesis and synthesis of some fats, proteins, and fatty acid degradation, etc.
PC1–7*	Chooses urea synthesis from among the various alternatives and creates a goal to study urea synthesis using the tissue slice method.
HSC1	Considers alternative hypotheses on urea synthesis, viz., amino acids may produce urea, pyrimidines may do so, cynates may be precursors to urea, etc.
DM4*	Considers it likely that amino acids may produce urea.
EP1	Considers various amino acids as alternatives.
DM5–8*	Chooses alanine.
HG8	Assigns to alanine the properties of the class, amino acid.

Table 6.2
General Heuristics in KEKADA

CATEGORY OF HEURISTICS	DOMAIN-INDEPENDENT	NO	DOMAIN-SPECIFIC	NO
PROBLEM CHOOSERS	PC0-8	9		
PROBLEM GENERATORS	PG1	1		
DECISION-MAKERS	DM1-4	4	DM5-10	6
EXPERIMENT-PROPOSERS	EP1,EP6,EP7	3	EP2-5,EP8	5
EXPECTATION-SETTERS	ES1-4	4		
HYPOTHESIS-GENERATORS	HG1,3,8	3	HG2,4,5,6,7	5
HYPOTHESIS-MODIFIERS	HM4-5	2	HM1-3,B1-	15
CONFIDENCE-MODIFIERS	CF3,CF4,CF5	3	CF1,2	2
HYPOTHESIS/STRATEGY CHOOSERS	HSC1,HSC2	2		
BACKGROUND KNOWLEDGE			DOMAIN-SPECIFIC	
TOTAL		31		33

Source: Kulkarni and Simon (1988), p. 172. Reprinted with the permission of the Ablex Publishing Corporation.

EP2–3   Decides for an experiment on alanine and on ammonia. Decides for an experiment on both combined together.

ES1–3*   Sets expectations for these experiments.

E1,
ES4,
CF1–2*   Asks user for the results of experiments, modifies confidences.

PG1,
PC8   Notes the result of the experiment on aniline as surprising, and makes it focus of attention, creates the following hypotheses:

HG5,
B1–11*   Studies alanine to urea reaction, *decides that intermediate exists.*

HG2   *Some essential substance is missing from the tissue slice preparation.*

HG3   *The reason for surprise may be one of the subreactions.*

HG1*   *The phenomenon may be common to some or all elements of a class.*

[seq0]

[Begin seq0]

HSC1	Evaluates the alternatives.
DM4, 9*	Decides to consider the hypothesis that an absence of a substance may be causing the surprise.
EP6	Guesses the substances which may be present—various substances involved in carbohydrate mechanism.
DM5*	Chooses glucose.
ES3	Sets expectations for the experiment.
E1, ES4	Asks user for output for an experiment on aniline and glucose.
CF3	Modifies failed-effort slot in hypothesis.

[End seq0]

[Repeats seq0 for various substances.]

HM4	Makes inactive the existential hypothesis that there may be a substance missing.
HSC1	Evaluates the alternatives.
DM4, 9*	Decides to consider the hypothesis that the cause of the process may be in one of the subprocesses.
HSC2, DM1	Decides to study the subprocess of urea synthesis from ammonia.
EP7, ES1, E1, ES4, CF4–5*	Carries out experiments on urea formation on ammonia under various conditions of pH, aerobicity and in various organs, study quantitative relations.

[seq1]

[Begin seq1]

HSC1	Evaluates the alternatives.
DM4*	Decides to consider the third hypothesis: that the surprise may be limited to a class.
EP1	Decides to list possible amino acids for consideration.
DM5– 8*	Chooses cysteine.

HG8   Assigns properties of the class to cysteine.

EP2–3   Decides for an experiment on cysteine and on ammonia. Decides for an experiment on both combined together.

ES1–3,   Sets expectations for these experiments. Asks user for the results of the
E1,   experiment. Modifies the confidences in hypotheses.
ES4,
CF1–2*

[End seq1]

[Repeats seq1 on other amino acids, last one being ornithine.]

PG1,   Notices the ornithine effect and makes it the focus of attention. Creates
PC8   following hypotheses.

HG7   New clue is created for *mixed action of both the inputs.*

HG4*   *Hypotheses about who donates what to the reaction.*
HG5,

B1–11*   *Intermediate exists.*

HG4*   *Possibility that ornithine or ammonia is catalyst.*

HG1*   *Possibility that the phenomenon may be common to a class of substances.*

HG6*   *Possibility of relation to similar reactions.*

[seq2]

[Begin seq2]

HSC1   Evaluates the alternatives.

DM4–   Decides to study the scope of the phenomenon. Considers that the
9*   phenomenon may be common to amino acids.

EP1   Considers various amino acids.

DM5–   Decides on an amino acid as the choice.
8*

HG8   Assigns properties of the class to that amino acid.

EP2–3   Decides for an experiment on the amino acid leucine and on ammonia, separately and combined.

ES1–3,   Sets expectations for these experiments. Asks user for the results of
E1,   experiments. Changes the implied failure in hypotheses about how urea is
ES4,   formed to reduce the failed-effort slot in the hypothesis asserting that the
CF–3*   phenomenon may be common to a class.

[End seq2]

[Repeats [seq2] for various amino-acids]

HM4   Removes the description that some amino acids might produce urea.

[seq3]

[Begin seq3]

HSC1   Evaluates the alternatives.

DM4–   Decides to study the hypothesis that the scope to the surprise may be
9*   common to some or all amines.

EP1   Considers various amines.

DM5–   Decides on putrescine. Decides for an experiment on putrescine and
8*   ammonia.

HG8   Assigns the properties of its class to putrescine.

ES3,   Sets expectations for these experiments. Asks user for the results of
E1,   experiments. Reduces the failed-effort slot in the hypothesis asserting that
ES4,   the phenomenon may be common to a class.
CF3

[End seq3]

[Repeats [seq3] for various amines.]

HM4   Removes description that some amines might produce urea.

[Repeats [seq3] for various carboxylic acids.]

HM4   Removes description that some carboxylic acids might produce urea.

HSC1   Evaluates the various alternatives.

DM10   User decides to study the hypothesis that source of NH_2 group in urea is
           ammonia.

EP4,   Carries out the experiment after setting expectations.
ES1,
E1

HM6   Concludes that the source of amino group is NH_3.

HSC1   Evaluates the various alternatives.

DM10   User chooses to study the related reaction: arginine reaction.

EP8,   Two possible hypotheses are created: *arginine may be intermediate, or*
DM10   *there may be a class of substances exhibiting reaction similar to arginine*
        reaction. Considers the second hypothesis.

EP1   Considers substances in guanidine class.

DM5*   Chooses guanidine as substance for reaction.

EP1   Decides for the reaction on guanidine and ammonia.

HG8   Assigns properties of the class to guanidine.

ES3,   Carries out the experiment. Reduces the confidence in the existential
E1,   hypothesis.
ES4,
CF3

HSC1–   Chooses the possibility that ornithine is catalyst.
DM10

EP5   Decides for an experiment to verify catalysis.

E1   Carries out experiment to check catalysis.

HM1   Concludes that ornithine acts as a catalyst.

B1–11* Balances the catalysis reaction.

HG5   *Creates hypothesis that there exists intermediate in the reaction.*

HM2,   *Creates candidates for intermediate.* Balances the reactions. Counts the
B1–11* number of inputs. Evaluates the intermediates. Chooses arginine.

HG5   *Creates a hypothesis that there exists intermediate in the reaction.*

(User, when asked to carry out a survey, creates elements corresponding to citrulline and other substances.)

> *Considers candidate substances* which are structurally intermediate between the inputs and the outputs of the ornithine to arginine reaction. Balances the reactions. Counts the number of inputs. Evaluates the plausibility of the candidate substances and chooses citrulline from them. (Kulkarni and Simon, 1988, pp. 160–164; italics added)

The log of KEKADA's behavior depicts in detail pathways to discovery that parallel Holmes's (1980) description of Krebs's sequence of discovery steps (discussed in a previous section). KEKADA's parallel behavior to that of Krebs is clearly discernible in Figure 6.4, which groups the details of the log into larger units that delineate the course of the research and the stages of the ornithine discovery.

Figure 6.4
Progress of KEKADA in the Discovery

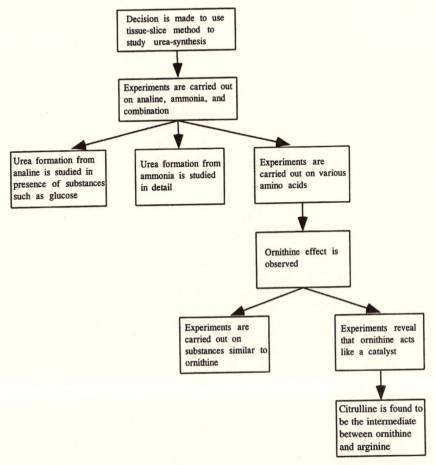

Source: Kulkarni and Simon (1988), p. 165. Reprinted with the permission of the Ablex Publishing Corporation.

Kulkarni and Simon (1988) conclude that not only does KEKADA succeed in its simulation but that it also "constitutes a theory of Krebs's style of experimentation":

In the introduction, we argued that Holmes's reconstruction of Krebs's discovery of ornithine cycle is reliable data on which to build a theory of discovery. Now, if we compare the course of work of Krebs with that of KEKADA, we find that there are only minor differences in the initial knowledge with which KEKADA and Krebs started. Apart from these differences, KEKADA follows the same strategy of experimentation as Krebs and its motivations for carrying out various experiments are the same as the motivations

of Krebs whenever these are indicated by evidence in the diaries and retrospective interviews. As KEKADA accounts for the data on Krebs's research, it constitutes a theory
of Krebs's style of experimentation. Next we must ask how general this theory is. (Kulkarni and Simon, 1988, p. 171)

KEKADA as a General Simulator of the Scientific Discovery Process

From the point of view of Kulkarni and Simon (1988), the processes of
scientific discovery, whether those of Krebs or those of any other scientist, can
be represented as a goal-directed series of problem-solving steps guided by do-
main-directed knowledge and heuristic operators that are both domain-specific
and domain-general. The KEKADA system simulates this theory of the nature
of the scientific discovery process.

(1) KEKADA contains many general heuristics that are applicable in a large number
of situations. [Table 6.2] shows that KEKADA has 31 domain-independent and
33 domain-specific heuristics. The domain-independent heuristics are some that
scientists in various disciplines continue to use in making discoveries. Of domain-
specific heuristics, DM5 to DM10 are actually applications to chemistry of more
general domain-independent heuristics. Of the other domain-specific heuristics,
for all except B*, DM9 and EP3 we have historical evidence (Baldwin, 1947;
Fruton, 1972; Holmes, 1980; personal communication; Luck, 1932) that they were
in common use in the study of metabolic reactions in biochemistry in the early
20th century, before 1931 and for some years later. Thus, they constituted accepted domain-specific strategies which a newcomer like Krebs was likely to
know after a brief introduction to the field. The B* heuristics are also quite general
in their applicability, for they can be used to balance not only the reactions in
this discovery, but many other reactions as well.

(2) As is shown in the log [in the previous section], most of KEKADA's heuristics
are used a number of times in the particular scenario given. EP8, HG2, HG7, and
HM1 are the only domain-specific heuristics that are fired only once, but their
potential utility in other research situations is clear.

(3) Some of KEKADA's heuristics were also used in different forms by AM, a mathematical discovery system, in the course of a wide variety of discoveries (Davis
& Lenat, 1980).

(4) Thanks to Holmes (1980, personal communication), we now have data on a second major discovery of Hans Krebs, that of glutamine synthesis. A hand simulation indicates that the path that Krebs followed there is wholly consistent with
the current theory. We will report in more detail on the KEKADA simulation of
the research on glutamine synthesis in another study.

These considerations show that although KEKADA was handcrafted to fit our knowledge of the procedures Krebs used in his discovery of the urea cycle, the structure and
the heuristics it embodies constitute a model of wider applicability. (Kulkarni and Simon,
1988, pp. 171, 173).

PHILOSOPHICAL AND PSYCHOLOGICAL
IMPLICATIONS OF SCIENTIFIC DISCOVERY SYSTEMS

At the beginning of this section, it is stated that the general logic of computational theories of scientific discovery includes a set of general assumptions. The research of Kulkarni and Simon (1988) on the KEKADA system is now used to examine these assumptions and, to that extent, to evaluate the logic of computational theories of scientific discovery.

The assumption that the processes of creativity in scientific discovery has a knowable character can be supported once it is granted that some degree of confidence can be placed in Holmes's (1980) account, and that Krebs's logs and recollections of the onset, course, and outcome of his experimentation possess an acceptable level of completeness and reliability. The assumption that the creative processes of scientific discovery are definable can be supported given KEKADA's definitional heuristics, which include the capacity for planning and executing experiments, the recognition of surprising experimental results, and the consequent revision of hypotheses and continuation of the control strategies of systematic experimentation.

The assumption that scientific discovery processes represent subsets of general problem-solving strategies is supported by the two-space (instant space and rule space) model of problem solving (Simon and Lea, 1974) which provided the general superstructure for the development of the control logic in the KEKADA system. KEKADA's success in replicating Hans Krebs's scientific discoveries appears to support the understanding of scientific discovery as a special case of the two-space problem-solving theory.

The assumption that scientific discovery processes can be modeled by the standard heuristics of computational problem-solving systems is supported by the use in KEKADA of the familiar artificial intelligence methodology of the production system. In addition, KEKADA's possession of a large set of general heuristics, potentially applicable to scientific discovery problems beyond those of Krebs, lends credence to the assumption that a computational system such as KEKADA can model general aspects of the process of scientific discovery.

The assumption that a computational system such as KEKADA can make original and independent discoveries is difficult to evaluate. To KEKADA, as to Krebs, the discoveries were new. To the scientific world, KEKADA's discoveries were replications and rediscoveries. The metabolic processes of the ornithine cycle were disclosed by Krebs, and that disclosure was repeated by KEKADA. The developers (Kulkarni and Simon, 1988) cannot claim for KEKADA the status of making an original contribution to contemporary knowledge in the field of biochemistry.

The general logic of the computational theory of scientific discovery processes should be contrasted with theories of human scientific discovery that characterize or require the existence of intrinsic motivation. Theories of the nature of human creativity (Sternburg, 1988) are in general agreement that the conditions for creativity require inherent interest in the subject and love for the creative task:

> Guiding our investigations is what we have termed the *intrinsic motivation principle of creativity*:
>
> People will be most creative when they feel motivated primarily by the interest, enjoyment, satisfaction, and challenge of the work itself—not the external pressures.
>
> In essence, we are saying that the love people feel for their work has a great deal to do with the creativity of their performances. This proposition is clearly supported by accounts of the phenomenology of creativity. Most reports from and about creative individuals are filled with notions of an intense involvement in and unrivaled love for their work. Thomas Mann, for example, described in one of his letters his passion for writing (John-Steiner, 1985), and physicists who were close to Albert Einstein saw in him a similar kind of intensity. In the words of the Nobel Prize-winning inventor Dennis Gabor, "no one has ever enjoyed science as much as Einstein" (John-Steiner, 1985, p. 67). (Hennessey and Amabile, 1988, p. 11)

> I want to know how God created this world. I am not interested in this or that phenomenon, in the spectrum of this or that element. I want to know His thoughts, the rest are details. . . . Once the validity of this mode of thought has been recognized, the final results appear almost simple; any intelligent undergraduate can understand them without much trouble. But the years of searching in the dark for a truth that one feels, but cannot express; the intense desire and the alterations of confidence and misgiving, until one breaks through to clarity and understanding, are only known to him who has himself experienced them. (Einstein, quoted in Ferris, 1988, p. 177)

Clearly, computational theories of discovery do not require that the computational system possess intrinsic motivation as a necessary condition for creativity. The heuristic mechanisms of computational systems are sufficient.

Finally, it is not clear that the use of a scientist's laboratory logs and recollections is adequate for areas of science that, unlike the rather applied bench experimentation of Krebs, depend upon complex reflection, deep theory, and thought experimentation, as exemplified in the creative processes of Albert Einstein. It remains to be seen whether the intellectual levels of advanced theoretical science can be encompassed by computational theories of scientific discovery.

> There is no inductive method which could lead to the fundamental concepts of physics . . . in error are those theorists who believe that the theory comes inductively from experience. (Einstein, 1933)

The unconscious processes (Feldman, 1988; Hadamard, 1949; Langley and Jones, 1988; Torrance, 1988) that lead to great insights of scientific discovery in astronomy, mathematics, biology, and molecular genetics remain a scientific enigma whose decipherment may depend on advances in the neural sciences in conjunction with psychological and computational approaches.

Just as the mind in its many facets stands as the major "general" target for current neurobiological work, creative efforts are among the most important "specifics" in need of elucidation. Numerous electrophysiological and neuroradiological tools now make feasible studies of individual differences. . . .

One other point worth stressing is that neurobiologists can now expect to receive aid from researchers working at the other side of the cognitive-scientific interface. Many psychologists and artificial intelligence researchers working at the level of "domain" or "intelligence" are now probing cognitive processes in great detail; an account in terms of underlying neurophysiological or neurochemical processes is no longer remote. And when it comes to the study of particular human faculties, ranging from language to vision, there is again a cadre of workers prepared to see their work analyzed in terms of underlying biological systems. (Gardner, 1988, p. 318)

A complete science of the nature of scientific discovery processes cannot beg the question of the heart of the discovery process by using different terminologies equivalently limited to only a descriptive function, but must possess a theory capable of predicting, under specified conditions, the emergence of new creative insights. The possibility of such a theory remains a beckoning and honorable destiny.

SCIENTIFIC PROBLEM TYPES AND COMPUTATIONAL DISCOVERY SYSTEMS

Scientific research involves an intricate set of interrelated problems. The problems range from data and observation to technique and experimentation to theory formation and revision. A schematic analysis of these problem types, developed by Root-Bernstein (1989), is presented in Table 6.3.

To what extent have artificial intelligence approaches to the problems of scientific discovery encountered and solved the types of problems described by Root-Bernstein (1989)? I have constructed Table 6.4 "Scientific Problem Types and Computational Discovery Systems" as a parallel to Root-Bernstein's table. The table which I have constructed suggests that computational discovery systems have made considerable progress in dealing with types of problems encountered in standard scientific research.

Table 6.3
Problem Types

Type	Examples	Method of Solution
Definition	What is energy? What species is this?	Invention of concept or taxonomy
Theory	How do we explain the distribution of the species? What causes objects to fall?	Invention of theory
Data	What information is needed to test or build a theory?	Observation, experiment
Technique	How can we obtain data? How do we analyze it? How may the phenomenon best be displayed?	Invention of instruments and methods of analysis and display
Evaluation	How adequate is a definition, theory, observation, or technique? Is something a true anomaly or an artifact?	Invention of criteria for evaluation
Integration	Can two disparate theories or sets of data be integrated? Does Mendel contradict Darwin?	Reinterpretation and rethinking of existing concepts and ideas
Extension	How many cases does a theory explain? What are the boundary conditions for applying a technique or theory?	Prediction and testing
Comparison	Which theory or data set is more useful?	Invention of criteria for comparison
Application	How can this observation, theory, or technique be used?	Knowledge of related unsolved problems
Artifact	Do these data disprove a theory? Is the technique for data collection appropriate?	Recognition that problem is insoluble as stated

Source: Root-Bernstein (1989), p. 61.

Table 6.4
Scientific Problem Types and Computational Discovery Systems

Type	Examples	System and Reference
Definition	How can taxonomies be constructed from primitive observations? How can hierarchies of concepts be formed from primitive taxonomies?	AM (Lenat, 1979); BACON (Langley & Zytkow, 1989); GLAUBER (Langley et al., 1983)
Theory	How can qualitative and quantitative theory formation be achieved?	PHINEAS (Falkenhainer, 1990)
Data	How can data required for theory formation and revision be systematically collected?	IDS (Nordhausen & Langley, 1990)
Technique	How can data be analyzed and conceptualized?	ABACUS (Falkenhainer & Michalski, 1986)
Evaluation	How can the validity of theories and experimental findings (including anomalies) be determined?	KEKADA (Kulkarni & Simon, 1988)
Integration	Can conflicting theories be resolved?	ECHO (Thagard, 1989)
Extension	How can the limits of a theory be determined?	FAHRENHEIT (Langley Zytkow, 1989)
Comparison	How can the relative merits of two theories be ascertained?	ECHO (Thagard & Nowak, 1990)
Application	How can established theory be applied to exploration of novel problems?	PHINEAS
Artifact	How does surprising experimental data modify current theory?	KEKADA (Kulkarni & Simon, 1990)

7

The Development of Efficient Learning Systems

KNOWLEDGE AND STRATEGY IN LEARNING AND PROBLEM SOLVING

It is a truism that the pathways of experience lead from being an apprentice to being a master. In recent decades, cognitive psychology and artificial intelligence have attempted to define this transition from novice to expert. Elio and Scharf (1990) developed EUREKA, a computer model of the changes in strategy approach and knowledge organization that take place as the status of novice gives way to the attainment of mastery.

The General Logic of EUREKA

The cognitive theory of psychological knowledge schemata provides the general logic for EUREKA.

In the model described below, we propose that interrelated prototypes or schemas emerge with experience. These structures functionally organize related domain-specific expectations, inferences, and methods for solving problems. Furthermore, we assume that the shift in problem-solving strategy is a by-product of the changing content and inter-association of these schemas. (Elio and Scharf, 1990, p. 582)

In EUREKA, there is a provision for reclassification, modification, and retrieval of strategic knowledge. EUREKA's knowledge can evolve as it experiences and solves physics problems. Knowledge develops in the direction of increasingly abstract categories of physics concepts and principles and sophisticated problem-solving methods.

Our model of strategy and knowledge organization shifts is implemented in a system called EUREKA, using a MOP [Memory Organization Packets]-based representation. The model assumes that some knowledge about physics concepts, equations, and inference rules is initially available in a form that does not specify their usefulness or relevance to any particular type of problem. EUREKA uses this textbook knowledge in conjunction with a means-ends problem-solving strategy to solve force and energy physics problems. After EUREKA solves a problem, the entire problem-solving episode—a set of features, inferences, and solution steps—is stored in a P-MOP [Problem Memory Organization Packet] network that represents long-term memory for previous problem-solving experiences. When a new problem-solving experience is integrated into the P-MOP, it is compared with previous problem-solving knowledge represented on the P-MOPs and indices among P-MOPs. Common portions of the solution method and inferences are abstracted and moved onto newly created P-MOPs organized by new indices. The indices that organize this long-term memory knowledge determine what is retrieved during solution and for generalization. These indices are based on features of the problem. Initially, superficial commonalities and differences of the problems (e.g., inclined plane, pulley) are the types of knowledge abstracted in P-MOPs. *As EUREKA solves more problems, implicit physics concepts (aspects of the problem not explicitly mentioned in the problem statement), like energies and forces, emerge as the important distinguishing features. These features eventually become the dominant retrieval paths among associated solution methods and domain inferences that have been abstracted as commonalities on P-MOPs. This evolving organization of problem prototype knowledge and the discriminating features organizing it are what underlies the shift in EUREKA's problem-solving strategy and the quality of its solutions.* (Elio and Scharf, 1990, pp. 548–585; italics added)

EUREKA's Initial Physics Knowledge

EUREKA is initially provided with physics-textbook knowledge. The knowledge is neither systematic nor organized in order to simulate the level of comprehension that a novice physics student would have.

The unorganized knowledge is a set of equations and concepts that a novice might know from studying a textbook chapter on force and energy problems. Concepts include real-world objects (e.g., inclined plane, body), relations among objects (e.g., on) and measurable quantities for describing objects and relations between them (e.g., acceleration, friction). This knowledge is unorganized with respect to its potential usefulness to problem solving. For example, we assume that novices could give an equation for Newton's second law even if they could not immediately recognize its applicability to a particular problem. (Elio and Scharf, 1990, p. 585)

EUREKA's Problem Solver

The means-ends strategy is used by EUREKA's problem solver to derive a required quantity in a physics problem. If the means-ends strategy fails,

EUREKA possesses an interesting meta-strategy that redirects the focus of attention toward a reconstrual of parts of the problem or of their interrelationship.

EUREKA's problem solver is based on a means-ends strategy that uses the textbook knowledge and the P-MOP knowledge to solve problems. The problem solver also includes an implicit meta-strategy for establishing a focus of attention. This focus of attention directs EUREKA to consider aspects of the problem other than the desired quantity whenever the means-ends approach gets stuck in deriving the problem's desired quantity. These other aspects include relations among objects and features of objects. We call the results of a solution process a problem-solving experience. A problem-solving experience contains retrieved equations, inference rules, derived quantities, inferred concepts, and a kind of "train-of-thought" recording of how the solution method evolved. The entire experience, including any dead ends that were investigated during solution, is then stored in the P-MOP network. (Elio and Scharf, 1990, p. 585)

EUREKA's Memory Network

The most interesting feature of the P-MOP network is its dynamic character that reflects changes in the underlying conceptual schemata, as EUREKA develops its strategic knowledge.

The P-MOP network represents EUREKA's long-term memory for past problem-solving experiences as a set of constantly changing problem-type schemas. When given a new problem to solve, EUREKA's problem solver consults the P-MOP network for knowledge that might be relevant to the current problem. Initially, there is no long-term memory knowledge, so the problem solver must rely on the means-ends strategy in conjunction with the textbook knowledge network. Problem-type schemas evolve in the P-MOP network as EUREKA solves each problem and integrates the new problem-solving experience into its existing P-MOP network. After a few problems, the schemas this P-MOP network represents contain few solution methodologies and domain inference rules, primarily organized by surface features the problem had in common. As the P-MOP network accommodates more problem-solving experiences, indices reflecting known concepts and abstract problem features such as "potential energy of the body is known," "the body is moving at time 2," and "there is a normal force acting on the body," emerge as organizing features that lead to more complete solution methodologies and associated domain inference rules. EUREKA's solutions to problems begin to simulate what Larkin et al. (1980) call a knowledge-development approach through the influence of these more expertlike schemas in the P-MOP network. (Elio and Scharf, 1990, pp. 585–586)

Problem Representation in EUREKA

The nature of problem representation in EUREKA will be described in this section. For each of two physics problems given to EUREKA, the form of representation and the content of the associated P-MOP will be presented. The first physics problem posed to EUREKA was: "A body of mass 2 slugs is on an inclined plane that has an angle of 30 degrees from the horizontal. The coefficient of friction is 0.3. Find the acceleration of the body." (Elio and Scharf, 1990, p. 586)

For this physics problem, Elio and Scharf (1990) describe its representation and processing in EUREKA in the following account:

EUREKA does not take problems in this natural language form. [Figure 7.1] gives the exact form of Problem 1 given to EUREKA. The problem representation is organized around objects. It also includes the known and desired quantities of the problem. We use the predicate *presence-of* to denote the presence of abstract entities such as forces. The interpretation of *presence-of (body 1, gravity-x-axis)* is "There is a force present that is called gravity-x-axis and it is acting on body 1." We include the forces due to gravity in the initial problem representation. In this problem, the reference frame is specified such that the x-axis is along the inclined plane in the direction of motion and the y-axis is perpendicular to the x-axis.

As EUREKA solves a problem, the problem's representation becomes "enhanced" with inference rules, facts, and solution methodologies. [Figure 7.1] shows the additional knowledge that EUREKA added to Problem 1's representation as it developed a solution. The first type of new knowledge is inference rules that were retrieved from the textbook knowledge network during solution (we explain how this is done later). If the conditions of an inference rule are present as features in a problem, then the representation is augmented with the inference rule and the conclusion of the rule. For example, the inference rules in [Figure 7.1] conclude that normal and frictional forces are acting on the body. We refer to the conclusions of these types of inferences as abstract physics concepts.

The second type of new information in the enhanced representation is derived quantities. These are values of quantities found during the solution process by using equations with known quantities. In this example, seven quantities were derived. The enhanced representation also contains a solution method, drawn in [Figure 7.1a] as a tree structure. The root node of the solution method tree is the desired quantity in the problem. Reading the [Figure 7.1b] solution method tree in a top-down, left-to-right fashion gives the solution process: acceleration along the x-axis, sum of forces along the x-axis, gravity along the x-axis, normal force along the y-axis, sum of forces along the y-axis, and gravity along the y-axis. We describe how EUREKA chooses a focus of attention in the section on the problem solver. The solution method also records which equations were used at each step. *It is this enhanced problem representation (i.e., [Figure 7.1a and b] combined) that is subsequently stored in the P-MOP network.*

This enhancement process is an important kind of transformation. The problem that is ultimately stored in the P-MOP network contains many new concepts and quantities inferred during solution. (Elio and Scharf, 1990, pp. 586–588; italics added)

Elio and Scharf (1990) emphasize EUREKA's special inference ability:

In the case of EUREKA, indexing the enhanced problem representation effectively means that a problem's descriptors are determined by the problem-solving process and not by the problem statement's original form. For example, an inference that there is a force acting along the x-axis introduces a new, additional descriptor for some problem situation. *Thus, EUREKA is not limited to describing and learning problem schemas in terms of the descriptors found in the problem statement, but rather will learn schemas*

Figure 7.1
Problem 1's Initial Representation (a) and Additional Information Added During the Solution Process (b)

Objects	body1,surface1
Relations	on(body1,surface1)
Features	moving(body1,time2), inclined(surface1), feature (friction (body1,surface1))), mass(body1)
Knowns	(body1,mass), (surface1,incline-angle), gravity, coefficient-friction, (body1, acceleration-y-axis)
Presence-of	(body1,acceleration-x-axis)
Desired	(body1,gravity-x-axis), (body1,gravity-y-axis)

(a)

Presence-of	(body1,friction-x-axis), (body1,normal-y-axis)
Derived	(body1,gravity-x-axis), (body1,sum-of-forces-y-axis) (body1,gravity-y-axis), (body1,normal-y-axis) (body1,friction-x-axis), (body1,sum-of-forces-x-axis) (body1,acceleration-x-axis)
Inference Rules	If a body is on a surface that has friction, Then infer the presence of a frictional force action on the body along x axis If a body is on something, Then infer the presence of a normal force acting on the body along the y axis
Soin-Method	

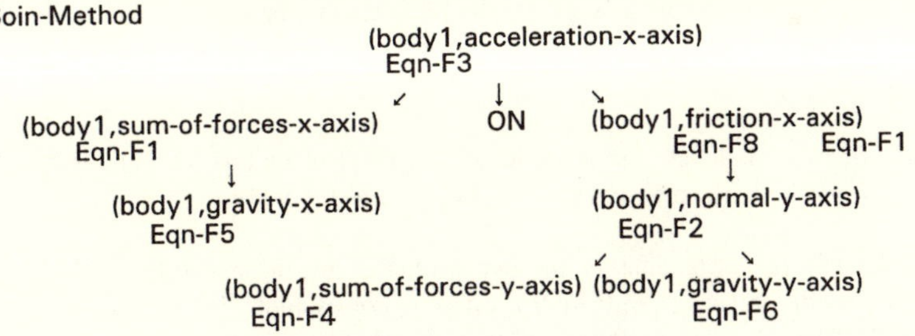

(b)

Source: Elio and Scharf (1990). Reprinted with the permission of the Ablex Publishing Corporation.

based on inferred concepts using its textbook and existing P-MOP knowledge. (Elio and Scharf, 1990, p. 588; italics added)

The P-MOP in EUREKA

The P-MOP is a crucial component of the EUREKA system. Elio and Scharf (1990) summarize its major characteristics in the following account:

Two types of knowledge are organized in the P-MOP network: Specific problem-solving experiences, a term we use interchangably with enhanced problem representations (see [Figure 7.1]), and P-MOPs, which represent a collection of common features (domain inference rules, solution methods, and problem features). When we say that a P-MOP "organizes" other P-MOPs and specific experiences, we mean that (a) the P-MOP contains information common to a number of other P-MOPs and specific experiences and (b) these other structures are accessible from this P-MOP via indices or retrieval paths that represent their differences from each other.

The root node of the P-MOP network is a P-MOP that defines a "generic physics problem." This is shown as P-MOP1 in [Figure 7.2]. Following Kolodner's (1983b) terminology, a P-MOP has a set of *norms* that represent commonalities of the knowledge it organizes. The norms on P-MOP1 are a collection of predicates for specifying how physics problems can be described, namely in terms of things that are known and desired, objects, features of objects, and relations among objects.

Problem-solving experiences are organized according to their differences from the norms appearing on a P-MOP. As the root node of the network, P-MOP1 organizes incoming problem-solving experiences according to how they differ from its norms, that is, differences in knowns, objects, object relations, and so forth. Each difference from a norm is called an *index*. An index is a predicate-value pair, such as *desired (acceleration, body1)*, that points to the representation of a specific problem-solving experience or to another P-MOP. A predicate must appear as a norm before it can serve as an index. As we explain below, any predicate that appears in an enhanced problem representation, in addition to the ones initially defining P-MOP1, can become norms on a P-MOP. Once a predicate is recognized as a potential commonality and becomes a norm on a particular P-MOP, it is also eligible to become an index to organize similar problem-solving knowledge from that P-MOP.

Each time EUREKA finishes a problem, it stores the final enhanced problem representation into the P-MOP network. [Figure 7.2] shows what the network would look like after Problems 1 and 2 have been solved and their enhanced representations integrated into the P-MOP network. The English version of Problem 2 is:

A body of mass 3 slugs is on a frictionless inclined plane that had an angle of 40 degrees from the horizontal. Find the acceleration of the body.

The enhanced representations of the two problems are indexed from P-MOP1 according to their differences from P-MOP1's norms. For example, Problem 1's representation and Problem 2's representation differ from P-MOP1's *feature* norm, which only says that objects have features, but not what those features actually are. To minimize the complexity of the figure, different indices pointing to the same knowledge structure are shown beside a single line. Thus, there are two different indices from P-MOP1 to Problem 1's enhanced representation.

P-MOP2 in [Figure 7.2] represents the commonalities and discriminating features of the two problem-solving experiences. Both problems involve a moving body on an inclined surface, a gravity force, a normal force acting on the body, several known quantities, and the acceleration of the body along the plane as the desired quantity. These are the norms of P-MOP1. Because the inference rule, *If a body is on an object, then there is a normal force acting on the body along the y-axis*, is used in the solution of both problems, it is also stored on P-MOP2. In addition to containing commonalities between these two problems, P-MOP2 also keeps track of the differences for indexing these

Figure 7.2
The P-MOP Representation of Problems 1 and 2

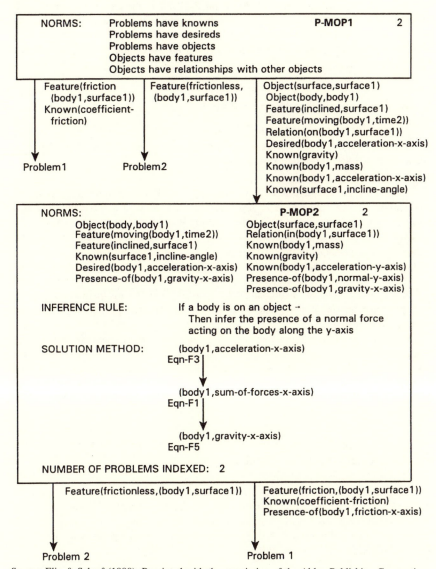

Source: Elio & Scharf (1990). Reprinted with the permission of the Ablex Publishing Corporation.

problems. In this example, features regarding friction are the differences. Problem 2 is indexed from P-MOP2 by the feature that the surface is frictionless. Problem 1 is indexed in three ways from P-MOP2. Indices serve as directed retrieval paths for accessing knowledge structures from each other in the network. The information in one knowledge structure is reached from another by meeting the specifications of the index connecting them.

The P-MOP restructuring mechanisms, which are discussed in greater detail below, also compare the solution methods of the two problems and store common solution steps on the P-MOP. In this case, only part of the solution method was common between the two problems. The solution method shown on P-MOP2 is the entire solution method EUREKA developed for Problem 2. Because friction was not common between the two problems, the portion of Problem 1's solution that dealt with friction does not appear on P-MOP2 but instead remains on Problem 1's enhanced representation. (Elio and Scharf, 1990, pp. 588–591)

The Textbook Network in EUREKA

EUREKA's textbook network is presented in detail in Appendix A. In this section, an overview will be given of three types of knowledge found in the network: concepts, inference rules, and equations.

Concepts in the textbook network include physical objects, features of objects, and relationships between objects. *Body* is an example of a physical object with *mass* as a feature; it may have the relation *on* with another object that is a surface. Forces, like gravitational, frictional, and normal force, and energies, such as potential and kinetic energy, are also concepts in the textbook network.

Inference rules are implications of the form P→Q, where P is a set of conditions that must be present in the problem representation in order to add Q to the problem representation. For example, the two conditions necessary for inferring friction using Inf-A in Appendix A are that a body must be a surface and that there is friction between the body and the surface.

The third type of knowledge contained in the textbook are equations describing kinematic, force, and energy relationships. The equations contain a left-hand side, a right-hand side, and possibly one or more constraints. For example, the constraint of Eqn-E14 in Appendix A requires that the object of interest be on a surface. Constraints of an equation must appear in the problem representation for the equation to be used. (Elio and Scharf, 1990, pp. 591–592)

The nature of the interrelationships among concepts, inference rules, and equations is summarized in the following account:

Concepts are associated with each other through simple a-kind-of relations and with the inference rules and equations in which they participate. A concept is associated with an equation if it appears anywhere in the equation. Besides these associational relations, we have no further assumptions about the representations of this type of textbook knowledge. (Elio and Scharf, 1990, p. 592)

The Focus of Attention in EUREKA

To solve a physics problem, EUREKA must derive a desired quantity. The focus of attention mechanism constitutes EUREKA's control over its set of cognitive maneuvers between and within concepts, inferences, and equations. The cognitive control exercised by the focus of attention is one of the more interesting features of the EUREKA system. Following a general description, the detailed operations of the focus of attention will be illustrated by reference to the first physics problem discussed earlier in this section.

The focus of attention is important because it derives the retrieval of inferences and equations from the textbook knowledge network and their incorporation into the evolving problem representation. For each focus of attention, EUREKA retrieves all associated inference rules and relevant equations. If the conditions of an inference rule are satisfied by features of the problem representation, both the rule and its conclusion are added to the problem representation. Typically, if EUREKA wishes to use an equation to solve for some quantity and that equation contains other unknown quantities, then one of those unknown quantities becomes the new focus of attention. Thus, the focus of attention also drives the creation of goal-subgoal trees that record the relations between each focus of attention and the associated equations EUREKA has retrieved. These goal-subgoal structures represent the evolving solution method and are also added to the problem representation. If EUREKA uses all of its equations for its focus of attention and has not solved the problem, it selects a new focus of attention from other features in the problem representation, some of which may have resulted from inferences. These features in turn might enable EUREKA to continue its equation-retrieval process. A problem is solved when its desired quantity has been derived. (Elio and Scharf, 1990, p. 593)

Elio and Scharf (1990) present the following account of the focus of attention mechanism as applied to the first physics problem:

EUREKA's first step in solving Problem 1 is to set its focus of attention to be the desired quantity, which is acceleration of the body along the x-axis. This creates a goal that is added to the problem representation. EUREKA next retrieves all inferences from the textbook knowledge that are associated with the current focus of attention. In this case, there are none associated with acceleration. EUREKA then retrieves from the textbook network all equations that have the focus of attention as a variable. In order to be used, equations must have their constraints satisfied and must not contain more than one unknown variable other than the focus of attention. This leaves only Eqn-F3; sum-of-forces-x-axis=mass*acceleration-x-axis.

Having retrieved this equation, EUREKA works on deriving the remaining unknowns so the equation can be solved for acceleration. The mass of the body appears as a known quantity in the problem representation, so the next focus of attention is sum-of-forces-x-axis. At this stage of the problem, the goal-subgoal structure in the solution method indicates that (a) the first focus of attention was acceleration-along-x-axis, (b) Eqn-F3 was retrieved and selected to solve for this quantity, and (c) the next focus of attention was sum-of-forces-x-axis [Figure 7.1b].

The focus of attention is not sum-of-forces-x-axis. EUREKA finds no inferences associated with this concept but does not retrieve four equations from the textbook knowledge network. Only equation Eqn-F1 (see Appendix B) has all its constraints satisfied and does not contain more than one unknown. As mentioned previously, this equation's right-hand side is constructed by a procedure that sums all of the forces along the x-axis. Gravity along the x-axis is the only force contained in the current problem representation. Therefore, the Eqn-F1 is instantiated as sum-of-forces-x-axis=gravity-x-axis and the next focus of attention is gravity-x-axis.

Gravity is not associated with any inferences but does not appear in Eqn-F5. At this point in the growing problem representation, all variables in this equation appear as known quantities. As a result, gravity-x-axis is marked as derived and added to the problem representation. This goal is popped, EUREKA goes back to Eqn-F1, and the focus of attention reverts to sum-of-forces-x-axis (see [Figure 7.1]). Recall that Eqn-F1 is a vector summation of forces along the x-axis, without specifying what these forces are. The only force EUREKA knows about at this point is gravity along the x-axis. It formulates the equation using this as the only force and asks the teacher if all the relevant forces have been identified. The force due to friction is missing, so the teacher responds ''no'' and EUREKA knows it cannot solve this equation correctly at this time. Note that the teacher does not specify what is missing. Over time, EUREKA learns what the relevant forces are for this type of problem, so when it asks about these equations after some experience, the teacher will respond ''yes [you have all the relevant forces there].'' Getting back to the example, there are no other equations associated with the current focus of attention, sum-of-forces-x-axis. Therefore, EUREKA changes its focus of attention back to the parent goal, acceleration-along-x-axis. However, there are no other eligible equations for deriving acceleration.

Once EUREKA has arrived back at its top goal, the desired quantity, with no answer and no more equations to use, it must find a new focus of attention. There are a number of other aspects about the problem that could serve as focuses of attention and possibly get the solution moving again. Specifically, there are four leads EUREKA considers in this order: recently inferred concepts that were not in the original problem representation, relations among objects in the problem, features of objects in the problem, and the objects themselves. This approach to finding a new focus of attention constitutes an implicit meta-strategy and serves to keep EUREKA on its current tangent, even though it has run out of equations. Intuitively, it seems reasonable that the most recent changes to the representation should influence the solution method, but we have no data on whether a meta-strategy favoring recently inferred concepts is a correct characterization of novice problem-solving behavior.

At this point in Problem 1's enhanced representation, there are no newly inferred concepts. The next lead to follow is relations, so EUREKA arbitrarily selects the relation *on* and retrieves five associated inference rules. Two of these five inference rules have their conditions met in the current representation:

Inf-A	If	a body is on a surface and there is a friction between the body and the surface
	Then	there is the presence-of-friction force acting on the body along the x-axis
Inf-B	If	a body is on an object
	Then	there is the presence-of a normal force acting on the body along the y-axis

The problem representation is augmented with the conclusions of these rules. EUREKA then goes to the textbook knowledge network to retrieve equations but the concept *on* has no associated equations. Because this is a dead end, another focus of attention is needed. The problem representation now has newly inferred concepts, so EUREKA arbitrarily makes one of them, friction-x-axis, the new focus of attention and proceeds to retrieve associated inferences and equations.

EUREKA continues in this manner until the original desired quantity is derived and the problem is solved. This yields the solution tree shown in [Figure 7.1]. At this point, the enhanced problem representation, including the solution tree in [Figure 7.1], is stored in the P-MOP network. (Elio and Scharf, 1990, pp. 595–596)

EUREKA's Novice and Expert Protocols

Elio and Scharf (1990) offer the following protocols for understanding what EUREKA might be doing differentially when it solves problems as a novice and as an expert:

Although we did not program EUREKA to simulate a verbal protocol during problem solving, it is easy to depict such a protocol using the structures in [Figures 7.3a and 7.3b] and Problem 1 as an example. As a novice solving Problem 1, EUREKA has no prior knowledge in the P-MOP network, so its solution is based strictly on means-ends analysis. The protocol it could give as it constructed the solution method in [Figure 7.1] might go as follows:

EUREKA: I need an equation to solve for acceleration. Eqn-F3 is a possibility. Sum-of-forces is an unknown in Eqn-F3.

I need an equation to solve for sum-of-forces. Eqn-F1 is a possibility.

Gravity is an unknown in Eqn-F1. I need an equation to solve for gravity.

Eqn-F5 is the best possibility. I know all the other quantities in Eqn-F5, so I can solve for gravity.

I substitute gravity into Eqn-F1 and believe that I know all the forces needed to solve for the sum-of-forces. Is this correct?

Teacher: No, you haven't identified all the forces.

EUREKA: So I can't solve Eqn-F1 and I have no other ways to get acceleration right now.

I notice that the body is ON something. If a body is on something, then there is a frictional force acting on that body. I could try solving for friction. The equations I know for doing that are. . . .

and so on.

In order to generate a protocol for this same problem after the problem-solving knowledge in [Figure 7.3a and 7.3b] developed, EUREKA could mention constraints that are matched (indices traversed), deep features that are inferred (inference rules on P-MOPs), and possible solution methods (also found on P-MOPs). For Problem 1, P-MOP1 does not provide any useful information. P-MOP10 can be reached via a number of inclined-plane indices, so the expert solution protocol to Problem 1 might begin with any one of them as the first constraint satisfied:

EUREKA: There is an on-relationship between the body and the surface [*one possible path to P-MOP10*]. There is a normal force acting on the body [*inference rule on P-MOP10*].

Figure 7.3a
The P-MOP Network After All Ten Problems Are Solved

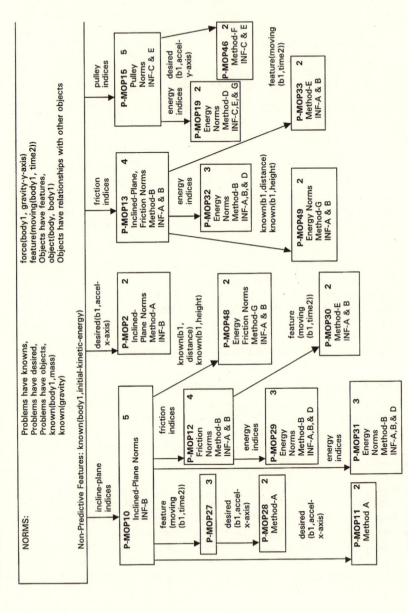

Source: Elio and Scharf (1990).

Figure 7.3b
The P-MOP Network After All Ten Problems Are Solved

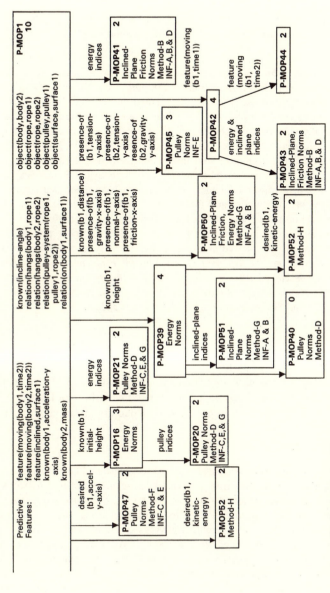

Source: Elio and Scharf (1990).

The coefficient of friction is known [*one of several indices to P-MOP12 which is preferred because it indexes the most experiences*].

I know there is a normal force and a frictional force acting on the body [*inference rules on P-MOP12*] and I know how to solve for normal force acting on this body [*Method B on P-MOP12*].

The body is also in motion along a surface [*moving to P-MOP30*], which means that the frictional force can be found by [*Method E on P-MOP30*].

At this point, P-MOP30 indexes two problems, one of which is Problem 1. Having reached Problem 1's representation (see [Figure 7.1]), EUREKA would only need the leftmost subtree because it has already figured out that there are normal and frictional forces acting on the body and what methods would be appropriate for deriving them. Even if the solution to Problem 1 were completely forgotten, EUREKA would have generated a nearly complete solution in this forward-working manner. We think it is important that the qualitative shift in solution methods comes not from retrieving past solution trees, but from remembering and recalling relevant inferences about the problem scenarios which trigger principles, which in turn have associated contexts that specify conditions of applicability and further tests. P-MOPs 1, 10, 12, and 30 used in this hypothetical protocol comprise what we consider to be a complete configuration of constraints. The norms found on the P-MOPs, particularly those that are also predictive features, can also be viewed as expectations for the type of problem EUREKA is currently working on. *The hypothetical protocols for Problem 1 illustrate how a shift to a knowledge-development strategy is supported by the kind of knowledge abstracted in the P-MOP network and the manner in which it is organized and restructured with experience.* (Elio and Scharf, 1990, pp. 619–620; italics added)

Elio and Scharf (1990) point out that as a result of EUREKA's experience with additional problems beyond those of Problems 1 and 2, its strategic knowledge organization increases in sophistication, as shown in the complex networks of Figures 7.3a and 7.3b compared with those of Figures 7.1a and 7.1b; EUREKA has moved from novice knowledge organization to expert knowledge organization.

The problem-solving trace and protocols demonstrated how EUREKA's final knowledge organization evolves from a novice-like organization based on surface features to an expert-like organization characterized by known quantities and abstract physics entities. In its novice stages, EUREKA has no option but to use means-ends analysis to solve problems. When a few problem-solving experiences are indexed, the initial P-MOP network is organized around surface features. As more problems are solved, known quantities and inferred physics entities become the discriminating and characteristic features upon which organizational structure is based. *EUREKA begins to prefer indices about known quantities and abstract physics entities like forces because, over time, they emerge as the best discriminating features of problem-solving knowledge.* (Elio and Scharf, 1990, p. 621; italics added)

PHILOSOPHICAL AND PSYCHOLOGICAL
IMPLICATIONS OF THE EUREKA PROGRAM

Elio and Scharf (1990) have demonstrated how, in EUREKA, knowledge concerning the domain of elementary physics problems is acquired, organized, reorganized, and abstracted with consequent augmentation of the system's power. Unlike expert systems in general, which are only performance motivated, EUREKA provides a detailed developmental account of its transitional progress as it achieves the status of an expert problem solver. Important advances in the understanding of how human novices become human experts could be achieved by a comparison of EUREKA, serving as a computational model, with research protocols produced by human subjects.

8

The Development of Independent Robots

SUBSETS OF ENVIRONMENTAL ATTRIBUTES AND ROBOTIC ATTRIBUTES

For robots, as for any organism, behavior is a function of its own attributes and the attributes of the environment. Therefore, the ultimate objective of a robot that can make its autonomous way in the world is constrained by the subset of world attributes that frame the robot's behavior and delimit the problem faced by the designer of robotic systems.

The ultimate objective of developing a self-directed robot that can flexibly adapt to changing environmental circumstances is dramatically different from the achieved goal of designing narrowly dedicated intelligent systems.

Autonomy. This goal holds that a system is intelligent if it can, on its own initiative, do things in the real world. This is to be contrasted with, say, merely planning in some abstract place, or performing in a simulated world, or advising a human who then goes off and does things. The idea is that the real world is always so much more complex than our models of it, that it is only a fair test of the programs we claim to be intelligent. (Lenat and Feigenbaum, 1991, p. 209)

Varieties of Robots

In recent years, there has been a burgeoning of research and development activity in robotics. University, industrial, and governmental laboratories, have created sophisticated robotic designs with worldwide applications.

A robot named ORACLE is shearing sheep in Western Australia. One called RM3 is washing, debarnacling, and painting the hulls of ships in France. Several dozen brain operations have been performed at Long Beach Memorial Hospital in California with the help of a robot arm for precision drilling of the skull. . . . The U.S. defense department is using undersea robots built by Honeywell to disarm mines in the Persian Gulf and other locations. Thousands of robots are routinely used in bioengineering laboratories to perform the extremely delicate operations required to snip and connect minute pieces of DNA. And walking robots are used in nuclear power plants to perform operations in areas too dangerous for humans. . . . The next generation of robots will take several more steps in replicating the subtlety of humans perceptual ability and movement while retaining the machines inherent advantages in speed, memory, precision, repeatability, and tireless operation. Specialized chips are being developed that will provide the massively parallel computations required for substantially higher levels of visual perception. Equally sophisticated tactile sensors are being designed into robot hands. Manipulators with dozens of degrees of freedom will combine the ability to lift both very heavy objects and delicate ones without breaking the latter. These robots' "local" intelligence will be fully integrated into the computerized control systems of a modern factory. (Kurzwell, 1990, p. 317)

A Sophisticated Robot: Wabot-2

The computer musician, Wabot-2, comprehends and performs musical scores and thereby demonstrates a sophisticated integration of central and sensory motor information processing.

A particularly impressive robot called Wabot-2 (Waseda Robot; . . .) was developed in the mid-to-late 1980's by Waseda University in Tokyo and refined by Sumitomo Electric [Roads, 1986]. This human-size (and humanlike) 200-pound robot is capable of reading sheet music through its camera eye and then, with its ten fingers and two feet, playing the music on an organ or synthesizer keyboard. It has a total of 50 joints and can strike keys at the rate of 15 per second, comparable to a skilled keyboard player. Its camera eye provides relatively high resolution for a robot. Using a charge-coupled device (CCD) sensing array, it has a resolution of 2,000 by 3,000 pixels (by comparison, the eyes of a person with good eyesight can resolve about 10,000 by 10,000 points). Wabot-2 also has a sense of hearing: it can track the pitch of a human singer it is accompanying and adjust the tempo of its playing accordingly. Finally, the robot has rudimentary speech-recognition and synthesis capabilities and can engage in simple conversations. There are severe limitations on the complexity of the musical score that it can read, and the music must be precisely placed by a human assistant. Nonetheless, Wabot-2 is an impressive demonstration of the state of the robotic art in the late 1980's. (Kurzwell, 1990, pp. 318–320)

ROBOTIC INTELLIGENCE AND THE WORLD

The competent performance of Wabot-2 rests on the application of well-recognized artificial intelligence methods, and most researchers would concur that further advances in robotic intelligence generally would depend on continued application of these methods. However, the MIT artificial intelligence researcher Rodney Brooks takes the position that these methods are generally unnecessary and that mobile robot intelligence can be engineered without regard to the central artificial intelligence method of symbolic or conceptual representation. In the following section, the theory and research included in ''Intelligence Without Representation'' (Brooks, 1991) will be discussed, and, then, a brief commentary will be offered.

Robotic Intelligence: Overview of the Brooks Position

Brooks (1991) summarizes his theoretical position and research in the following account:

Artificial intelligence research has foundered on the issue of representation. When intelligence is approached in an incremental manner, with strict reliance on interfacing to the real world through perception and action, reliance on representation disappears. In this paper, we outline our approach to incrementally building complete intelligent creatures. The fundamental decomposition of the intelligence system is not into independent information processing units which must interface with each other via representations. Instead, the intelligence system is decomposed into independent and parallel activity producers which all interface directly to the world through perception and action, rather than interface to each other particularly much. The notions of central and peripheral systems evaporate—everything is both central and peripheral. Based on these principles we have built a very successful series of mobile robots which operate without supervision as creatures in standard office environments. (Brooks, 1991, p. 139)

Creating Artificial Intelligence: The Approach of Brooks

Brooks (1991) argues for an incremental and experimental approach to the development of artificial intelligence and against the value of representational models of the world.

In this paper I . . . argue for a different approach to creating artificial intelligence:

—We must incrementally build up the capabilities of intelligence systems, having complete systems at each step of the way and thus automatically insure that the pieces and their interfaces are valid.

—At each step we should build complete intelligence systems that we let loose in the real world with real sensing and real action. Anything less provides a candidate with which we can delude ourselves.

We have been following this approach and have built a series of autonomous mobile robots. We have reached an unexpected conclusion (C) and have a rather radical hypothesis (H).

(C) When we examine very simple level intelligence we find that explicit representations and models of the world simply get in the way. It turns out to be better to use the world as its own model.

(H) Representation is the wrong unit of abstraction in building the bulkiest parts of intelligent systems.

Representation has been a central issue in artificial intelligence work over the last fifteen years only because it has provided an interface between otherwise isolated modules and conference papers. (Brooks, 1991, p. 140)

Autonomous Mobile Robots: Goals and Characteristics

Brooks (1991) summarizes his purpose in developing autonomous mobile robots and outlines their characteristics in the following account:

I wish to build completely autonomous mobile agents that coexist in the world with humans, and are seen by those humans as intelligent beings in their own right. I would call such agents creatures. This is my intellectual motivation. I have no particular interest in demonstrating how human beings work, though humans, like other animals, are interesting objects of study in this endeavor as they are successful autonomous agents. I have no particular interest in applications; it seems clear to me that if my goals can be met then the range of application for such creatures will be limited only by our (or their) imagination. I have no particular interest in the philosophical implications of creatures, although clearly there will be significant implications. . . .

First, let us consider some of the requirements for our creatures.

—A creature must cope appropriately and in a timely fashion with changes in its dynamic environment.

—A creature should be robust with respect to its environment; minor changes in the properties of the world should not lead to a total collapse of the creature's behavior; rather one should expect only a gradual change in the capabilities of the creature as the environment changes more and more.

—A creature should be able to maintain multiple goals and, depending on the circumstances it finds itself in, change which particular goals it is actively pursuing; thus it can both adapt to surroundings and capitalize on fortuitous circumstances.

—A creature should do something in the world; it should have some purpose in being. (Brooks, 1991, p. 146).

Autonomous Mobile Robots: Logic of Their Construction

In the following section, Brooks (1991) describes his approach to the construction of autonomous mobile robots and points out the advantages of his incremental approach.

Each activity, or behavior producing system individually connects sensing to action. We refer to an activity producing system as a layer. An activity is a pattern of interactions within the world. Another name for our activities might well be skill. Emphasizing that each activity can at least post facto be rationalized as pursuing some purpose. We have chosen the word activity, however, because our layers must decide when to act for themselves, not befriend subroutines to be invoked at the beck and call of some other layer.

The advantage of this approach is that it gives an incremental path from very simple systems to complex autonomous intelligence systems. At each step of the way it is only necessary to build one small piece, and interface it into an existing, working, complete intelligence.

The idea is to first build a very simple complete autonomous system, and test it in the real world. Our favorite example of such a system is a creature, actually a mobile robot, which avoids hitting things. It senses objects in its immediate vicinity and moves away from them, halting if it senses something in its path. It isn't still necessary to build the system by decomposing it into parts, but there need be no clear distinction between the "perception subsystem", a "central system", and an "action system". In fact, there may well be two independent channels connecting sensing to action (one for initiating motion, and one for emergency halts), so there is no single place where perception delivers a representation of the world in the traditional sense.

Next we build an incremental layer of intelligence which operates in parallel to the first system. It is pasted onto the existing debugged system and tested again in the real world. This new layer might directly access the sensors and run a different algorithm on the delivered data. The first level autonomous system continues to run in parallel, and unaware of the existence of the second level. For example, in [Brooks, 1986] we reported on building a first level of control which let the creature avoid objects and then adding a layer which instilled an activity of trying to visit distant visible places. The second layer injected commands to the motor control part of the first layer directing the robot towards the goal, but independently the first layer would cause the robot to veer away from previously unseen obstacles. The second layer monitored the progress of the creature and sent updated motor commands, thus achieving its goal without being explicitly aware of objects, which had been handled by the lower level of control. (Brooks, 1991, pp. 146–147)

Autonomous Mobile Robots: The Problem of Representation

In the following account, Brooks (1991) asserts that his robots operate without need for central representation, which is replaced by direct perception and action:

With multiple layers, the notion of perception delivering a description of the world gets blurred even more as a part of the system to a perception is spread out over many pieces which are not particularly connected by data paths or related by function. Certainly there is no identifiable place where the output of perception can be found. Furthermore, totally different sorts of processing of the sensor data proceed independently and in parallel, each affecting the overall system activity through quite different channels of control.

In fact, not by design, but rather by observation we note that a common theme in the ways in which our layered and distributed approach helps our creatures meet our goals is that there is no central representation.

—Low level simple activities can instill the creature with reactions to dangerous or important changes in its environment. Without complex representations and the need to maintain those representations and reason about them, these reactions can easily be made quick enough to serve their purpose. The key idea is to sense the environment often, and so have an up-to-date idea of what is happening in the world.

—By having multiple parallel activities, and by removing the idea of a central representation, there is less chance that any given change in the class of properties enjoyed by the world can cause total collapse of the system. Rather one might expect that a given change will at most incapacitate some but not all of the levels of control. Gradually as a more alien world is soon entered (alien in the sense that the properties that hold are different from the properties in which the individual layers were debugged), the performance of the creature might continue to degrade. By not trying to have an analogous model of the world, centrally located in the system, we are less likely to have built-in a dependence on the model being completely accurate. Rather, individual layers extract only those aspects of the world which they find relevant— projections of representation into a simple subspace, if you like. Changes in the fundamental structure of a world have less chance of being reflected in every one of those projections than they would have of showing up as a difficulty in matching some query to a central single world model.

—Each layer of control can be thought of as having its own implicit purpose (or goal if you insist). Since there are active layers, running in parallel and with access to its sensors, they can monitor the environment and decide on the appropriateness of their goals. Sometimes goals can be abandoned when circumstances seem unpromising, and other times fortuitous circumstances can be taken advantage of. The key idea here is to be using the world as its own model and to continuously match the preconditions of each goal against the real world. Because there is separate hardware for each layer we can match as many goals as can exist in parallel, and do not pay any price for higher numbers of goals as we would if we tried to add more and more sophistication to a single processor, or even some multi-processor with a capacity bounded network.

—The purpose of the creature is implicit in its higher level purposes, goals, or layers. There need be no explicit representation of goals at some central (or distributed) process selects from to decide what is most appropriate for the creature to do next. . . .

Just as there is no central representation there is not even a central system. Each activity producing layer connects perception to action directly. It is only the observer of the creature who imputes a central representation or central control. The creature itself has none; it is a collection of competing behaviors. Out of the local chaos of their interactions there emerges, in the eye of an observer, a coherent pattern of behavior. There is no central purpose for locus of control. Minksy [1986] gives a similar account of how human behavior is generated.

Note carefully that we are not claiming that chaos is a necessary ingredient of intelligent behavior. Indeed, we advocate careful engineering of all the interactions within the system (evolution has the luxury of incredibly long time scales and enormous numbers of individual experiments and thus perhaps was able to do without this careful engineering).

We do claim however, that there need be no explicit representation of either the world or the intentions of the system to generate intelligent behaviors for a creature. Without such explicit representations, and when viewed locally, the interaction may indeed seem chaotic and without purpose.

I claim there is more than this, however. Even at a local level we do not have traditional AI representations. We never use tokens which have any semantics that can be attached to them. The best that can be said in our implementation is that one number is passed from a process to another. But it is only by looking at the state of both the first and second processes that the number can be given any interpretation at all. An extremist might say that we really do have representations, but that they are just implicit. Within appropriate mapping of the complete system and its state to another domain, we could define a representation that these numbers and topological connections between processes somehow encode.

However we are not happy with calling such things a representation. They differ from standard representations in too many ways.

There are no variables (e.g. see [Minsky, 1986] for a more thorough treatment of this) that need instantiation in reasoning processes. There are no rules which need to be selected through pattern matching. There are no choices to be made. To a large extent the state of the world determines the action of the creature. Simon [1969] noted that the complexity of behavior of a system was not necessarily inherent in the complexity of the creature, but perhaps in the complexity of the environment. He made this analysis in his description of an ant wandering a beach, but ignored its implications in the next paragraph when he talked about humans. We hypothesize (following Edgars and Chapman) that much of even human mobile activity is similarly a reflection of the world through very simple mechanisms without detailed representations. (Brooks, 1991, pp. 147–149)

Autonomous Mobile Robots: The Subsumption Architecture

Brooks (1991) has constructed a series of robots, each dependent on a subsumption architecture of finite state machines.

We have built a series of four robots based on the methodology of task decomposition. They all operate in an unconstrained dynamic world (laboratory and office areas in the MIT Artificial Intelligence laboratory). They successfully operate with people walking by, people deliberately trying to confuse them, and people just standing by watching them. All four robots are creatures in the sense that on power-up they exist in the world and interact with it, pursuing multiple goals determined by their control layers implementing different activities. This is in contrast to other mobile robots that are given programs or plans to follow for a specific mission. . . .

All the robots implement the same abstract architecture, which we call the subsumption architecture, which embodies the fundamental ideas of decomposition into layers of task achieving behaviors, an incremental decomposition perceived by the end of their world. Details of these implementations can be found in [Brooks, 1986].

Each layer in the subsumption architecture is composed of a fixed topology network of simple finite state machines. Each finite state machine has a handful of states, one or two internal registers, one or two internal timers, and access to simple computational machines, which can compute things such as vector sums. The finite state machines run asynchronously, sending and receiving fixed length messages (1-bit messages on the two small robots, and 24-bit messages on larger ones) over wires. . . .

There is no central locus of control. Rather, the finite state machines are data-driven by the messages they receive. The arrival of messages or the expiration of designated time periods cause the finite state machine to change state. The finite state machines have access to the contents of the messages and might output them, test them with the predicate and conditionally branch to a different state, or pass them to simple computation elements. There is no possibility of access to global data, nor dynamically established communication links. There is thus no possibility of global control. All finite state machines are equal, yet at the same time they are prisoners of their fixed topology connections.

Layers are combined through mechanisms we call suppression (once the name subsumption architecture) and inhibition. In both cases as a new layer is added, one of the new wires is side-tapped into an existing wire. A predefined time constant is associated with each sidetap. In the case of suppression the sidetapping occurs on the input side of the finite state machine. If a message arrives on the net wire it is directed to the input port of the finite state machine as though it had arrived on the existing wire. Additionally, any new messages on the existing wire are suppressed (i.e., rejected) for the specified time period. For inhibition the sidetapping occurs on the output side of the finite state machine. A message on the new wire simply inhibits messages being emitted on the existing wire for the specified time period. Unlike suppression the new message is not delivered in their place.

As an example, consider the three layers of [Figure 8.1]. These are three layers of control that we have run on our first mobile robot for well over a year. The robot has a ring of twelve ultrasonic sonars as its primary sensors. Every second these sonars are run to give twelve radial depth measurements. Sonar is extremely noisy due to many objects being mirrors to sonar. There are thus problems with specular reflection and return paths following multiple reflections due to surface schema with low angles of incidents (less than 30 degrees).

In more detail the three layers work as follows:

(1) The lowest level layer implements a behavior which makes the robot (the physical embodiment of the creature) avoid hitting objects. It both avoids static objects and moving objects, even those that are actively attacking it. The finite state machine labeled SONAR simply runs the sonar devices and every second emits an instantaneous map with the readings converted to polar coordinates. This map is passed on to the COLLIDE and FEEL FORCE finite state machine. The first of these simply watches to see if there is anything dead ahead, and if so sends a halt message to the finite state machine in charge of running the robot forward—if that finite state machine is not in the correct state the message may well be ignored. Simultaneously, the other finite state machine computes a repulsive force on the robot, based on an inverse squared law, where each sonar return is considered to indicate the presence of a repulsive object. The contributions from each sonar are added to produce an overall force acting on the robot. The output is

Figure 8.1
Layers of Control

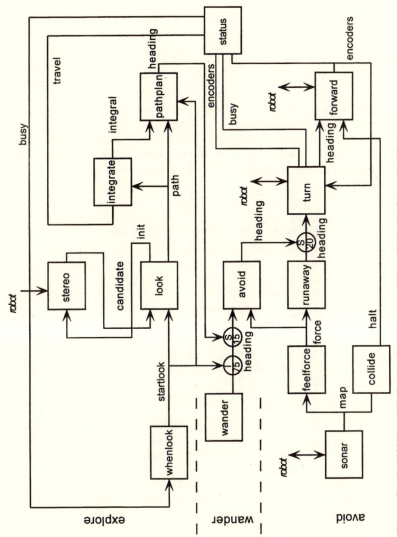

Source: Brooks (1991), p. 152. Reprinted with the permission of Elsevier Science Publishers.

passed to the runaway machine which thresholds it and passes it on to the turn machine which orients the robot directly away from the summed repulsive force. Finally, the forward machine drives the robot forward. Whenever this machine receives a halt message while the robot is driving forward, it commands the robot to halt.

This network of finite state machines generates behaviors which let the robot avoid objects. If it starts in the middle of an empty room it simply sits there. If someone walks up to it the robot moves away. If it moves in the direction of other obstacles it halts. Overall, it manages to exist in a dynamic environment without hitting or being hit by objects.

(2) The next layer makes the robot wander about, when not busy avoiding objects. The WANDER finite state machine generates a random heading for the robot every ten seconds or so. The AVOID machine treats that heading as an attractive force and sums it with the repulsive force computed from the sonar. It uses the results to suppress the lower level behavior, forcing the robot to move in a direction close to what WANDER decided but at the same time avoiding the obstacles. Note that if the TURN or FORWARD finite state machines are busy running the robot the new impulse to wander will be ignored.

(3) The third layer makes the robot try to explore. It looks for distant places, then tries to reach them. This layer suppresses the wander layer, and observes how the bottom layer diverts the robot due to obstacles (perhaps dynamic). It corrects for any divergences and the robot achieves the goal.

The WHENLOOK finite state machine notices when the robot is not busy moving, and starts up the FREE SPACE FINDER (labeled STEREO in [Figure 8.1] finite state machine. At the same time it inhibits wandering behavior so that the observation will remain valid. When a path is observed it is sent to the PATHPLAN finite state machine, which injects the commanded direction to the AVOID finite state machine. In this way, lower level optical avoidance continues to function. This may cause the robot to go in a direction different to that desired by PATHPLAN. For that reason the actual path of the robot is monitored by the INTEGRATE finite state machine, which sends updated estimates to the PATHPLAN machine. This machine then acts as a difference engine forcing the robot in the desired direction and compensating for the actual path of the robot as it avoids obstacles.

These particular layers were implemented in our first robot. See [Brooks, 1986] for more details. Brooks and Connell [1986] report on another three layers implemented on that particular robot. (Brooks, 1991, pp. 150–154)

Comparison of Subsumption Architecture and Standard Artificial Intelligence Approaches

In the following section, Brooks (1991) compares the theory and embodiment of subsumption architecture with a series of standard artificial intelligence approaches including connectionism, neural networks, productions rules, and blackboard architecture:

The subsumption architecture with its network of simple machines is reminiscent, at the surface at least, with a number of mechanistic approaches to intelligence, such as connectionism and neural networks. But it is different in many respects from these endeavors, and also quite different from many other post-Dartmouth traditions in artificial intelligence. We very briefly explain those differences in the following sections.

It Isn't Connectionism

Connectionists try to make networks of simple processors. In that regard, the things they build (in simulation only—no connectionist has ever driven a real robot in a real environment, no matter how simple) are similar to the subsumption networks we build. However, their processing nodes tend to be uniform in their looking (as the name suggests) for revelations for understanding how to connect them correctly (which is usually assumed to mean richly at least). Our nodes are all unique finite state machines and the density of connections is very much lower, certainly not uniform, and very low indeed between layers. Additionally, connectionists seem to be looking for explicit distributed representations to spontaneously arise from their networks. We harbor no such hopes because we believe representations are not necessary and appear only in the eye or mind of the observer.

It Isn't Neural Networks

Neural networks is the parent discipline of which connectionism is a recent incarnation. Workers in neural networks claim there is some biological significance to the network nodes, as models of neurons. Most of the models seem widely implausible given the paucity of modeled connections relative to the thousands found in real neurons. We claim no biological significance in our choice of finite state machines as network nodes.

It Isn't Production Rules

Each individual activity producing layer of our architecture could be viewed as an implementation of a production rule. When the right conditions are met in the environment a certain action will be performed. We feel that analogy is a little like saying that any FORTRAN program with IF statements is implementing a production rule system. A standard production system really is more—it has a rule base, from which a rule is selected based on matching preconditions of all the rules to the same database. The preconditions may include variables which must be matched to individuals in the database. Our layers run in parallel and have no variables or need for matching. Instead, aspects of the world are extracted and these directly trigger or modify certain behaviors of the layer.

It Isn't a Blackboard

If one really wanted, one could make an analogy of our networks to a blackboard control architecture. Some of the finite state machines would be localized knowledge sources. Others would be processes acting on those knowledge sources by finding them on the blackboard. There's a simplifying point in our architecture however: all the processes know exactly where to look on the blackboard as they are hardwired to the correct place. I think this forced analogy indicates its own weakness. There's no flexibility at all on where a process can gather appropriate knowledge. Most advanced blackboard architectures make heavy use of the general sharing and availability of almost all knowledge. Furthermore, in spirit at least, blackboard systems tend to hide from a consumer of knowledge who the particular producer was. This is the primary means of abstraction in blackboard systems. In our system we make such connections explicit and permanent. (Brooks, 1991, pp. 154–155)

Autonomous Mobile Robots: Further Development

In the following section, Brooks (1991) sketches his guiding concepts for further research in the development of autonomous mobile robots.

Since our approach is a performance based one, it is the performance of the systems we build which must be used to measure its usefulness and to point to its limitations.

We claim that as of mid-1987 our robots, using the subsumption architecture to implement complete creatures, are the most reactive real time mobile robots in existence. Most other mobile robots are still at the stage of individual experimental runs in static environments, or at best in completely mapped static environments. Ours, on the other hand, operate completely autonomously in complex dynamic environments at the flick of their own switches, and continuing until their batteries are drained. We believe they operate at a level closer to simple insect level intelligence than to bacterial level intelligence. Our goal (worth nothing if we don't deliver) is simple insect level intelligence within two years. Evolution took 3 billion years to get from single cells to insects, and only another 500 million years to get from there to humans. This statement is not intended as a prediction of our future performance, but rather to indicate the nontrivial nature of insect level intelligence.

Despite this good performance to date, there are a number of serious questions about our approach. We have beliefs and hopes about how these questions will be resolved, but under our criteria only performance truly counts. Experiments in building more complex systems takes time, so with the caveat that the experiments described below have not yet been performed we outline how we see our current endeavor progressing. Our intent in discussing this is to indicate that there is at least a plausible path forward to more intelligent machines from our current situation.

Our belief is that the source of activity producing layers over the control we are developing (mobility, vision, and survival related tasks) are necessary prerequisites for higher level intelligence in the style we attribute to human beings.

The most natural and serious questions concerning limits of our approach are:

—How many layers can be built in this subsumption architecture before the interactions between layers become too complex to continue?

—How complex can the behaviors be that are developed without the aid of central representation?

—Can higher level functions such as learning occur in these fixed topology networks of simple finite state machines?

We outline our current thoughts on these questions.

How Many Layers?

The highest number of layers we have run on a physical robot is three. In simulation we have run six parallel layers. The technique of completely debugging a robot and all assisting activity producing layers before designing and adding a new one seems to have been practical until now at least.

How Complex?

We are currently working towards a complex behavior pattern on our fourth robot which will require approximately 14 individual activity producing layers.

The robot has infrared proximity sensors for local obstacle avoidance. It has an on-board manipulator which can grasp objects at ground and tabletop levels, and also determine a rough weight. The hand has depth sensors mounted on it so that homing in on the target object in order to grasp it can be controlled directly. We are currently working on a structured light laser scanner to determine rough depth maps in a forward looking direction from the robot.

The high level behavior we are trying to instill in these creatures is to wander around the office areas of our laboratory, find open office doors, and retrieve empty soda cans from cluttered desks and crowded offices and return them to a central repository.

In order to achieve this overall behavior a number of simpler task achieving behaviors are necessary. They include: avoiding objects, following walls, recognizing doorways and going through them, aligning on large landmarks, heading in a homeward direction, learning homeward bearings at landmarks and following them, locating table-like objects, approaching such objects, scanning table tops for cylindrical objects of roughly the height of a soda can, serving the manipulator arm, moving the hand above sensed objects, using the hand sensor to look for objects of soda can size sticking up from a background, grasping objects if they are light enough, and depositing objects.

Individual tasks may not be coordinated by any central controller. Instead they can index off of the state of the world. For instance, the grasp behavior can cause the manipulator to grasp any object of the appropriate size seen by the hand sensor. The robot will not randomly grasp just any object however, because it will only be when other layers or behaviors have noticed an object of roughly the same shape on top of a table-like object that the grasping key will find itself in a position where its sensing of the world tells it to react. If, from above, the object no longer looks like a soda can, the grasp reflex will not happen and other lower level behaviors will cause the robot to look elsewhere for new candidates.

Is Learning and Such Possible?

Some insects demonstrate a simple type of learning that has been dubbed "learning by instinct" [Gould and Marler, 1986]. It is hypothesized that honey bees, for example, are prewired to learn how to distinguish certain classes of flowers, and to learn routes to and from the home hive and sources of nectar. Other insects, butterflies, have been shown to be able to learn to distinguish flowers, but in an information limited way [Lewis, 1986]. If they are forced to learn about a second sort of flower, they forget what they already know about the first, in a manner that suggests that the total amount of information that they know remains constant.

We have found a way to build fixed topology networks of our finite state machines which can perform learning, as an isolated subsystem, at levels comparable to these examples. At the moment of course we are in the very position we lambasted most AI workers for earlier in this paper. We have an isolated module of the system working, and inputs and outputs left dangling.

We are working to remedy the situation, but experimental work with physical creatures is a nontrivial and time consuming activity. We find that almost any predesigned piece of equipment or software has so many preconceptions of how they are to be used built into them, that they are not flexible enough to be part of our complete systems. Thus, as of mid-1987, our work in learning is held up by the need to build a new type of video camera and high speed lower power processing box to run specially developed vision algorithms at ten frames per second. Each of these steps is a significant engineering endeavor which we are undertaking as fast as resources permit.

Of course, talk is cheap.

The Future

Only experiments with real creatures and real worlds can answer the natural doubts about our approach. Time will tell. (Brooks, 1991, pp. 156–158)

Commentary on the Brooks Thesis

Brooks is extending the general thesis that activity or behavior generally across robots, animals, and humans is not dependent upon conceptual, representational, strategic thought, planning, and reasoning, but rather is a function of automatic mechanistic (finite state machines) responses to environmental contingencies. The thesis is reminiscent of Gibsonian ecological views (Gibson, 1979), which the organism by means of its genetically determined autonomous nervous system can smoothly adapt, without cogitation, to the general demands and specific survival pressures of changing environmental situations. The thesis is also reminiscent of Skinnerian radical behaviorism (Skinner, 1938), that schedules of environmental reinforcement control behavior in all organisms. Clearly, the thesis of Brooks and the theories of Gibson and Skinner are too broad and universalistic in their range of application, but quite useful and pertinent in specific domains. But even within the domain of robotics, the demands for an adequate artificial intelligence theory for the relatively cognitive performance of the computer musician Wabot-2 differ from the demands for the performance of an autonomous mobile robot. A system of the future that combines cognition and mobility will require an adroit combination of design elements drawn from the Brooks thesis and the symbolic conceptual representations of traditional artificial intelligence.

PHILOSOPHICAL AND PSYCHOLOGICAL IMPLICATIONS OF INTELLIGENT ROBOTS

From ancient times to the present, two modes of intellectual orientation characterize the creation of robots: the animistic orientation and the technological orientation.

The Animistic Orientation to Robots

In classical Greece, the animistic orientation is epitomized in the striving of the sculptor Pygmalion to create from a block of stone a beautiful woman, Galatia. In modern Japan, the animistic orientation is expressed in the anthropomorphic computer musician Wabot-2 (described in the previous section).

In the animistic orientation, a lifelike theatrical effect on the audience is sought, imagination is engaged and criticism suspended.

The Technological Orientation to Robots

In classical Greece, the technological orientation is epitomized by steam-and water-driven mechanisms that control the opening and closing of sacred temple doors. In the modern world, the technological orientation is manifest in the hundreds of thousands of computer-controlled robots operating in industrial, military, and scientific settings (described in a previous section).

In the technological orientation, productive results are sought, economic values are predominant, and personification is unnecessary.

9

Human Level Language Comprehension and Language Generation

LANGUAGE COMPREHENSION AND ARTIFICIAL INTELLIGENCE

The Limitations of Language-Comprehension Systems

The field of artificial intelligence has two separable but often intertwined objectives: (1) the matching or surpassing of human cognition; and (2) the advancement of computer cognition. With respect to the domain of language, the objectives have included both the development of natural language-understanding systems and natural language-processing systems. Language-processing systems would no more understand language than symbolic integration-processing systems understand mathematics. These systems process first-order logic or other representations, and correct processing is all that can be claimed. Language-processing systems are constituted of structures that manipulate representations of objects and events. The constituted structures do not understand natural language, and their manipulation of representations accord to them the proper appellation of information-processing automata. The thesis that natural language-understanding systems are automata that process information, and that they are not cognizant comprehenders of language, will be examined in the course of the following discussion of a number of artificial intelligence programs.

The ELIZA System and Psychotherapeutic Comprehension

Table 9.1 is a sample of a conversation between ELIZA and a young woman (Weizenbaum, 1976). In the conversation, ELIZA simulates the role of a client-

Table 9.1
A Conversation between ELIZA and a Young Woman

[1]	Men are all alike.
[2]	IN WHAT WAY
[3]	They're always bugging us about something or other.
[4]	CAN YOU THINK OF A SPECIFIC EXAMPLE
[5]	Well, my boyfriend made me come here.
[6]	YOUR BOYFRIEND MADE YOU COME HERE
[7]	He says I'm depressed much of the time.
[8]	I AM SORRY TO HEAR YOU ARE DEPRESSED
[9]	It's true. I am unhappy.
[10]	DO YOU THINK COMING HERE WILL HELP YOU TO NOT BE UNHAPPY
[11]	I need some help, that much seems certain.
[12]	WHAT WOULD IT MEAN TO YOU IF YOU GOT SOME HELP
[13]	Perhaps I could learn to get along with my mother.
[14]	TELL ME MORE ABOUT YOUR FAMILY
[15]	My mother takes care of me.
[16]	WHO ELSE IN YOUR FAMILY TAKES CARE OF YOU
[17]	My father.
[18]	YOUR FATHER
[19]	You are like my father in some ways.
[20]	WHAT RESEMBLANCE DO YOU SEE
[21]	You are not very aggressive but I think you don't want me to notice that.
[22]	WHAT MAKES YOU THINK I AM NOT VERY AGGRESSIVE
[23]	You don't argue with me.
[24]	WHY DO YOU THINK I DON'T ARGUE WITH YOU
[25]	You are afraid of me.
[26]	DOES IT PLEASE YOU TO BELIEVE I AM AFRAID OF YOU
[27]	My father is afraid of everybody.
[28]	WHAT ELSE COMES TO MIND WHEN YOU THINK OF YOUR FATHER
[29]	Bullies.
[30]	DOES THAT HAVE ANYTHING TO DO WITH THE FACT THAT YOUR BOYFRIEND MADE YOU COME HERE

Source: Weisenbaum, quoted in Boden (1977), pp. 106–107.

centered psychotherapist (Rogers, 1951). ELIZA gives the impression of understanding the language and personal problems of her client.

ELIZA's statements are produced from a stock of stereotyped phrases that mimic the psychotherapeutic techniques of the recognition, reflection, and clarification of the client's feelings and beliefs. ELIZA's internal representational structure matches key words or phrases in a client's statements with its stock of phrase templates and generates statements that give the appearance of sensitive listening and understanding.

For example, in Table 9.1 (lines 27 and 28), ELIZA identifies the key word "father" in the client's statement, "My father is afraid of everybody," converted "my" to "your," selected one of its stock phrases, "What else comes to mind when you think of," and produced the response, "What else comes to mind when you think of your father?" In lines 7 and 8, the key word "depressed" in "He says I'm depressed much of the time," triggers ELIZA's synthetic response, "I am sorry to hear you are depressed," using the stock phrase, "I am sorry to hear."

Inspection of Table 9.1 reveals the application of other stock phrases: "Do you think coming here will help you not to be" (line 10); "What would it mean to you" (line 12); "What makes you think" (line 22); "Does it please you to believe" (line 26).

ELIZA also has in her repertory a routine that gives the appearance of an incisive interpretation or conceptual integration by referring to an earlier statement (line 6), preceding it with the stock phrase, "Does that have anything to do with the fact that," and producing, "Does that have anything to do with the fact that your boyfriend made you come here" (line 30). ELIZA possesses many other schemes such as the transmutation of the client input type, "Everybody . . . me," into ELIZA's output type, "Who in particular . . . you" (where the filler for the ellipses might be: dislikes, bothers, makes fun of, talks about, ignores), and the recasting of the client input type, "Besides I . . ." or, "The reason why I . . ." into ELIZA's output type, "What is the real reason that you . . ."

In her "psychotherapeutic conversations," ELIZA succeeds in giving the semblance of humanity, as Weizenbaum (1976, pp. 190–191) comments:

After all, I reasoned, a psychiatrist can reflect the patient's remark, "My mommy took my teddy bear away from me," by saying, "Tell me more about your parents," without really having to know anything about teddy bears, for example . . .

Nevertheless, ELIZA created the most remarkable illusion of having understood in the minds of the many people who conversed with it. . . . This illusion was especially strong and most tenaciously clung to among people who knew little or nothing about computers. They would often demand to be permitted to converse with the system in private, and would, after conversing with it for a time, insist, in spite of my explanations, that the machine really understood them.

It is then easy to understand why people conversing with ELIZA believe, and cling to the belief, that they are being understood. The "sense" and the continuity the person conversing with ELIZA perceives is supplied largely by the person himself. He assigns meanings and interpretations to what ELIZA "says" that confirm his initial hypothesis that the system does understand.

The SHRDLU System and Its Micro-World Comprehension

Table 9.2 presents an interview with SHRDLU (Winograd, 1972). In a simulated micro-world of toy objects on a tabletop, SHRDLU's simulated robot arm manipulates the objects and displays these manipulations on a video screen. In addition, SHRDLU carries on by teletype a conversation with a human participant regarding its micro-world behavior.

The protocol in Table 9.2 contains examples of SHRDLU's ability to reason, to respond to questions, follow commands, and learn new concepts. The first section of the protocol (lines 1–6) is an example of SHRDLU's ability to recognize ambiguity and to request clarification before responding to a command: "Grasp the pyramid" is an ambiguous command because there is more than one pyramid in SHRDLU's micro-world.

The second section of the protocol (lines 7–16) is an example of SHRDLU's ability to give reasoned responses to questions that contain fairly complex constructions: "Is at least one of them narrower than the one which I told you to pick up?" The third section of the protocol (lines 17–22) contains examples of SHRDLU's processing of temporal concepts, such as "before," "when," "while," and of explanatory concepts, such as "why." The fourth section of the protocol (lines 23–30) demonstrates the processing of a new concept: (1) identification of the concept ("Sorry, I don't know the word steeple"); (2) acquisition of the concept ("A steeple is a stack that . . ."); and (3) application of the concept ("Build one"—"OK").

SHRDLU keeps a record of the structure of the conversation that enables it to make use of context in determining a specific referent. For example, in the second section of the protocol (lines 7–16), SHRDLU is able to determine that the "pyramid" in the interviewer's question ("What is the pyramid supported by?") refers to its own previous response "The blue pyramid and the blue block" (line 8). SHRDLU keeps track of descriptive qualities in its interviewer's responses to use in interpretation of a referent for "it." For example, if the interviewer had previously referred to "the blue block," the "it" in a subsequent query ("What color is it?") must refer to some other block. Regarding SHRDLU's conversational limitations, Winograd (1973, p. 158) comments:

[SHRDLU fails to address] all the implications of viewing language as a process of communication between two intelligent people. A human language user is always engaged in a process of trying to understand the world around him, including the person he is talking to. He is actively constructing models and hypotheses, and makes use of them in the process of language understanding.

[Since SHRDLU] keeps track of when things have been mentioned, it can check a possible interpretation of a question to see whether the asker could answer it himself from his previous sentences. If so, it assumes he probably means something else. We could characterize this as two sorts of knowledge. First, it assumes that a person asks questions for the purpose of getting information that he doesn't already have, and second, it has a very primitive model of what information he has on the basis of what he has

Table 9.2

A Conversation with SHRDLU (a Simulated Robot) Concerning Its Behavior in a Micro-World

[1]	pick up a big red block.
[2]	OK.
[3]	grasp that pyramid.
[4]	I DON'T UNDERSTAND WHICH PYRAMID YOU MEAN.
[5]	find a block which is taller than the one you are holding and put it into the box.
[6]	OK.
	. . .
[7]	what does the box contain?
[8]	THE BLUE PYRAMID AND THE BLUE BLOCK.
[9]	what is the pyramid supported by?
[10]	THE BOX.
[11]	how many blocks are not in the box?
[12]	FOUR OF THEM.
[13]	is at least one of them narrower than the one which I told you to pick up?
[14]	YES, THE RED CUBE.
[15]	can the table pick up blocks?
[16]	NO.
	. . .
[17]	had you touched any pyramid before you put the green one on the little cube?
[18]	YES, THE GREEN ONE.
[19]	when did you pick it up?
[20]	WHILE I WAS STACKING UP THE RED CUBE, A LARGE RED BLOCK AND A LARGE GREEN CUBE.
[21]	Why?
[22]	TO GET RID OF IT.
	. . .
[23]	does a steeple . . .
[24]	SORRY, I DON'T KNOW THE WORD "STEEPLE".
[25]	a "steeple" is a stack which contains two green cubes and a pyramid.
[26]	I UNDERSTAND.
[27]	are there any steeples now?
[28]	NO.
[29]	build one.
[30]	OK.

Note: The micro-world consists of a table top, a box, and blocks of various shapes, sizes, and colors. In the protocol, SHRDLU's responses are in uppercase letters, and the human participants' responses are in lowercase letters.

Source: Winograd, quoted in Gardner (1985).

Table 9.3
The English Notation for the Plot of Shakespeare's *Macbeth*

[Macbeth is a noble] before [Macbeth is a king].

Macbeth marry Lady-Macbeth.

Lady-Macbeth is a woman--has-property greedy ambitious.

Duncan is a king.

Macduff is a noble--has-property loyal angry.

Weird-sisters is a hag group--has-property old ugly weird--number 3.

Weird-sisters predict [Macbeth murder Duncan].

Macbeth desire [Macbeth kind-of king]

      [cause [Macbeth murder Duncan]].

Lady-Macbeth persuade [Macbeth murder Duncan].

Macbeth murder Duncan [coagent Lady-Macbeth--instrument-knife].

Lady-Macbeth kill Lady-Macbeth.

Macbeth murder Duncan [cause [Macduff kill Macbeth]].

Source: Winston (1980). Reprinted with the permission of the Association of Computing Machinery.

said. A realistic view of language must have a complex model of this type, and the heuristics in our system touch only the tiniest bit of the relevant knowledge.

SHRDLU is a language-processing automaton. It is not a cognizant language comprehender. SHRDLU does not possess the knowledge necessary to understand its own conversation with its human participant. SHRDLU does not initiate actions, but performs in response to the prompts of its human controller.

A conversation with SHRDLU about its micro-world does not represent a microcosm of conversation between human beings. Human conversation is reciprocal in character, motivated in purpose, situation-related, expansive or constrained, technical or general, serious or playful, informative or misleading, on one level or several levels, natural or stilted, designed to impress or to be impressed, and, unlike SHRDLU, a manifestation of general intelligence.

System for the Comprehension of Shakespearean Plays

An implemented system developed by Winston (1980) contained representation of the plots of five Shakespearean plays and determined similarities among them by using a set of matching or analogy algorithms. Table 9.3 presents the

Table 9.4
Matched Scores between Five Shakespearean Plays

	MA	HA	JU	OT	TA
Macbeth	78	49	45	21	9
Hamlet	49	108	35	22	9
Julius Ceasar	45	35	91	28	8
Othello	21	22	28	71	10
Taming of the Shrew	9	9	8	10	50

Note: Higher scores indicate closer matches. Mean-diagonal score (play matched with itself) equals eight.
Source: Winston (1980). Reprinted with the permission of the Association of Computing Machinery.

plot of *Macbeth*. The implemented system used similarities in properties, classification memberships, and causal relationships (murdering a king to become king) to calculate a matching score of correspondence between plots. Table 9.4 presents the matrix of matching scores among the five plays: four tragedies (*Macbeth, Hamlet, Julius Caesar, Othello*) and one comedy (*The Taming of the Shrew*).

Table 9.4 indicates that the implemented system separated the comedy from the cluster of the four tragedies and that within the cluster, *Macbeth* and *Hamlet* are the most closely matched. The matching algorithm that compared *Macbeth* and *Hamlet* calculated the number of matching points to be assigned to corresponding plot elements of each tragedy. Among the corresponding plot elements (analogies) were: Both were motivated to become kings themselves; Macbeth and Claudius murder kings (Duncan and the ghost), and they themselves are the victims of murderers (Macduff and Hamlet); and the wives (Lady Macbeth and Gertrude) are implicated in the tragedies.

The implemented system (Winston, 1980) does not analyze Lady Macbeth's lines to determine her complex motivations in persuading Macbeth to murder

Duncan; neither can it empathize with her ensuing guilt stricken reactions. Thus, in no sense does the system understand the language, characters, or the analogy of the plot to that of *Hamlet*. The impression of understanding Shakespearean plots is an illusory anthropomorphism referred to in the discussion of ELIZA (above) and applicable to the BORIS system discussed below (Lehnert et al., 1983).

The BORIS System and Narrative Comprehension

Lehnert et al. (1983) developed BORIS, a program that exhibits "in-depth understanding" of narratives about friendship and adultery. Like the SAM program (Schank and Reisbeck, 1981) that used script-based representations and the PAM program that used goal-based representations, BORIS uses sets of fixed representations that employ fixed rules for assigning meaning to significant human relationships. Its understanding, therefore, is a kind of mechanical stimulus-response structure that cannot allow for interpretations of situations and meanings that were not thought of by the human programmers of BORIS. The representational structure of BORIS contains rules that stipulate (1) Whenever two persons are alone in a bedroom, assume that sex is going on; and (2) the reaction of a husband to coming upon a scene of his wife in an adulterous relationship is "surprised." Exceptions to these fixed stipulations are not hard to find. Two persons alone in a bedroom may be consulting about replacing the wallpaper; and the stipulation "surprised," on the one hand, arbitrarily narrows the range of serious emotional and cognitive meanings and, on the other hand, would not allow for the jocular substitution of "amazed" for the husband's reaction and the reservation of "surprise" for the adulterous pair (as in the story about Noah Webster's retort to his wife's, "Why, Mr. Webster, I am surprised," on finding him with his young secretary on his knee: "No, madam, I am surprised, you are amazed").

The BORIS system processes data about significant human experiences and answers questions about a human interest story correctly, but it has no understanding. The understanding resides with its human programmers, and BORIS is a mechanistic intermediary. People interacting with BORIS or reading a protocol of its answers to questions about a story concerned with divorce may infer that BORIS is using human psychological processes and fail to realize that BORIS is using programmed data structures and procedural operations. People may be most deceived where BORIS uses a set of templates called TAUs (thematic affective units) to capture the theme or moral of the story. Table 9.5 presents some of the TAUs that BORIS uses in processing events in a divorce story. Table 9.6 presents an interactive question-and-answer session in which BORIS is examined regarding its "comprehension" of the emotional climax of the divorce narrative.

To process this one story about divorce the BORIS program uses fifteen types

Table 9.5
TAUs Used by BORIS in Processing and the Events in the Divorce Story That They Represent

---

TAU-DIRE-STRAITS: Paul doesn't know who to turn to.

TAU-RED-HANDED: Paul catches Sarah in bed.

TAU-BROKEN-OBLIGATION: Sarah has been having an affair.

TAU-HIDDEN-BLESSING: Paul realizes his problems are solved.

Source: Lehnert et al. (1983). Reprinted with the permission of Elsevier Science Publishers.

of knowledge structures that operate interactively and at multiple levels. Examples of these knowledge structures are scripts (Cullingford, 1981), goals (Wilensky, 1978), plans (Schank and Abelson, 1977), settings (Dyer and Lehnert, 1980), objective primitives (Lehnert and Burstein, 1979), affects (Dyer, 1981), themes (Wilensky, 1978), interpersonal relationships (Schank and Abelson, 1977), events (Dyer, 1981), physical states (Schank, 1975), social acts (Schank and Carbonell, 1979), MOPS (memory organization packets; Schank, 1975), and TAUs (thematic affective units; Dyer, 1981).

BORIS, as a language processor, is technically advanced, but, as its programmers indicate, the generality of the mechanisms in BORIS when applied to stories different than the one that BORIS "mastered" remains a formidable research problem. For example, what scale of augmentation of BORIS would be required for it to process themes of marital jealousy and adultery in such classics as Hawthorne's (Spector, 1981) *The Scarlet Letter* and Shakespeare's (Quiller-Couch, 1969) *Othello*.

A Parallel Processing System for Language Comprehension

Waltz and Pollack (1985) have conducted research concerned with the development of a massively parallel and strongly interactive natural language processing (NLP) system. They take the position that in the traditional serial model of processing input, syntactic, lexical, and contextual sources of language knowledge deviates from the nature of human language comprehension which follows an integrative model. The reason for the deviation is the reliance by computer scientists on the now forty-year-old von Neumann computer and its associated programming languages. Waltz and Pollack (1985) report the development of

Table 9.6
A Paragraph from the Divorce Story That Was Processed by BORIS

BORIS Divorce-1

Processing Paragraph 5

> When Paul walked into the bedroom and found Sarah with another
> man he nearly had a heart attack. Then he realized what a
> blessing it was. With Richard there as a witness, Sarah's
> divorce case was shot. Richard congratulated Paul and
> suggested that they celebrate at dinner. Paul was eager to
> comply.

READY TO ACCEPT Q/A

> Why did Richard drive Paul home?
>
> SO PAUL COULD CHANGE HIS CLOTHES.
>
> What happened to Paul at home?
>
> PAUL CAUGHT SARAH COMMITTING ADULTERY.
>
> How did Paul feel?
>
> PAUL WAS SURPRISED.
>
> Why did Sarah lose her divorce case?
>
> SARAH COMMITTED ADULTERY.
>
> Why did Richard congratulate Paul?
>
> PAUL WON HIS DIVORCE CASE.

Note: In the interactive question and answer protocol BORIS's answers are in uppercase.
Source: Lehnert et al. (1983). Reprinted with the permission of Elsevier Science Publishers.

several parallel processing components of a complete language-processing system that permits implementation of their theory of integrated natural language
processing. The structure of their model will be presented.

The processes of spreading activation and lateral inhibition are fundamental
in the Waltz and Pollack model. Spreading activation algorithms direct breadth-
first searches for shortest path (Collins and Loftus, 1975; McClelland and Rumelhart, 1980; Quillian, 1968) in semantic networks. The spreading activation

process requires a compensatory damping or lateral inhibition process because activation may result in the futile exploration of distantly related search paths. The excessive spread of activation is damped by the spread of lateral inhibition.

Thus, in the structure of the Waltz and Pollack parser, there are inhibition links between nodes containing distinct phrases, nodes containing distinct lexical forms, nodes containing distinct word senses, and nodes containing discordant case role categories. There are activation links between sentence phrases and their constituent elements, specific words and their meanings, sets of roles and role fillers, and concordant syntactic and semantic meaning impositions. The composition of inhibition links and activation links in the parser produces, over a set of iterated cycles of language processing, a predominance of node patterns marked by consistency in language meaning.

As indicated earlier, the von Neumann computer, as a serial processor, is not an adequate model of human language comprehension. Interestingly, von Neumann (1951) presciently indicated that parallel computers would be required for the adequate modeling of human cognition. The massively parallel and strongly interactive language-processing system developed by Waltz and Pollack (1985) is not a von Neumann machine, but constitutes a development directly in line with von Neumann's advanced theory of the parallel, rather than serial, nature of human cognition.

ARTIFICIAL INTELLIGENCE AND THE PRAGMATICS OF LANGUAGE GENERATION

> It never happens that [the automaton] arranges its speech in various ways, in order to reply appropriately to everything that may be said in its presence, as even the lowest type of a man can do.
>
> Descartes, quoted in Wilson (1969), p. 138

> Explanations by human experts, in general, are tailored to their audiences. The details of reasoning as related to another expert in the same domain will be different from those related to a layman. This requires a kind of intelligent behavior not apparent in the explanation facilities of current expert systems.
>
> Hayes-Roth, Waterman, and Lenat (1983), p. 49).

The problem of how to inculcate flexibility in a language generation program so as to take account of pragmatics, that is, the intentionality intended by the speaker and interpreted by the hearer, was investigated by Hovy (1990). In this section, the general logic, principles, features, behavioral examples, and limitations of PAULINE (Hovy, 1990) will be described, and, then, in a commentary section, general issues of artificial intelligence approaches to the pragmatics of language generation will be examined.

The General Logic of PAULINE

Two general principles govern the development of PAULINE: the principle of rhetorical strategies and the principle of interweaving of generation processes. Beyond the rules themselves, it is important to note that they are inclusive of both computers and humans and that, although any one program such as PAULINE may be confined to a given topic in its elaborative details, the general rules hold and guide the program's development and execution. Hovy (1990) summarizes his general research questions in the following section:

> This paper addresses the question "why and how is it that we say the same thing differently to different people, or even to the same person in different circumstances?" We vary the content and form of our text in order to convey more information than is contained in the literal meanings of our words. This information expresses the speaker's interpersonal goals toward the hearer and, in general, his or her perception of the pragmatic aspects of the conversation. This paper discusses two insights that arise when one studies this question: the existence of a level of organization that mediates between communicative goals and generator decisions, and the interleaved planning-realization regime and associated monitoring required for generation. To illustrate these ideas, a computer program is described which contains plans and strategies to produce stylistically appropriate texts from a single representation under various settings that model pragmatic circumstances. (Hovy, 1990, p. 153)

Hovy (1990) presents the theoretical assumptions underlying the development of PAULINE in the following account:

> In order for generator programs to produce similarly varied, information-bearing text, such programs must have some means of representing relevant characteristics of the hearer, the conversation setting, and their interpersonal goals. These are the *pragmatic* concerns. In addition, they must contain choice points in the grammar that enable topics to be said in various ways. These are the *syntactic* concerns. Finally, they require criteria by which to make the decisions so that the choices accurately reflect the pragmatic aspects and convey appropriate additional information. These are called here the *rhetorical* concerns. . . .
>
> This paper describes how the program PAULINE (Planning and Uttering Language in Natural Environments) produces stylistically appropriate texts from a single story representation under various settings that model pragmatic circumstances.
>
> PAULINE addresses simultaneously a wider range of problems than has been tried in any single language generation program before (with the possible exception of Clippinger [1974]). It contains about 12,000 lines of LISP code, and produces varied and sophisticated text. As is to be expected, no part of PAULINE provides a satisfactorily detailed solution to any problem; to a larger or smaller degree, each of the questions it addresses is solved by a set of simplified, somewhat ad hoc methods. In fact, some methods have been studied in much greater detail by other NLP researchers. Others remain as projects for the future.
>
> However, this does not invalidate the content of the work. *This research uncovered*

two principal insights about the nature of language generation that do not depend directly on the details; they will hold for any language generator sophisticated enough to try to achieve a number of communicative goals in a single text. While the details of any particular module will not be defended too hard, nor even the exact extent of each module, the following will be defended to the end: the existence of a level of organization mediating between communicative goals and generator decisions, containing entities called here rhetorical goals; and the monitoring of the modules' operation in an interleaved planning-realization regime. The lessons learned here are going to apply to any large and complex enough generator—human or computer. (Hovy, 1990, pp. 155–156; italics added)

Pragmatic Characteristics of PAULINE

PAULINE contains pragmatic representations of the characteristics of speaker-hearer interactions. These pragmatic characteristics are described in the following section:

In order to study the relationship between pragmatic considerations and computer language generation, one requires something concrete enough to program. To characterize the pragmatics of its conversation, PAULINE used a list of features. . . . The precise names and values of these features are not a serious claim; the (pragmatic!) justification is that they are the kinds of features necessary for language generation. Any language processing program addressing these questions will have features that, on some level, resemble them. In this representation of pragmatics, each feature was given a fixed number of possible values, usually lying on a scale. In a few cases, features were conflated and the result merely given a set of distinct values; this could eventually be refined. PAULINE's characterization of the *conversation setting* and *interlocutor characteristics* is:

- conversational atmosphere (setting):
    —time: much, some, little
    —tone: formal, informal, festive
    —conditions: good, noisy
- speaker:
    —knowledge of the topic: expert, student, novice
    —interest in the topic: high, low
    —opinions of the topic: good, neutral, bad
    —emotional state: happy, angry, calm
- hearer:
    —knowledge of the topic: expert, student, novice
    —interest in the topic: high, low
    —opinions of the topic: good, neutral, bad

—language ability: high, low

—emotional state: happy, angry, calm

• speaker-hearer relationship:

—depth of acquaintance: friends, acquaintance, strangers

—relative social status: dominant, equal, subordinate

—emotion: like, neutral, dislike

In addition, PAULINE can have the following *interpersonal goals*:

• hearer:

—affect hearer's knowledge: teach, neutral, confuse

—affect hearer's opinions of topic: switch, none, reinforce

—involve hearer in the conversation: involve, neutral, repel

—affect hearer's emotional state: anger, neutral, deactivate

• speaker-hearer relationship:

—affect hearer's emotion toward speaker: respect, like, dislike

—affect relative status: dominant, equal, subordinate

—affect interpersonal distance: intimate, close, distant . . .

PAULINE uses the following stylistic rhetorical goals, with values along the indicated ranges:

—formality (highfalutin, normal, colloquial): highfalutin language is used for speeches

—simplicity (simple, normal, complex): simple text has short sentences and easy words

—timidity (timid, reckless): willingness to spend time to consider including opinions

—partiality (impartial, implicit, explicit): how explicitly you state your opinions

—detail (details only, interpretations, both): too many details can be boring to non-experts

—haste (pressured, unplanned, somewhat planned, planned): when there's little time . . .

—force (forceful, normal, quiet): forceful text is energetic and driving

—floridity (dry, neutral, flowery): flowery text contains unusual words

—color (facts only, with color): colorful text includes examples and idioms

—personal reference (two ranges, for speaker and hearer): amount of direct reference to the interlocutors

—open-mindedness (narrow-minded, open-minded): willingness to consider new topics

—respect (four values): being arrogant, respectful, neutral, or cajoling

Of course, it is impossible to list all possible styles. Every speaker has an idiosyncratic set of techniques, often tailored to particular hearers, for using language to achieve his or her interpersonal goals. Thus, this work should not be interpreted as claiming to describe exhaustively any language user's stylistic knowledge. Rather, it is intended as a description of the general *function of style* in a generator—the expression of rhetorical goals, which in turn serve the speaker's general communicative goals in the text; and of a useful *method of definition of style*—as constraints on the decisions the generator has to make. (Hovy, 1990, pp. 160–161, 163)

Architecture of PAULINE

Hovy (1990) provides the following succinct description of the architecture of PAULINE:

PAULINE has the architecture shown in [Figure 9.1]. Its input is represented in a standard case-frame-type language based on conceptual dependency (Schank, 1972, 1975; Schank & Abelson, 1977) and is embedded in a property-inheritance network (see Bobrow & Winograd, 1977; Charniak, Riesbeck, & McDermott, 1980). The shantytown example consists of about 120 elements. No intermediate representation (say, one that varies depending on the desired slant and style) is created. Its grammar is described in Hovy (1988). The program consists of about 12,000 lines of T, a scheme-like dialect of LISP developed at Yale. (Hovy, 1990, pp. 169–170)

Interpretation in PAULINE

In the following section, Hovy (1990) provides a conceptual analysis of the problem of text interpretation in general and examples of PAULINE's interpretative behavior:

In [the following] example, PAULINE produces a number of versions describing a hypothetical primary election between Carter and Kennedy during the 1980 Democratic Presidential nomination race. In the election, Kennedy narrows Carter's lead. The underlying representation comprises about 80 distinct units. When PAULINE is given as input the outcome for each candidate, straightforward generation produces:

(f) IN THE PRIMARY ON 20 FEBRUARY CARTER GOT 1850 VOTES. KENNEDY GOT 2185.

However, PAULINE can notice that both outcomes relate to the same primary, and can say instead:

(g) IN THE PRIMARY ON 20 FEBRUARY, KENNEDY BEAT CARTER BY 335 VOTES.

Figure 9.1
Program Architecture

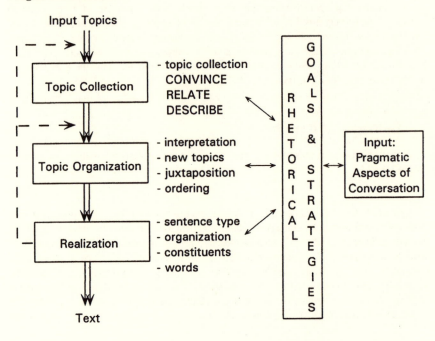

Source: Hovy (1990), p. 169. Reprinted with the permission of Elsevier Science Publishers.

(or any of a number of similar sentences using "beat," "win," and "lose"). But why stop there? If PAULINE examines the input further, it can notice that Carter's current delegate count is greater than Kennedy's, that this was also the case before the primary, and that this primary is part of a series that culminates in the final election, the nomination. In other words, PAULINE can recognize that what happened in this primary was:

(h) IN THE PRIMARY ON 20 FEBRUARY, KENNEDY NARROWED CARTER'S LEAD BY GETTING 2185 VOTES TO HIS 1850.

If we want good text from our generators, we have to give them the ability to recognize that "beat" or "lose" or "narrow lead" can be used instead of only straightforward sentences (f).

This ability is more than a simple grouping of the two outcomes. It is an act of generator-directed inference, of interpretation, forming out of two topics a new topic, perhaps one that does not even exist in memory yet. And the new topic is not simply a generator construct, but is a valid concept in memory. The act of determining that "beat" is appropriate *is* the act of interpreting the input as an instance of BEAT—denying this is to imply that "beat" can logically be used where BEAT is not appropriate, which is a contradiction. This is not an obvious point; one could hold that the task of finding "beat" to satisfy a syntactic or pragmatic goal is a legitimate generator function, whereas the task of instantiating it and incorporating it into memory is not. However, it is clearly inefficient for a generator to interpret its input, say it, and then simply forget it again!— especially when there is no principled reason why generator inferences should be distinct from other memory processes.

Thus, after interpretation, the newly built instance of the concept should be added to the story representation, where it can also be used by other processes, or by the generator the next time it tells the story. In this way the content of memory can change as a result of generation. This is consistent with the fact that you often understand a topic better after you have told someone about it: the act of generating has caused you to make explicit and to remember some information you didn't have before.

Immediately, this view poses the question: *which process is responsible for making these inferences*? The two possible positions on this issue reflect the amount of work one expects the generator to do. According to the strict minimalist position—a position held by most, if not all, generator builders today—the generator's responsibility is to produce text that faithfully mirrors the input topics with minimal deviation: each sentence-level input topic produces a distinct output sentence (though perhaps conjoined with or subordinated to another). This inflexible attitude gave rise to the JUDGE texts (a) and (b). To circumvent this problem, in practice, most generator builders employ in their program a number of special-purpose techniques, such as sophisticated sentence specialists that are sensitive to the subsequent input topics. This is a tacit acknowledgement that the strict position does not hold. However, on renouncing the hard-line position, one must face the question *how much generator-directed inference are you prepared to do*?

I do not believe that a simple answer can be given to this question. The issue here is economic: a tradeoff exists between the time and effort required to do interpretation (which includes finding candidate interpretations, making them, and deciding on one) on the one hand, and the importance of flowing, good text on the other. Greater expense in time and effort produces better text. Thus pragmatic criteria are appropriate for treating this question. Hence a reasonable answer is: *I'll do as much inference as I can do, given the available time, the pragmatic constraints on what I want the hearer to know, and the richness of my memory and my lexicon*. Of these three factors, the most difficult is clearly the pragmatic constraints on what the hearer is to be told. When does the hearer need to know the details of the topic? What is the effect of saying only interpretations? Or of saying both? The answer can be summarized as: if you can trust the hearer to make the interpretations himself, then all you need say are the details. Thus, if the hearer is a political pundit who is following the nomination race with interest, then clearly (f) is better, since he or she can draw the conclusion without difficulty, and, in addition, now has precise numerical information. If, in contrast, the hearer has only minimal knowledge about or interest in the nomination procedure, then (h) is better, since it removes the burden of details and the task of doing the interpretation. What must you say, however, if the hearer is interested and has a limited amount of knowledge—say, he or she is a student of a political process—or is knowledgeable but unlikely to make the right interpretation—say, he or she is a strong Kennedy supporter, whereas you are pro-Carter? In both these cases you must ensure that the hearer understands how you expect him or her to interpret the facts. So you give the details *and* the interpretations:

> (I) KENNEDY NARROWED CARTER'S LEAD IN THE PRIMARY ON 20 FEB-RUARY. HE GOT 2185 VOTES AND CARTER GOT 1850.

These considerations can be stated as rules, using the terms defined above to characterize the pragmatic aspects of conversations and the goals of speakers. PAULINE uses these rules to activate the rhetorical goal *detail* that controls the level of detail of topics generated. The goal takes one of the values *details, interpretations, all* (both details and interpretations):

> —Set the goal's value to *details* if the hearer is likely to understand the details or wants to hear the details. This rule bears on information about the hearer: Is the hearer's knowledge level marked *expert*; or is the hearer's interest level marked *high*?

> —Otherwise, set it to *all* if the hearer is likely to make the wrong interpretations of the details, that is, when the hearer's knowledge level is marked *student* or *novice*; the atmosphere (time) is not marked *little*; and the hearer's sympathies and antipathies for the central topic of the conversation are not the opposite of the speaker's.

> —Otherwise, set it to *interpretations*.

In addition to these considerations, the value of the goal can be affected by the desire not to upset the hearer:

> —Then, set the value to *interpretations* if it is better to avoid painful topics, to ensure that painful aspects (the details, the interpretation, or the inferences used to make it) can simply be left out. This rule translates as follows: Is speaker-hearer depth of acquaintance marked *strangers*, or is speaker-hearer relative social status marked *subordinate*, or is desired effect of hearer's emotion toward speaker marked *like*, or is desired effect of interpersonal distance marked *close*, or is desired effect on hearer's emotional state marked *calm*?

> *In summary, you must be as specific as the hearer's knowledge of the topic allows: if you are too specific he or she won't understand, and if you are too general you run the risk of seeming to hide things, or of being uncooperative. In the first case, you violate the goal to be intelligible, and in the second, you violate the goal to avoid unacceptable implications. In either case, you violate Grice's maxim of quantity to say neither more or less than is required (Grice, 1975).* (Hovy, 1990, pp. 175–178; italics added)

Affect in PAULINE

It is interesting that PAULINE can process, within limits, the affective aspects of interpersonal communications. In the following section, Hovy (1990) describes the concepts and rules that guide PAULINE's affective behavior:

In order to slant the text to fit the hearer's opinions, the speaker must be able to determine what the hearer is likely to find sympathetic, what he or she is likely to dislike, and what he or she is likely not to care about much. PAULINE uses three values of affect: GOOD, BAD, and NEUTRAL. (Of course, *affect* here simply denotes something akin to ''like.'' But even with this limited denotation, three values are sufficient to give the program interesting behavior. In this regard it is similar to the work on narrative summarization in Lehnert [1982].)

PAULINE's affects derive from two sources: provided by the user and defined as intrinsic to certain representation elements. To give PAULINE opinions, the user must specify one or more representation elements as *sympathies* or *antipathies*. (In PAULINE, this is simply implemented by having a sympathy and an antipathy list. Elements on these lists will be characterized as GOOD and BAD respectively.) The second source of affect is defined for those generic representation elements that carry some intrinsic affect in the example domain. For example, in neutral context, the concept ARREST is BAD, the university's goal to be reasonable and fair is GOOD, and all other concepts, such as STUDENTS and CONSTRUCTION, are NEUTRAL.

In order to compute an opinion about any arbitrary piece of input representation, PAULINE has the ability to combine its given affects and concepts' intrinsic affects and to propagate affect along relations to other concepts. Though their exact form obviously depends on the design of the representation, the basic rules are:

(1) affect is preserved when combined with NEUTRAL;

(2) like affects combine to GOOD;

(3) unlike affects combine to BAD;

(4) affect inverts when propagated along certain relations (e.g., the *patient* of BAD is GOOD). A special rule for affect propagation is defined for each such relation. (Hovy, 1990, pp. 182–183)

Partiality and Impartiality in PAULINE

Hovy (1990) presents a conceptual analysis of the conditions for the expression of partial and impartial opinions and the implementation of this analysis by a set of rules in PAULINE.

When should the speaker exhibit partiality? In general, since his or her sympathies and antipathies reflect so accurately the speaker's disposition toward the world, any opinion with which the hearer disagrees implies distance between them—perhaps even censure on the part of the speaker. Thus, to simplify, when the speaker's opinion agrees with the hearer's, expressing it will tend to make them closer; when it disagrees, expressing it may cause problems. Furthermore, partiality can be expressed explicitly, using clauses that state the speaker's opinion, or implicitly, using techniques such as phrasal juxtaposition and stress words. The rules PAULINE uses to activate its rhetorical goal of partiality are:

(1) Set the value of the goal to *explicit* if the speaker's and hearer's affects for the topic agree and desired effect on hearer's emotion toward speaker is marked *like*;

or desired effect on interpersonal distance is marked *close*; or tone is marked *informal*.

(2) Set it to *implicit* if the speaker's and hearer's affects for the topic agree and desired effect on interpersonal distance is marked *distant*, since being lukewarm about the agreement with the hearer separates them; or speaker-hearer relative social status is marked *dominant*, for the same reason; or desire to involve hearer is marked *repel*, that is, if the speaker does not want to make the hearer too involved in the conversation.

(3) Otherwise, set it to *impartial* if their affects agree, or if their affects disagree and desired effect on hearer's opinion is marked *none*, hearer's knowledge level is marked *expert*, and speaker's knowledge level is marked *student* or *novice*, and desired effect on hearer's emotion toward speaker is marked *respect* or *like*, since when the speaker cares about an expert hearer's opinion, he or she will not want to exhibit partiality and lack of knowledge.

(4) Set the value of the goal to *explicit* if the speaker's and hearer's affects for the topic disagree and desired effect on hearer's opinion is marked *switch*; or desired effect on hearer's emotional state is marked *anger*; or desired effect on hearer's emotion toward speaker is marked *dislike*; or desired effect on interpersonal distance is marked *distant*.

(5) Otherwise, set it to *implicit* if their affects disagree and desired effect on hearer's opinion is marked *switch*; or desire to involve hearer is marked *involve* or relative social status is marked *subordinate* (that is, when the hearer is subordinate to the speaker).

Having determined a value for this goal of partiality, PAULINE uses the following strategies of style that act as criteria at decision points to make text partial (both *explicit* and *implicit*):

(1) *topic inclusion*: include explicit expressions of opinion (if *explicit*)

(2) *topic organization*: make appropriate interpretations of topics, as discussed below (if *implicit*)

(3) *topic/phrase organization*: juxtapose topics in affect-imputing phrases (*explicit* and *implicit*)

(4) *sentence inclusion and organization*: include appropriate descriptive adjunct groups, adverbial and adjectival (*explicit*)

(5) *sentence constituent inclusion*: include appropriate affect-laden adjectives and adverbs; and include stress words (*explicit* and *implicit*)

(6) *word choice*: select nouns and verbs that carry affect (*explicit* and *implicit*)

In contrast, in order to make its text as impartial as possible, the program uses inverse strategies. . . .

In the shantytown example of [Table 9.7], PAULINE is given three input topics (the building of the shanties, their being taken down, and Yale's permission for them to be rebuilt). When the program has the goal to switch the hearer's opinions to correspond

Table 9.7
Partiality

For Protesters	For University	Decision Strategy
[AS A REMINDER TO] YALE UNIVERSITY TO DIVEST FROM COMPANIES DOING BUSINESS IN SOUTH AFRICA, [A LARGE NUMBER OF] [CONCERNED] STUDENTS	IN APRIL, [A SMALL NUMBER OF] [ ] STUDENTS [TOOK OVER] BEINECKE PLAZA	interp: *support* adj choice: enhancer interp: *tactics*
ERECTED A SHANTYTOWN NAMED WINNIE MANDELA CITY ON BEINECKE PLAZA IN APRIL.	AND ERECTED A SHANTYTOWN NAMED WINNIE MANDELA CITY	topic: given in input
	[IN ORDER TO FORCE] YALE UNIVERSITY TO DIVEST FROM COMPANIES DOING BUSINESS IN SOUTH AFRICA.	interp: *coercion*
	YALE [REQUESTED] THAT THE STUDENTS BUILD IT ELSEWHERE, BUT THEY REFUSED TO LEAVE.	verb choice: leniency topic: pro-university
	SO THE UNIVERSITY GAVE IT PERMISSION TO EXIST UNTIL THE MEETING OF THE YALE CORPORATION, BUT [EVEN] AFTER THAT THEY [STILL] REFUSED TO MOVE.	topic: pro-university adv choice: enhancer adv choice: enhancer topic: pro-university interp: *abnormal-circ*
[AT 5:30 AM ON APRIL 14,] [YALE HAD] OFFICIALS [DESTROY] IT; ALSO, AT THAT TIME, THE UNIVERSITY [HAD] THE POLICE ARREST 76 STUDENTS AFTER THE LOCAL COMMUNITY'S [HUGE] [OUTCRY].	OFFICIALS [HAD TO] [DISASSEMBLE] THE SHANTYTOWN	interp: *coercion* verb choice: force topic: given in input interp: *coercion*
	[ ]. FINALLY,	topic: pro-protesters topic: pro-protesters
		interp: *support*
YALE PERMITTED THE STUDENTS TO RECONSTRUCT THE SHANTYTOWN	YALE, [BEING CONCILIATORY] TOWARD THE STUDENTS, [NOT ONLY] PERMITTED THEM TO, RECONSTRUCT IT [BUT ALSO] ANNOUNCED THAT A COMMISSION WOULD GO TO SOUTH AFRICA IN JULY TO STUDY THE SYSTEM OF APARTHEID.	interp: *conciliation* phrase juxta: enhancer topic: given in input phrase juxta: enhancer topic: pro-university

Source: Hovy (1990), p. 186. Reprinted with the permission of Elsevier Science Publishers.

to its own, it activates the CONVINCE topic collection plan. When PAULINE is speaking as a university supporter, the *good results* step of the plan causes it to collect, as additional topics, the university's offer of an alternative site for the shanties and the protesters' refusal to move, since these topics are (a) direct results of the building of the shanties and are (b) GOOD from the program's point of view, for they serve the university's goal to be lenient and show the protesters' intransigence. When on the other hand it is speaking as protester, the same step causes it to collect the item representing the students' arrest. Other steps of the plan provide other topics. Eventually, having performed the collection, PAULINE begins topic organization with the initial input and the topics it has collected. . . .

[PAULINE] has limited inferential capability. It also has a list of rules that prescribe how the generator should proceed to find forms of expression for input topics with certain characteristics, and that indicate what aspects of these topics can be used to create an appropriate slant. The goals that activate these rules are called the *rhetorical goals of opinion*. When the program is given sympathies that oppose the hearer's sympathies, and when the pragmatic value for effect on hearer's opinion of the topic is *switch*, PAULINE activates these goals, which can be paraphrased as:

—*State outright* that our side is good and theirs is bad.

—Show how our side has *good goals*, by describing how (a) we help other people; (b) we want a solution to the conflict; and (c) our goals are good according to accepted standards.

—Explain how our side does *good actions* to achieve the goals: (a) the actions are not unreasonable or nasty; (b) they are good according to accepted standards; and (c) they are performed in the open.

—Specifically, describe our side's *response to the opponent*: (a) negotiations that have taken place and (b) how we have moderated our demands.

—Finally, show how *other people* believe that we are good, by describing (a) their active support and (b) their statements and recommendations to that effect.

A similar list exists for the inverse goal, to show how bad the opponents' side is. Both lists contain a large number of specific inferences and explicit suggestions for sentences. For example, a strategy to make the opponents look bad is:

—Show how *they are unreasonable*: (a) they started the whole affair; (b) they coerce others into doing things; (c) they have little support; (d) they don't seem to want a solution; (e) their demands/goals are beyond reasonable expectations; (f) they are only in it for their own good; (g) they are immoral, unfair; (h) they use distasteful/ugly tactics, misuse their rights, or overstep the bounds of propriety; (i) they disseminate false or misleading information about the dispute; (j) they have a hidden agenda; (k) they won't discuss/negotiate the issue; (l) they won't moderate their stance, are un-conciliatory, intransigent.

These strategies are encoded as top-down interpretation inferences. They fire when the input sentence topics have characteristics that match their activation conditions; the left-hand sides are patterns of representation element types and their right-hand sides cause the generator to select the appropriate forms of expression. In somewhat more detail, the inferences *coercion* and *limited support* (see [Table 9.8]) can be paraphrased as (the terms in capitals are elements of the representation language; MTRANS denotes the act of transferring information; PTRANS the act of transferring physical objects; and ATRANS the act of transferring control over something; see Schank, 1972; Schank and Abelson, 1977):

—*Coercion*: they force their will on others (corresponding to the university speaker's "in order to force"):

Table 9.8
Case 1 (to an acquaintance): *colloquial, impartial, details, somewhat planned*

Text	Decision	Rhetorical goal value
Topic: central topic	RELATE plan	
[ ] CARTER AND KENNEDY WERE	no adjuncts before	*colloquial*
THE CANDIDATES IN A PRIMARY		
[IN MICHIGAN] [ON 20 FEBRUARY].	adjuncts after subject	*colloquial, planned*
Topic: result	RELATE plan	
CARTER [LOST]	neutral verb	*impartial*
TO KENNEDY BY [1335] VOTES.	neutral details	*impartial, details*
Topic: outcome with good affect for Kennedy	RELATE plan	*impartial*
AT PRESENT, KENNEDY		
HAS A BETTER CHANCE		
OF [GETTING] THE NOMINATION	informal word	*colloquial*
THAN [ ] BEFORE.	elide *he had*	*colloquial*
Topic: outcome with good affect for Carter	RELATE plan	*impartial*
CARTER IS ALSO CLOSER	separate sentence	*colloquial*
TO [GETTING] THE	informal world	*colloquial*
NOMINATION THAN [ ] BEFORE.	elide *he was*	*colloquial*
Topic: actor's goals (twice)	RELATE plan	
BOTH CARTER AND KENNEDY [WANT]	informal verb	*colloquial*
TO [GET] THE NOMINATION	informal verb	*colloquial*

Source: Hovy (1990), p. 191. Reprinted with permission of Elsevier Science Publishers.

If the current topic is an ACTION,

AND its affect is BAD,

AND the action serves one of the

opponent's goals,

AND the goal's desire is to have

some other party do some act,

THEN imply that the opponents force their

will on them (using verbs and phrases

such as "force," "make them do").

—*Limited support*: they claim to have more support than they have (corresponding to the university speaker's adjective "a small number"):

IF the current topic claims support (an

MTRANS of a SUPPORT),

AND the ACTOR's affect is BAD,

AND the SUPPORT contains a number

of people,

THEN minimize that number, by using

adjectives such as "a small

number," "a few."

Different inferences are applied at different times in the generation process. This depends on the kinds of effect they have on the processing and is controlled by the grammar. Inferences that call for the candidate topic(s) to be interpreted and completely replaced by other topics (such as interpreting a request as a coercion) are run during the topic organization phase; inferences that suggest appropriate adjectives ("a large number," "a small group") are run when noun phrases are built; those that prescribe specific verbs when predicates are constructed. . . . Thus, in addition to stressing affective concepts, a speaker can strengthen his or her case by imputing affect to neutral concepts too! This is, for example, what PAULINE does to produce

NOT ONLY DID YALE UNIVERSITY PERMIT THE

STUDENTS TO REBUILD THE SHANTYTOWN, BUT YALE

ANNOUNCED THAT A COMMISSION WOULD GO TO SOUTH

AFRICA TO STUDY THE SYSTEM OF APARTHEID.

when defending the university (see [Table 9.7]). For PAULINE, the commission visit topic is simply NEUTRAL, whereas permission to rebuild, because it serves the goal to be reasonable (which is intrinsically GOOD) is GOOD. When juxtaposed in this way, *both* sentences seem GOOD for Yale—exactly what PAULINE wants. . . .

The juxtaposition of topics is controlled by the active rhetorical goals of opinion. In the shantytown example, for instance, the program's first goal is to introduce the topic. Its topic collection strategies provide it with two topics (the shanty construction and the protectors' intention) that are related by a SUBGOAL-TO relation. As at any decision point, the active rhetorical strategies of style are queried: should the relation between the two topics be used to conjoin them into a compound sentence? The answer is *yes*, since the relevant topic organization strategy, activated for both *explicit* and *implicit* values of partiality, calls for the use of affect-imputing enhancer and mitigator phrases. What is an appropriate way to express a SUBGOAL-TO relation? Here the inferences of opinion come into play, making decisions about the appropriateness of various interpretations of the two topics and their relationship. When sympathetic toward the university, one inference that matches the construction and its goal, which has the desired state that Yale divest from the companies, is that of *coercion*, described above. This strategy spawns the instruction to say a newly-formed interpretation, CAUSE-TO-DO, with the protesters' intent as attached topic, and the conjunction "in order to force." In contrast, when PAULINE is speaking as a protestor, the strategy *we are lenient, offer passive resistance* causes it to join the topics using the phrase "as a reminder to." (When the program has no opinions, it would simply use a neutral phrase such as "in order to" or "so as to.") All these phrases are in the lexicon, indexed in a discrimination net linked to the relation SUBGOAL-TO.

Nouns and verbs often carry affective value themselves. The words in PAULINE's lexicon are organized in discrimination nets to provide enhancing and mitigating alternatives when required. For example, the representation primitive MTRANS indexes to, amongst others, the verbs "order," "tell," "ask," and "request"; and DECONSTRUCT to "tear down," "disassemble," and "remove." See [Table 9.7]. (Hovy, 1990, pp. 182–190)

Table 9.9
Case 2 (to a friend): *colloquial, implicit, all (details and interpretations), planned*

Text	Decision	Rhetorical goal value
Topic: results with good affect for Kennedy	CONVINCE plan	*implicit*
[ ] KENNEDY	no adjuncts before	*colloquial*
[DIMINISHED] CARTER'S [LEAD]	interpretation	*all, planned*
BY [GETTING]	informal verb	*colloquial*
[ALL OF]	enhancer adj	*implicit*
[21850] VOTES	details	*all*
[IN THE PRIMARY] [IN MICHIGAN]	adjuncts after subject	*colloquial*
Topic: reminding	indexed off interp	*planned*
IN A SIMILAR CASE, CARTER DECREASED	reminding	*implicit, planned*
UDALL'S LEAD IN A PRIMARY		
IN 1976, AND HE [EASILY]	enhancer adv	*implicit*
[TROUNCED] UDALL TO BE NOMINATED	enhancer verb	*implicit*
BY [2600] DELEGATES	details	*all*
Topic: outcome with good affect for Kennedy	CONVINCE plan	*implicit*
[I AM REAL GLAD THAT]	informal opinion	*colloquial, explicit*
KENNEDY IS [NOW] CLOSER TO	adjunct after, informal	*colloquial*
[GETTING THE NOMINATION THAN	informal verb	*colloquial*
[ ] BEFORE.	elide *he was*	*colloquial*

Source: Hovy (1990), p. 192. Reprinted with the permission of Elsevier Science Publishers.

A Further Example of PAULINE's Performance

In the following section, Hovy (1990) provides another interesting example of PAULINE's pragmatic generation of language:

In summary, compare PAULINE's generation of the Carter Kennedy example under three pragmatically different scenarios. In all three cases, the input is the same; the differences in the text result from the different values for the active rhetorical goals, which result from the different initial pragmatic settings. Only the effects of the rhetorical goals of formality, detail, partiality and haste will be discussed here (see Hovy [1987] for more details).

Case 1. Neither interlocutor has opinions about the topic (causing partiality to be set to *impartial*); both have the usual knowledge of the electoral process (making detail be *details*); the level of formality is *colloquial*; and when the program is given enough time, haste is activated with the value *somewhat planned*. The result appears in [Table 9.8].

Case 2. The hearer is a *friend* and social *equal* (therefore again *colloquial* formality) who is not as expert as the sibling (i.e., knowledge level is *student*, which makes detail be *details and interpretations*). But now both interlocutors have opinions: PAULINE's sympathy is for Kennedy and the hearer's is for Carter (so that partiality is *implicit*). The program is given as much time (mainly to make interpretations) as it needs: haste is *planned*. The result appears in [Table 9.9].

Case 3. PAULINE is a Carter supporter and is speaking to its boss, an irascible Kennedy man. They are making a long-distance telephone call, which gives the program

Table 9.10

Case 3 (to the boss): *colloquial, implicit, interpretations, pressured*

Text	Decision	Rhetorical goal value
Topic: results and outcomes for Carter	CONVINCE plan	*implicit*
. . . .	no time for mitigation	*pressured*

Source: Hovy (1990), p. 192. Reprinted with the permission of Elsevier Science Publishers.

little time and makes conversational conditions *noisy* (activating the haste goal with the value *pressured*). Furthermore, the program is *distant* from its boss, does not wish to anger him (desired emotional effect is *calm down*), and still wants to make him feel socially *dominant* (resulting in *implicit* partiality and *interpretations* for detail). But to its boss ([Table 9.10]), the program says nothing!

This text came as a surprise. Investigation showed that the lack of time prevented any of the strategies for implicitly stating opinions from being applied: no topic collection plan was activated; no search for mitigating interpretations took place; the lack of a second topic meant no topic juxtaposition was possible; no rhetorical goals of opinion were present to guide mitigating adverb and adjective selection and appropriate word choice. Therefore, the goal to present the topic only in mitigated (implicit opinion) form couldn't be satisfied, and no sentence could be generated. (Hovy, 1990, pp. 191–192)

Limitations of PAULINE

In the following section, Hovy (1990) evaluates PAULINE from several perspectives and emphasizes the general applicability to other language generation systems of the two basic assumptions underlying theory and performance of the PAULINE system.

The question "why and how is it that we say the same thing in different ways to different people, or even to the same person in different circumstances?" is interesting from a number of perspectives. From a cognitive perspective, it highlights speakers' goals and personal interrelationships in communication; from a linguistic perspective, it raises interesting questions about the information content of language; and from an engineering-AI perspective, it illustrates the need for principled reasons by which a program that can realize the same input in various ways can make its selections.

As described in this paper, the answer deals with the pragmatic nature of communication—a big and complex field of study. In order to begin to study how pragmatics is used in generation, a number of assumptions about plausible types of speaker goals and the relevant characteristics of hearers and of conversational settings must be made. The specific pragmatic features used in PAULINE are but a first step. They are the types of factors that play a role in conversation; no claims are made about their literal veracity. Similarly, the strategies PAULINE uses to link its pragmatic features to the actual generator decisions, being dependent on the definitions of the features, are equally primitive; again, no strong claims are made about their existence in people in exactly the form shown. However, in even such a simple theory as this, certain lessons emerge, and these lessons, I believe, hold true no matter how sophisticated the eventual theory is. The lessons pertain primarily to the organization of pragmatic information in generation: the fact that interpersonal and situational information and goals are too general to be of immediate use; the resulting fact that intermediate strategies, here called rhetorical strategies, are required to guide generation; the fact that, in a model of generation that incorporates these goals, rhetorical planning and realization must be interleaved processes, where the interleaving takes place at the choice points.

The study of language generation by computer has traditionally been divided into two questions: *what shall I say?* and *how shall I say it?* The aim of this work is to illustrate the importance of a third question: *why should I say it?* If generators do not face up to this question, they will never be able to address the other two satisfactorily. (Hovy, 1990, p. 193)

Commentary

Pragmatics and Computation

The PAULINE program is an important contribution to artificial intelligence approaches that seek the emulation of human capacities for pragmatic language generation. The principles that enable PAULINE to adjust its knowledge and rhetorical style to different audiences, goals, and purposes are generalizable to other programs and other contexts.

The expansion of computational principles and programs to three additional areas of language pragmatics seems warranted: (a) conversational norms, (b) common ground enabling conversations, and (c) speech acts.

Computation and Conversational Norms

The area of conversational norms (Grice, 1975) may, in some respects, be especially amenable to computational approaches, simply because clear conversational norms and stipulations can be represented as production rules.

Computation and Common Grounds

In contrast to the precision of conversational norms, the variability of human conversation modes and contents constitutes a more formidable challenge to computational competencies. The constituents of linguistic common ground that permit effective human communication need to be established; it is these constituents and their concatenation that an expert computer conversationalist would need to emulate.

Computation and Speech Acts

The area of speech acts (Austin, 1962; Searle, 1969) comprises two levels of difficulty for computational approaches. Speech acts that convey meanings that are explicit, simple, and univocal in their implications can be computationally emulated more readily than speech acts that convey multiple messages, some explicit and some implicit, contradictory at different levels with open-ended interpretations.

PHILOSOPHICAL AND PSYCHOLOGICAL
IMPLICATIONS OF COMPUTATIONAL LANGUAGE
SYSTEMS

Language-processing automata, as developed in artificial intelligence research, have three general characteristics: (1) miniature domains of application; (2) limited representational structures; and (3) arbitrary and repetitive language processing. In interacting or "conversing" with these systems, people find that they must accommodate their own cognitive style, with its capacity for critical analysis and subtle interpretation, to the computer's capacity for predetermined, simplistic, and stereotyped productions.

However, the accommodation is never complete or final and often contains a type of noncritical fascination akin to the absorption in theatrical drama or the literary novel and poem (e.g., the ELIZA program; see the section on language comprehension and artificial intelligence in this chapter). In addition, people are often impressed with the ability of the program to give reasons for its behavior (e.g., the SHRDLU program; see the section on language comprehension and artificial intelligence in this chapter) or to give reasons for people's behavior (e.g., the Shakespeare analogy program, the BORIS program; see the section on language comprehension and artificial intelligence).

Computer programs are not autonomous agents, but rather structures of data and operations created by an autonomous human programmer. The programmer understands human language; the program does not.

The program responds to input queries, statements, or commands within the limits of the structure of its representations given to it by its human programmer. The correctness of a program's response to a given input does not signify understanding but correct mechanistic correspondences of input and program structures. The attribution of language comprehension to artificial intelligence programs is an act of illusory anthropomorphism comparable to the attribution of symphonic comprehension to digital music systems.

Computer systems that process language can, under the definition of physical symbol systems, be considered intelligent, as they input, process, and output symbols:

The Physical Symbol System Hypothesis (Newell and Simon, 1976) *states that a system will be capable of intelligent behavior if and only if it is a physical symbol system.* A physical symbol system is a system capable of inputting, outputting, storing, and modifying symbol structures, and of carrying out some of these actions in response to the symbols themselves. . . . Information processing psychology claims that intelligence is achievable physical symbol systems and only such systems. From that claim follow two empirically testable hypotheses: (1) that computers can be programmed to think, and (2) that the human brain is (at least) a physical symbol system. (Simon, 1990, p. 3)

Although computers and humans can, in some sense, be subsumed under the concept of physical symbol systems, imaginative, experimental research will need to be undertaken to advance computers beyond their currently quite limited ability to comprehend language at a sophisticated level. That advancement will depend in no small measure on probing research into the mechanisms of human language comprehension. Discovery of these mechanisms will permit their programming. The isolation of mechanisms will not be sufficient, however; and a theory of the nature of understanding will be necessary. The philosophical thrust of such a theory of understanding will need to explain the profound, though simply expressed, problem put forth by Einstein: "The hardest thing to understand is why we can understand anything at all" (Einstein, quoted in Minsky, 1986, p. 319).

10

Analogical Thinking

ARTIFICIAL INTELLIGENCE AND ANALOGICAL REASONING

Conceptual Components of Analogical Reasoning

In "Computational Approaches to Analogical Reasoning: A Comparative Analysis," Hall (1989) presents an abstract component model of the processes of analogical reasoning that is applicable to both artificial intelligence and human cognition.

This framework gives abstract process components that a relatively complete picture of analogical reasoning, computational or otherwise, would include:

1. *recognition* of a candidate analogous source, given a target description,
2. *elaboration* of an analogical mapping between source and target domains, possibly including a set of analogous inferences,
3. *evaluation* of the mapping and inferences in some context of use, including justification, repair, or extension of the mapping,
4. and *consolidation* of the outcome of the analogy so that its results can be usefully reinstated in other contexts.

These components provide a conceptual organization for comparing computational approaches to analogy. (Hall, 1989, p. 43)

Using the four-component process model as a guide, Hall (1989) compares sixteen computational studies of analogical reasoning. Hall (1989) summarizes these studies with respect to component processes of recognition and elaboration in the following account:

Contributions of Individual Studies to Processes of Recognition and Elaboration

Study	*Recognition*	*Elaboration*
Evans (1968) ANALOGY	given	object type and rule components, restrict object and rule mappings; relational mapping enabled by a fixed vocabulary of substitutions
Becker (1973) JCM	associative memory of schemata indexed by general concepts	kernel predicates map identically; node mismatch weighted by a linear combination of salience estimates; best candidate maximizes match score and schema confidence, minimizes cost
Kling (1971) ZORBA	given	partial mapping over theorem statements is extended by a type-restricted best-first search
Munyer (1981)	source formulas and derivations indexed by functional containment	extends unification through bottom-up, competitive reinforcement of a global mapping; requires consistent mappings at boundaries of the source derivation
Greiner (1988) NLAG	given a hint, generate a source problem and find an abstraction for solving it	find a target instance of the abstraction, inferring residual conjectures as needed
Brown (1977)	source domain given by tutorial context	incrementally extend a type-restricted mapping; map target problem into a source problem and solve it
McDermott ANA (1979)	manipulate target cues to trigger method indices; anticipate method failures	map source into existing or "stipulated" target objects; extend mapping to cover method subgoals
Carbonell (1983) ARIES	solution paths are indexed by states and constraints; a similarity metric screens candidate source sequences	map source and target sequences
Carbonell (1986)	similar initial reasoning triggers retrieval of a source derivation from dynamic memory	map source and target sequences
Simpson (1985) MEDIATOR	collect source remindings by traversing an episodic	mapping is distributed across index tests; align identical norm slots

Study	Evaluation	Consolidation
	tions in target; confirm plan predictions with user; remediate failures	
Winston (1978) FOX	a simile is given by a tutor or conjectured by the learner	prefer existing transfer frames, salient properties of the source, properties that are prototypical of the target class, or properties that continue the instructional context
Hobbs (1983a, 1983b) DIANA	a source schema is triggered by the appearance of target predicates	resolution of discourse problems aligns source and target concepts
Dyer (1983) BORRIS MORRIS	target planning failures trigger retrieval of a source narrative from dynamic memory	map narrative elements through a common planning
Winston (1986) MACBETH	recognize source by bottom-up voting through exhaustive type indexing; index rules by actors, acts, and objects	map a priori important relations before lower level relations
Burstein (1986) CARL	given source domain, a target example and reasoning context triggers retrieval of a source abstraction from dynamic memory	top-down relational mapping includes objects only as needed; can map nonidentical relations
Pirolli and Anderson (1985)	selects prior example under productions control; spreading activation retrieves declarative memory structures	mapping productions (some are learned) align code template components
Kedar-Cabelli (1985)	select a source instance and plan (not described); explain why the source instance satisfies the purpose	map the source explanation and plan to the target instance

(Hall, 1989, pp. 113–114)

Hall (1989) summarizes the set of computational studies in analogical reasoning with respect to the process components of evaluation and consolidation in the following section.

Contributions of Individual Studies to Processes of Evaluation and Consolidation

Study	Evaluation	Consolidation
Evans (1986) ANALOGY	drop unmatched relations and prefer candidates that preserve most source relations (A:B)	proposes rule proceduralization and generalization
Becker (1973) JCM	unmapped source kernels are treated as subgoals to be confirmed	store the target interpretation; weight adjustments introduce variables, drop conditions, and estimate a schema's worth
Kling (1971) ZORBA	pass target clauses to a separate resolution theorem prover	none
Munyer (1981)	implicit planning uses analogy as an evaluation function; explicit planning detects skewed analogies and finds plan repair steps; both succeed when a logically valid derivation is found	record the target derivation; generalize formulas and derivational sequences; delete redundant or unsuccessful derivations
Greiner (1988) NLAG	verify that inferred facts solve the target problem, are consistent with existing knowledge, and are acceptable to the user	add inferred facts to the domain theory
Brown (1977)	lift the source solution into the target domain; confirm transferred justifications, patching "bugs" as necessary	add successful descriptions, plans, justification, and code to the target domain repertoire
McDermott (1979) ANA	environment and user feedback confirms method expectations or signals method errors; repair by subgoaling on failure or selecting an alternate method	builds error detection and recovery productions; adds target instantiation of successful method production
Carbonell (1983) ARIES	MEA in T-space reduces differences between source and target sequences	store target solution sequence; generalize operator sequences; tune similarity metric and difference table; cluster over T-space failures

Study	Evaluation	Consolidation
Carbonell (1986)	check justifications for source steps in target description reconsider alternative source steps or prior failures; monitor a perseverance threshold	update case memory with target solution generalize target and source traces; justification points identify instances for learning search heuristics; decompose traces into general plan components
Simpson (1985) MEDIATOR	verify the source classification and plan preconditions in target; confirm plan predictions with user; remediate failures	memory update installs, inserts, and generalizes episodic structures
Winston (1978) FOX	check for violations of known target properties, confirm existing justification frames, or ask the tutor	transfer properties; construct transfer, justification, and typical-instance frames; conjecture additional properties or new similes
Hobbs (1983a) DIANA	preserve contextual coherence and satisfy pragmatic constraints	target schemata are extended; metaphors tire and die with repeated use
Dyer (1983) BORRIS MORRIS	find a coherent interpretation of the target narrative; confirm plan-based predictions	augment the target interpretation; reorganize existing memory structures to maintain discriminable access to the target narrative
Winston (1986) MACBETH	analogical inferences are confirmed directly by further analogies, by abductive inference, or by the teacher	record the target case; build general inference rules; augment rules to censor exceptions; index original case with rule
Burstein (1986) CARL	discard unsupported inferences; tutor gives feedback and corrections; multiple analogies correct misconceptions	integrate multiple causal abstractions in the target domain
Pirolli and Anderson (1985)	check inferred components against the target specification; test target code in the LISP environment; repair or abandon the current analogy	proceduralization and composition build general productions which supplant structural analogies
Kedar-Cabelli (1985)	justify explanatory inferences for target; replace structural attributes or plan steps as necessary	find a common explanatory structure for the refined concept

(Hall, 1989, pp. 114–115)

Process Component: Recognition of a Candidate Analogy

The construction of an analogy between a source and a target is initiated with a search for potentially applicable knowledge contained in the source. The search is typically guided by selective constraints as discussed by Hall (1989) in the following passage:

> Given an unfamiliar situation (the *target*), how does a reasoner connect this new situation with one or more familiar situations (*sources*) contained in a store of previous experience? From a computational perspective, search is implicated and an organization is usually imposed on the store of previous experience to help constrain search for a candidate source. From a cognitive perspective, a reasoner attends to familiar aspects of the target and uses these aspects to retrieve appropriate experiences from memory. By allowing partial similarity between target and candidate sources, a central problem of recognition is to impose constraints on the retrieval process but still allow recognition of analogically related sources. For example, strict organizational criteria that suppress tenuously related candidates might not allow recognition of relatively abstract inter-domain analogies. (Hall, 1989, p. 96)

In the following section, Hall (1989) compares computational studies with respect to how recognition constraints are established or imposed:

> The most effective but least ambitious solution to constraining recognition is to give the reasoner a source analog. Some studies do this as a simplifying assumption [e.g., Evans, 1968, Kling, 1971, or Pirolli and Anderson, 1985], while others give a hint about the source and rely on supporting mechanisms to complete recognition. For example, Kedar-Cabelli (1985) gives the learning purpose, the to-be-learned concept, and a target instance. The system then selects a prototypical source instance and a plan for using that instance to achieve the given purpose. Using a similar approach, Greiner (1985) gives an initial mapping (a hint) between source and target concepts, and then finds a source instantiation and an abstraction for solving it. Both approaches use the relation of an abstraction (or plan) to a source instance during later stages of analogical reasoning. Brown's (1977) reduction analogies, Winston's (1978) simile-based instruction, and Burstein's (1986) integration of multiple analogical models each place analogy in a tutorial context. In all three cases, the reasoner uses a hint and the ongoing tutoring context to recognize salient aspects of the source. For example, Burstein gives the analogy (e.g., a variable is like a box) and examples of its use, and CARL retrieves a source abstraction (e.g., a causal model of containment) to extend the analogy. (Hall, 1989, p. 96)

A prominent method of controlling constraint is indexing.

> Without giving the analogy directly, other source candidates compete for attention and require an organization that restricts their number. This organization is generally an indexing scheme that enforces selective retrieval. The reviewed studies use three general approaches: nonselective indexing, task-specific indexing, and task-independent indexing. In each, the question is what to choose as indices into the store of candidate sources.

Choosing an indexing scheme makes an explicit commitment to the kinds of analogies that can be recognized.

Nonselective indexing schemes approximate an associative memory for candidate sources. For example, Becker (1973) indexes candidate schemata through generic concept nodes, while Munyer (1981) indexes formulas around instances of functional containment. Each approach promises extensive search in a memory with relatively primitive organization. In practice, each applies additional constraints to the search process: Becker insists that mapped kernels occur in an appropriate position in the schema, and Munyer requires consistent formula mappings at either end of a candidate derivation. In both cases, recognition returns a set of candidate source analogs, and one (or several) are selected during elaboration and evaluation. For example, Munyer suggests an agenda control mechanism prioritized by the "degree of certainty" for competing analogical views.

Task-specific indexing schemes select distinguished elements of the representation and make an a priori commitment that these elements predict future contexts of use for the source. Winston's (1980) "classification-exploiting hypothesizing" resembles this scheme, although he mentions using relational indexing in the bottom-up voting mechanism. His later work (Winston, 1982) indexes acquires rules by the types of actors, acts, and objects found in their right-hand sides. Extracting type cues from the target problem, Winston retrieves sources which make predictions about those types. McDermott (1978) uses a similar strategy when indexing source method productions by types of objects and actions. As with nonselective approaches, both studies include further constraints on recognition. Winston (1980) weights his voting scheme in negative proportion to source concept prevalence and in positive proportion to the contextual salience of the target concept. McDermott, on the other hand, generates taxonomic variants of the target cue to make contact with method indices. In each case, differential focus on target elements refines cue extraction, allowing the reasoner to influence the recognition process by manipulating elements of the target description. Although task-specific indexing and cue extraction prove effective for the problems solved in these studies (e.g., painting or washing tables), these methods may not extend across more heterogeneous tasks and may not recognize more abstract analogical similarity between target and source domains.

Task-independent indexing schemes select more abstract representational elements for indices that organize memory. Carbonell's (1981, 1982) "invariance hierarchy" over semantic categories is an example of this approach. Examining metaphors and analogies in different domains, Carbonell ranks semantic categories by decreasing order of invariant transfer. The resulting hierarchy specifies that goals, plans and causal structure are usually preserved in an analogical mapping. Carbonell argues that this invariant hierarchy is important for recognizing analogies since memory can be organized around (i.e., indices are based on) precisely the knowledge structures that are likely to transfer without variation when reasoning by analogy. Thus, recognition proceeds by extracting goals, plans, or causal structure from the target and using these as indices into a memory for candidate sources. For example, Carbonell (1983) organizes a memory for solution sequences in ARIES around state descriptions (initial and goal states) and constraints, and then uses a similarity metric based on the same information to select among recognized candidates. Dyer (1983) also uses this indexing scheme to organize memory around instances of planning failures (TAUs). Planning difficulties in a target narrative serve as retrieval cues for recognizing adages and analogous narrative episodes. Likewise, Simpson (1985) recognizes analogous cases by comparing a target description with generalized episodes in a memory organized hierarchically around problem types and planning information. Traversing indices in episodic memory structures guides the recognition process through increasingly specific comparisons ending with retrieval of candidate cases. By indexing and retrieving over task-independent semantic categories, these approaches can support recognition and retrieval of genuinely novel metaphors or analogies.

Of these three indexing schemes, the task-independent approach might be preferred since it anticipates retrieval of useful source candidates and clearly allows recognition of analogies where target and source content are markedly different. . . . Also, as argued by Schank (1982), Dyer (1983), and Kolodner (1983a, 1983b), these approaches appear consistent with human studies of episodic memory organization and retrieval. On the other hand, task-independent indexing schemes could make overly strong a priori commitments to the utility of source situations, preventing access in some useful but unexpected contexts. This is especially true when the target is completely novel, since the reasoner may not be able to extract cues required for recognition of a useful analogy from a memory organized around abstract semantic categories. Evidence from studies of human analogical access (Gentner, 1987) suggests that recognizing an analogical source may depend on different principles than those that determine elaboration and evaluation. At present, it seems likely that analogical retrieval depends on interactions between several factors: what the reasoner attends to in the target situation, what is available in the store of source experiences, and the degree to which the reasoning context during recognition matches the encoding context for a stored source. These tradeoffs are open research questions for computational studies. As psychological models of memory organization and retrieval become more explicit, computational approaches to recognition may benefit; the converse may also be true. (Hall, 1989, pp. 97–98)

Process Component: Elaboration of Analogical Mapping

Elaboration is the process of mapping an analogy between source domain and target domain. In the elaborative process, constraints are exercised to yield an effective analogical mapping. Methods of constraints can be grouped as relational, semantic, and contextual.

The first class of preferences considers representations of the source and target, asking what aspects of those representations should be preserved. The most general approach, as evident in many studies, is to preserve the relational structure of the source representation. For example, Brown (1977) maps predicates from source to target domains only if those predicates have the same type and their arguments have a type-compatible mapping. With similar effect, Munyer (1981) uses a bottom-up approach in which local maps between arguments compete to reinforce predicate mappings higher in the representational network. In both cases, the relational structure of a source representation is preserved in the analogy mapping if a corresponding structure can be found in the target representation. This approach is also found in algorithms for computing inductive summaries over instances (e.g., Hayes-Roth, 1978) and has been studied systematically by Falkenhainer (Falkenhainer, Forbus, and Gentner, 1986, 1987) as a computational realization of Gentner's structure-mapping theory (Gentner, 1983).

The second class of preferences focuses on semantic categories of source and target knowledge, asking what semantic structures are commonly preserved in analogies and metaphors. These preferences range from task-specific restrictions to preserving more general informational categories in the analogical mapping. Evans' (1968) restriction of a one-to-one mapping of rule components and Pirolli and Anderson's (1985) compilation of mapping rules are examples of task-specific semantic preferences. Winston's promotion of salient source properties when comprehending similes (Winston, 1978) or his preference for salient relations (e.g., cause or enablement relations) in importance-dominated matching (Winston, 1980) are intermediate along this continuum. Carbonell's invariance hierarchy (1981, 1982) and Simpson's (1985) use of that hierarchy to organize memory and direct elaboration are examples of the most general preference for semantic categories. Whereas the first class of mapping preferences preserve relational structure in source and target descriptions, this class promotes semantic categories deemed important for the analogy a *priori*. . . .

The third class of preferences focuses on the contextual relevance of mapped material, asking which relational or semantic structures to preserve within the current reasoning context. Since an arbitrarily large collection of facts might be known of the source or target, some mechanism must focus on those facts which are important at the moment. Contextual relevance is a broad concept, and takes different forms in the studies reviewed here. For example, Burstein (1986) uses a tutorial context to select among alternative relational abstractions in the source domains. Also arguing for contextual constraints, Kedar-Cabelli (1985) uses a to-be-learned concept and its stated purpose (e.g., drinking hot liquids) to focus elaboration on explanatory inferences used with a source instance of the concept. Perhaps the strongest adherent to contextual relevance, Hobbs (1983a, 1983b) argues that resolving discourse problems in context finds a coherent metaphorical interpretation. (Hall, 1989, pp. 100–101; italics added)

Hall (1989) points out that although these classes of constraints as separately conceived have been subject to contention, harmony can be established by viewing them in an integrative framework.

In isolation, these three preference classes for elaborating an analogical mapping may seem incompatible. For example, relying solely on a preference for preserving semantic categories, a reasoner might attempt to map isolated and potentially irrelevant source goals, plans, or causal relations. These could be suppressed by a mapping strategy that preferred maximally coherent (or "systematic" [Gentner, 1983]) relational structures. In contrast, relying solely on a preference for relational structure, a reasoner might fail to map attribute-level information that is critical for achieving some goal. These and other arguments are leveled in detail by Holyoak (1985) and Gentner (1987) and are relevant for computational research.

From an integrative viewpoint, constraints provided by all three preference classes contribute to processes of analogical reasoning. When recognition and evaluation are considered as pre-and post-processes to elaboration, many of the more strident contrasts between these approaches fall away. For example, contextual constraints on recognition help to restrict the relational structures available for mapping, while evaluation processes give a posteriori force to a preference for semantic categories. *Since these categories tend to be represented as higher-order relational structures, the more parsimonious preference for preserving relational structure within elaboration may be a tenable approach, provided that contextual and semantic constraints surround the mapping process.* (Hall, 1989, p. 101; italics added)

In the elaborative process, inferential reasoning between source and target may range from simple mathematical confirmations as in proportional analogies to complex exploratory and hypothesis-testing behavior as in scientific discovery (Hesse, 1963) and as in personal problem solving such as found in the PLATO Dilemma Counseling System (Wagman, 1980a, 1984a, 1984b, 1988; Wagman and Kerber, 1980) wherein an analogous match is sought from a set of specific case dilemma solutions (source) to a troubling problem (target).

Comparing different approaches to analogy, elaboration of a mapping between target and source domains is clearly a process of varying complexity. In some studies, finding a mapping between target and source descriptions directly achieves the purpose of the analogy. For example, Evans' (1968) ANALOGY system generates a set of generalized rule candidates, choosing the one that best preserves a one-to-one, type-consistent mapping between source figures. Similar descriptions apply to most psychological studies of proportional analogies (e.g., Sternberg, 1977) and comparison-based theories of metaphor comprehension (e.g., Malgady and Johnson, 1980). In contrast, other studies describe elaboration as an active, incremental process. For example, Carbonell (1983, 1986) starts with a partial mapping over problem specifications (e.g., states and constraints) and then enters a complicated search space of plan transformations or replayed derivational steps to find a solution for the target problem. The repairs described by McDermott (1979) and Burstein (1986) or the justification for a new case described by Kedar-Cabelli (1985) suggest similar complexity when elaborating an effective analogy.

Simple, relatively homogenous correspondence as an end in itself supports a limited view of analogy: analogical comparisons finds a mapping which renders two superficially dissimilar situations virtually identical. In this view, the real work of analogy is in elaborating a consistent mapping, and analogical inference is either missing or given a limited role. *In contrast, more complex views of elaboration see analogy as an open-ended, experimental process. An elaborated mapping supports analogical inferences from a well-understood source domain into a less familiar target domain. These inferences are hypotheses that must be verified in the target domain, giving rise to an experimental interplay between elaboration and evaluation.* (Hall, 1989, pp. 101–102; italics added)

Process Component: Evaluation of the Analogy

In the evaluative process, mechanisms that confirm the validity or usefulness of the elaborated analogy are required. Hall (1989) describes a number of confirmation procedures in the following account.

The plausibility of analogical inferences can be confirmed by consulting prototypical expectations of the target domain or verifying the usefulness of inferences in some ongoing reasoning process. In either case, evaluation tests predictions about the target domain. As an example of confirmation using target expectations, Winston (1978) "filters" inferred target properties by checking that they fill slots or have values found in a "typical" target instance. In Winston's later work (1982), abductive reasoning verifies an analogical inference when its consequences are known in the target domain or provided by a tutor. In both cases, existing knowledge of the target is used to confirm predictions from the sources domain.

More ambitious evaluative strategies weigh the problem solving utility of analogical inferences. For example, Carbonell's (1983) transformational analogy mechanism uses a similarity metric to select T-operators which incrementally transform a source solution sequence into a larger solution sequence. Features used in this metric (e.g., comparisons of states or path constraints) encode knowledge of desirable or undesirable solution forms in the target domain. In a more general deductive framework, Greiner's (1985) NLAG must prove that an analogical conjecture is useful for solving the target problem. As an alternative to task-specific knowledge of the target domain, Burstein (1986) uses critical interactions between CARL and a tutor to collect feedback on analogy-driven solutions that includes corrections for wrong answers. In each approach, the success of an analogical inference in reaching a target solution is used to evaluate the analogy. (Hall, 1989, pp. 103–104)

Justification mechanisms constitute important methods in the evaluative process.

Taken in isolation, a fact or action suggested by an analogical inference may be plausible, but the reasons supporting that fact in the source domain may not be plausible when evaluated in the target domain. A common solution is to map source justifications of analogical inferences into the target domain and then to establish their validity. A justification gives a representational description of the "reasons" which support an inference or action in some domain. Becker (1973) gives an early example of this approach by collecting facts which justify a "motivated" analogical mapping. This motivation is to apply a schema in his prediction paradigm, and justifying facts are unmapped source kernels in either side of the schema (e.g., antecedent kernels in a forward application). Somewhat more direct, Winston's (1978) justification frames explicitly capture those aspects of a target description which must be present for a known analogy (i.e., a transfer frame) to be useful. For example, a justification frame for an analogy between a table and a cube to be used for a common purpose (e.g., to eat or write) might record that both target and source objects must be of medium size, have a flat top, and be level. Using functional justifications is extended by Winston et al. (1983) and used to good purpose by Kedar-Cabelli (1985). In purpose-directed analogy, an explanatory justification generated in the source domain (e.g., the structural reasons why a ceramic cup can be used to drink hot liquids) both confirms and constrains analogous reasoning in the target.

Replaying justifications is central to some computational studies of analogy. For example, Brown (1977) represents plan justifications as collections of assertions which relate steps in a solution plan to facts about the task domain found in a goal description. After generating a justified source solution, these assertions must be confirmed when the candidate solution is "inverse-mapped" into the target domain. If justifications cannot be confirmed, further elaboration of the existing analogy or introduction of a new analogy are attempted. Carbonell's derivational analogy method (1986) also replays justifications, stored as part of a derivational trace of decisions made when solving a source problem (e.g., programming quicksort in PASCAL). Given an analogous target problem (e.g., programming quicksort in LISP), the reasons for choosing among actions in the source derivation must be confirmed or replaced by alternative reasons for the derivational analogy to succeed. (Hall, 1989, p. 104)

The result of the evaluative process may be the detection of a faulty analogical bridge between source and target domains. The problem of repairing faulty analogies is discussed by Hall (1989) in the following account:

A number of studies use multiple analogies to repair inappropriate analogical inferences. For example, Burstein's (1986) CARL integrates multiple analogical models (e.g., physical containment and human memory) to repair incorrect predictions about simple assignment statements. Among the variety of studies using GRAPES simulations, [Anderson, Farrell, and Sauers (1984)] also model problem solving sessions in which the tutor presents a simplifying example to help repair incorrectly transferred LISP code. In both cases errors from inappropriate analogical inferences are repaired by introducing additional analogies. These must be integrated with the original analogy. In related psychological studies, Clement (1983) describes how expert problem solvers in physics use intermediate "bridging analogies" to help elaborate an analogical mapping between a target problem and a troublesome analogical source. *Each approach is computationally relevant and psychologically plausible, but integrating multiple analogies may introduce other difficulties. Multiple analogies, possible at differing levels of abstraction, must be combined into a useable concept, avoiding what Halasz and Moran characterize as a "baroque collection of special-purpose models"* [1982, p. 34]. (Hall, 1989, p. 105; italics added)

An integrated summary of the evaluative process component in analogical reasoning is given in the following passage:

In summary, analogical inferences must be treated, at best, as tentative hypotheses supported by a partial mapping between source and target domains. Domain interactions during evaluation confirm and repair analogical inferences extended during elaboration. Evaluation occurs at many levels: testing analogical predictions against expectations of what is typical of the target domain, verifying the utility of analogical inferences in some reasoning context, replaying justifications for analogical inferences in the target domain, and repairing inappropriate analogical inferences. *As a result of the evaluation process, parts of the analogical mapping may be changed or deleted, multiple analogies may be combined to suggest new hypotheses about the target domain, or the original analogy may be abandoned altogether in favor of an alternate line of reasoning.* (Hall, 1989, p. 106; italics added)

Process Component: Consolidation of the Analogy

The consolidation process component refers to the transfer of the verified knowledge contained in the analogy to subsequent problems.

The simplest form of consolidation directly records information successfully transferred from source to target domain. Of the reviewed studies that address consolidation, most perform this simple form of learning. For example, McDermott (1979) and Pirolli and Anderson (1985) record specific target productions; Hobbs (1983b) creates and extends a target schema; Winston (1980, 1982) records successful target cases; and Greiner (1985) augments the starting theory with useful target conjectures. In each approach, learned material is strongly context-specific with little or no generalization. When facing a new task which is identical to an earlier success, the earlier solution is applied directly without resorting to more costly inference mechanisms. *Although this simple learning scheme might seem limited, when coupled with powerful recognition and elaboration processes, it could achieve incremental performance improvements as the collection of source candidates provides wider domain coverage.* (Hall, 1989, p. 106; italics added)

A number of computational systems store and reuse analogical content and reasoning. For example, Winston (1978) stores transfer and justification frames. When reasoning about new similes, recognition first attempts to reuse an acquired transfer frame if related justification frames can be verified for the target. Using a similar approach, Pirolli and Anderson (1985) acquire task-specific mapping productions which supplant portions of later elaboration attempts. Other studies save the analogical mapping for the duration of an instructional context. For example, Brown (1977) and Burstein (1986) incrementally extend and repair a mapping as new tasks or feedback are given by a tutor. Although this may seem a matter of technical convenience, analogical reasoning is often an explicit component of tutorial interactions, and computational techniques of managing analogical comparisons (e.g., diagnosis or direct manipulation) can provide useful instructional or experimental tools.

To acquire knowledge with wider applicability, many studies form inductive summaries over target and source materials. Becker (1973), Winston (1982, 1986), and Pirolli and Anderson (1985) acquire generalized rules which consolidate inferences common to target and source. Becker's learner refines schemata through experience with a reactive environment; Winston's learner forms rules and censors from a series of predictive tasks presented by a tutor; and Pirolli's learner compiles analogical comparisons of declarative material into productions. Other studies use inductive mechanisms to form more complex plans or problem solving derivations common to target and source domains. For example, Carbonell (1983, 1986) consolidates successful transformational analogies into generalized solution sequences and derivational analogies into generalized plans and search heuristics. Similarly, Burstein (1986) argues for concept formation through analogies supported at varying levels of abstraction (e.g., causal inferences and plan steps) but includes learning from multiple analogical sources that cover different aspects of the target problem. (Hall, 1989, pp. 106–107)

Analogical Reasoning: Problems and Solutions

Research problems and proposed solutions in the area of computational analogical reasoning are collated in Table 10.1.

Process components of recognition, elaboration, evaluation, and consolidation developed and discussed in preceding sections not only reflect the academic topography of

Table 10.1
Problems and Solutions across Components of Analogical Reasoning

---

Recognition
Problem: Given a target and a store of *sources*, find a manageable but promising set of candidates.
Solutions: (1)   Give the source as a simplification [Kling, 1971] or in a tutorial context [Burstein, 1986].
        (2)   Organize the store of sources around an indexing scheme.
            (a) nonselective indexing [Becker, 1973],
            (b) task-specific indexing [Winston, 1982],
            (c) task-independent indexing [Dyer, 1983].

Elaboration
Problem: Given *target, source,* and mapping *preferences,* find a mapping and analogical inferences.
Solutions: (1)   Use an existing analogy map [Winston, 1978].
        (2)   prefer analogical mappings which:
            (a) preserve relational structure [Munyer, 1981],
            (b) preserve semantic categories [Simpson, 1985],
            (c) preserve contextual relevance [Kedar-Cabelli, 1985].

Evaluation
Problem: Given a mapping, analogical inferences, and a reasoning context, evaluate the analogy.
Solutions: (1)   Confirm analogical inferences:
            (a) test predictions against target domain knowledge [Winston, 1978],
            (b) weigh the utility of inferences in context [Greiner, 1985],
            (c) replay a justification in the target domain [Carbonell, 1986].
        (2)   Repair faulty analogical inferences:
            (a) post failures as subgoals [McDermott, 1979],
            (b) integrate multiple analogies [Burstein, 1986].
        (3)   Monitor global progress:
            (a) heuristic thresholding [Munyer, 1981],
            (b) treat failure as a new problem [Simpson, 1985].

Consolidation
Problem: Given a *target, source,* and evaluated analogical inferences, consolidate these to improve future performance.
Solutions: (1)   Record the target and outcome [McDermott, 1979].
        (2)   Record the analogical mapping [Winston, 1978].
        (3)   Record an inductive summary:
            (a) induce rules [Winston, 1986],
             (b) induce plan schema [Carbonell, 1983].
        (4)   Learn from failures:
            (a) record the failure to anticipate it later [McDermott, 1979],
            (b) record the failure remediation [Simpson, 1985],
            (c) refine analogy mechanisms [Carbonell, 1983].

Source: Hall (1989), p. 111. Reprinted with the permission of Elsevier Science Publishers.

work done in artificial intelligence and related disciplines, but these components also organize continuing research problems and proposed solutions. [Table 10.1] presents problems, proposed solutions, and citations to exemplary studies drawn from the comparative analysis of the preceding section.

Most work on analogical reasoning from a computational perspective addresses elaboration and evaluation, and alternative approaches to these problems can be clearly distinguished. Preferences for analogical mappings that preserve distinguished representational classes or contextually-relevant material constrain elaboration, while interactive constraints on confirmation, repair, and global monitoring of analogical inferences guide evaluation. As described in the preceding comparative analysis, these processes are strongly interdependent. In contrast, recognizing candidate analogs and consolidating information generated during their use have received less attention. However, differing approaches are also evident: alternative indexing schemes for organizing candidate sources constrain recognition, while a variety of analogically derived materials are learned during consolidation. Juxtaposed, these processes present a basic tension: recognizing analogies anticipates plausible inductive summarization, while consolidating confirmed analogical mappings attempts to predict future contexts of use.

Rather than solving basic problems in analogical reasoning, these approaches offer partial solutions, proposals, or refinements of larger problems. For example, replaying justifications for plan-level analogical inferences (Brown and Campione, 1985; Carbonell, 1986; and Kedar-Cabelli, 1985) refines the problem of elaboration and evaluating inferences at one level into a comparable problem at a lower level. For each analogy process component, the most ambitious and possibly most promising computational approaches have yet to be fully developed, implemented, or tested. Instead, implementations usually demonstrate carefully crafted solutions to isolated problems. Problems of scale and generality apply almost uniformly across the reviewed studies. This is less a criticism than an invitation to further analytical and empirical work. (Hall, 1989, pp. 111–112)

ANALOGICAL REASONING IN THE ACME SYSTEM

The Nature of Analogical Thinking

Thinking is sometimes deductive, sometimes inductive, and sometimes analogical. Deductive thinking has the character of formal logical representations and derivations; inductive thinking looks to the accumulated balance of positive and negative instances; analogical thinking seeks correspondences between the features of two sets of concepts or objects. Analogical thought can serve the purpose of setting forth an explanation by correspondence of elements in unknown situations with those in fully understood situations. Scientific discovery processes are often aided by analogical thought. In political, economic, and intellectual movements, analogies are widely used in argumentation and persuasion. Analogies in the form of expressive metaphors and similes are prevalent in classical literature and everyday language.

A theory of analogical thinking and a computational model of the theory has been developed by Holyoak and Thagard (1989). Their research will be described, and, then, the implications of their theory and model will be discussed in a commentary section.

The General Logic of Analogical Mapping by Constraint Satisfaction

The general logic of analogical mapping requires a set of criteria or constraints that delimit the essential correspondences or similitudes between two analogs, typically a source analog and a target analog. Three delimiting and interacting constraints are stipulated in the theory advanced by Holyoak and Thagard (1989):

The structural constraint of isomorphism encourages mappings that maximize the consistency of relational correspondences between the elements of the two analogs.

The constraint of semantic similarity supports mapping hypotheses to the degree that mapped predicates have similar meanings.

The constraint of pragmatic centrality favors mappings involving elements the analogist believes to be important in order to achieve the purpose for which the analogy is being used. (Holyoak and Thagard, 1989, p. 295; italics added)

The Analogical Constraint Mapping Engine Model of Analogical Mapping

Holyoak and Thagard (1989) developed Analogical Constraint Mapping Engine (ACME), a cooperative algorithm for analogical mapping that is directed toward the satisfaction of the sets of interactive constraints described in the previous section. The rationale for the use of a cooperative algorithm in analogical mapping is set forth in the following assertions:

Several properties of an information-processing task can provide cues that a cooperative algorithm may be appropriate. A cooperative algorithm for parallel constraint satisfaction is preferable to any serial decision procedure when: (a) a global decision is composed of a number of constituent decisions, (b) each constituent decision should be based upon multiple constraints, (c) the outcome of the global decision could vary depending upon the order in which constraints are applied and constituent decisions are made, and (d) there is no principled justification for preferring any particular order of constraints or of constituent decisions. Analogical mapping using constraints exhibits all of these features. (Holyoak and Thagard, 1989, pp. 306–307)

ACME (Analogical Constraint Mapping Engine), as a parallel architecture, constructs a network of nodes or units that represent hypotheses and produces an optimal mapping as an outcome of program processing. There are a number of general features in the design of ACME's network, its nodes, and hypotheses bearing out the relationship between the source analog and the target analog.

Each possible hypothesis about a possible pairing of an element from the source with a corresponding element of a target is assigned to a node or *unit*. Each unit has an *activation level*, ranging between some minimum and maximum values, which indicates the plausibility of a corresponding hypothesis, with higher activation indicating greater plausibility. Inferential dependencies between mapping hypotheses are represented by *weights* or *links* between units. Supporting evidence is given a negative weight. . . .

The input to the program consists of predicate-calculus representations of the source and target analogs, plus optional information about semantic similarity and pragmatic importance. It is assumed that a mapping may be computed either from a target analog to a source or vice versa. It is conjectured that the direction of the mapping will vary depending upon the use of the analogy and the knowledge of the analogist. If the source is much more familiar than the target, then it may be best to try to map source elements to target elements. On the other hand, if the source is much more complicated than the target or if the target contains highly salient elements, then the analogist may attempt to map from the target to the source. . . .

When given two structures as input, ACME automatically generates a network in accord with the constraints postulated by the theory. . . .

As units are established, links are formed between them to implement the constraint of structural consistency. All links are symmetrical, with the same weight regardless of direction. . . .

In addition to the units representing mapping hypotheses, the network includes two special units. The *semantic unit* is used to convey information about the system's prior assessment of the degree of semantic similarity between each pair of meaningful concepts in the target and source, and the *pragmatic unit* similarly is used to convey information about the pragmatic importance of possible correspondences. The semantic-similarity constraint is enforced by placing excitatory links from the semantic unit to all units representing mappings between predicates. The weights of these links are made proportional to the degree of semantic similarity between the mapped concepts. Similarly, the pragmatic-centrality constraint is represented by weights on links connecting the pragmatic unit to relevant mapping units. (Holyoak and Thagard, 1989, pp. 308–312)

General Applications of ACME

As the implementation of a general theory of analogical thinking, ACME should be able to apply its analogical mapping functions to analogical problem solving, analogical argumentation, analogical explanation, and analogical metaphor.

Major contexts for analogy use include problem solving, when the solution to one problem suggests a solution to a similar one; argumentation, when similarities between two situations are used to contend that what is true in one situation is likely to be true in the other; and explanation, when a familiar topic is used to provide understanding of a less familiar one. In addition, analogical reasoning is also used to understand formal analogies of the sort found in mathematics, as well as metaphors, which can be employed to serve both explanatory and more aesthetic functions. (Holyoak and Thagard, 1989, p. 318)

It is impressive that ACME does, in fact, apply its mapping algorithms to the many various contexts in which analogical reasoning takes place. Table 10.2

Table 10.2
Summary of Applications of ACME

Analogs	Number of Units	Number of Symmetric Links
Lightbulb/radiation problems (four versions) (Holyoak & Koh, 1987)	169-192	1373-1773
Fortress/radiation problems (Gick & Holyoak, 1980)	41	144
Cannibals and missionaries/farmer's dilemma problems (Gholson et al., 1986)	144	973
Contras interference	95	169
Politics interference (two versions)	55-67	308-381
Water-flow/heat-flow explanation (two versions) (Falkenhainer et al., 1986)	62-127	317-1010
Solar system/atom explanation (Falkenhainer et al., 1986)	93	733
Jealous animal stories (six versions) (Gentner & Toupin, 1986)	125-214	1048-1873
Addition/union	162	1468
Attribute mapping	43	220
Midwife/Socrates (three versions) (Kittay, 1987)	97-203	534-1702
Chemical analogies (8 different analogies) (Thagard et al., 1989)		

Source: Holyoak and Thagard (1989). Reprinted with the permission of the Ablex Publishing Corporation.

summarizes the types of analogies mapped by ACME and some network characteristics of each mapping.

ACME's analogical reasoning ability can be appreciated by considering two extremes in its range of applications. These are ACME's ability to process formal mathematical analogies on the one hand and literary metaphors on the other hand.

Application of ACME to a Formal Mathematical Analogy

ACME was posed the problem of discovering a formal analogy between two mathematical concepts: the addition of numbers and the union of sets. The analogy is formal in that it depends only on isomorphic or structural constraints and is devoid of semantic and pragmatic content.

[Table 10.3] presents a formal analogy between addition of numbers and union of sets. . . . Both addition and union have the abstract mathematical properties of commutativity, associativity, and the existence of an identity element (0 for numbers and ∅ for sets). ACME was given predicate-calculus representations of these two analogs, with no identical elements (note that number equality and set equality are given distinct symbols), and with all semantic weights set equal to the minimal value. This analogy is quite complex, as many propositions have the same predicates (sum or union), and many symbols representing intermediate results must be sorted out. Note that the representations given to the program did not explicitly group the components of each analog into three distinct equations. In the absence of any semantic or pragmatic information, only weights based upon isomorphism, coupled with the type restriction, provided information about the optimal mapping.

As the output in [Table 10.4] indicates, ACME settles to a complete solution to this formal mapping problem after 59 cycles. The model is thus able to derive a unique mapping in the absence of any overlap between the elements of the source and target. ACME's ability to deal with such examples is crucially dependent upon its parallel constraint-satisfaction algorithm. (Holyoak and Thagard, 1989, pp. 340–341)

Application of ACME to a Literary Metaphor

ACME's ability to map metaphors was tested by confronting it with two versions of a classical metaphor in which Socrates is the midwife of an idea. The correct version is the straightforward metaphor, but in the incorrect version misleading and confusing information is introduced. In the following account, the correct version is referred to as the isomorphic version.

The run reported in the first column of [Table 10.5] used the isomorphic version without any pragmatic weights. The network settles with a correct set of mappings after 34 cycles. Thus Socrates maps to the midwife, his student to the mother, the student's intellectual partner to the father, and the idea to the child. (Note that there is a homomorphic mapping of the predicates thinks _ about and tests _ truth to in _ labor _ with.) The propositions analogs are not essential here; deletion of them still allows a complete mapping to be discovered. (Holyoak and Thagard, 1989, p. 344).

In the nonisomorphic version or incorrect version, ACME's performance in mapping the metaphor is potentially degraded by the introduction of inappropriate data.

Table 10.3
Formal Isomorphism between Addition of Numbers and Union of Sets

Property	Addition	Union
Commutativity:	$N1 + N2 = N2 + N1$	$S1 \cup S2 = S2 \cup S1$
Associativity:	$N3 + (N4 + N5) =$	$S3 \cup [S4 \cup S5] =$
	$(N3 + N4) + N5$	$[S3 \cup S4] \cup S5$
Identity:	$N6 + 0 = N6$	$S6 \cup \varnothing = S6$

Predicate-Calculus Representations:

NUMBERS:

(sum (num1 num2 num10) n1)
(sum (num2 num1 num11) n2)
(num_eq (num10 num11) n3)
(sum (num5 num6 num12) n3)
(sum (num4 num12 num13) n5)
(sum (num4 num5 num14) n6)
(sum (num14 num6 num15) n7)
(num_eq (num13 num15) n8)
(sum (num20 zero num20) n9)

SETS:

(union (set1 set2 set10) s1)
(union (set2 set1 set11) s2)
(set_eq (set10 set11) s3)
(union (set5 set6 set12) s4)
(union (set4 set12 set13) s5)
(union (set4 set5 set14) s6)
(union (set14 set6 set15) s7)
(set_eq (set13 set15) s8)
(union (set20 empty-set set20) s9)

Source: Holyoak and Thagard (1989). Reprinted with the permission of the Ablex Publishing Corporation.

The nonisomorphic version contains the information that Socrates drinks hemlock juice, which is of course irrelevant to the metaphor. Far worse, the representation encodes the information that Socrates himself was matched to his wife by a midwife; and that Socrates' wife had a child with the help of this midwife. Clearly, this nonisomorphic extension will cause the structural and semantic constraints on mapping to support a much more superficial set of correspondences between the two situations. And indeed, in this second run, ACME finds only the barest fragments of the intended metaphoric mappings when the network settles after 105 cycles. Socrates' midwife now maps to the midwife

Table 10.4
Output After Running Addition/Union Analogy

Network has settled by cycle 59.

Test: TEST0 Total Times: 60

Mon May 2 10:40:03 EDT 1988

Analogy between numbers and sets.

Units not yet reached asymptote: 0

Goodness of network: 3.31

Calculating the best mappings after 60 cycles.

Best mapping of NUM10 is SET 10. 0.79

Best mapping of NUM2 is SET 2. 0.82

Best mapping of NUM1 is SET 1. 0.82

Best mapping of NUM11 is SET 11. 0.79

Best mapping of NUM12 is SET 12. 0.82

Best mapping of NUM6 is SET 6. 0.82

Best mapping of NUM5 is SET 5. 0.82

Best mapping of NUM13 is SET 13. 0.79

Best mapping of NUM4 is SET 4. 0.82

Best mapping of NUM14 is SET 14. 0.82

Best mapping of NUM15 is SET 15. 0.79

Best mapping of NUM20 is SET 20. 0.66

Best mapping of ZERO is EMPTY-SET. 0.66

Best mapping of NUM_EQ is SET_EQ. 0.57

Best mapping of SUM is UNION. 0.83

Source: Holyoak and Thagard (1989). Reprinted with the permission of the Ablex Publishing Corporation.

in the source, and Socrates' wife and child map to the source mother and child. Socrates himself simply maps to the father. Most of the other crucial objects and predicates (other than cause and helps, which map to themselves) have no good mappings. The only major pieces of the intended analogy that survive are the mappings between the student and the mother and between the idea and the child.

Note, however, that the original statement of the metaphor, "Socrates is a midwife of ideas," provides some direct pragmatic guidance as to the intended mappings. Clearly,

Table 10.5

Best Mappings, with Asymptotic Activation Levels, for Objects and Predicates in Three Versions of the Socrates/Midwife Metaphor

	Versions					
Cycles to Settle	Isomorphic Nonpragmatic 34		Nonisomorphic Nonpragmatic 105		Nonisomorphic Pragmatic 83	
Objects:						
Socrates	obj_midwife	.87	obj_father	.80	obj_midwife	.86
obj_student	obj_mother	.69	obj_mother	.69	obj_mother	.69
obj_partner	obj_father	.81	none		obj_father	.80
obj_idea	obj_child	.90	obj_child	.69	obj_child	.70
*obj_soc-midwife	--		obj_midwife	.84	none	
*obj_soc-wife	--		obj_mother	.69	obj_mother	.69
*obj_soc-child	--		obj_child	.69	obj_child	.65
*obj_hemlock	--		none		none	
Predicates:						
philospher	midwife	.58	none		midwife	.81
student	mother	.59	none		none	
intellectual_partner	father	.57	none		father	.57
idea	child	.59	none		child	.58
introduces	matches	.77	none		matches	.67
formulates	conceives	.72	conceives	.27	conceives	.31
thinks_about	in_labor_with	.36	none		none	
tests_truth	in_labor_with	.36	none		none	
knows_truth_or_falsify	gives_birth_to	.72	gives_birth_to	.72	gives_birth_to	.72
helps	helps	.77	helps	.79	helps	.80
cause	cause	.84	cause	.84	cause	.84
*poison	--		none		none	
*drink	--		none		none	
*father	--		father	.70	none	
*midwife	--		midwife	.70	none	
*mother	--		mother	.69	mother	.69
*child	--		child	.69	none	
*matches	--		matches	.78	none	
*conceives	--		conceives	.48	conceives	.43
*in_labor_with	--		in_labor_with	.74	in_labor_with	.74
*gives_birth_to	--		gives_birth_to	.46	gives_birth_to	.43

*Elements with an asterisk appeared only in nonisomorphic version. Elements that map to "none" have no mapping unit with activation greater than 20.

Source: Holyoak and Thagard (1989). Reprinted with the permission of the Ablex Publishing Corporation.

Socrates must map to the midwife, and the idea must map to something. This is precisely the kind of knowledge that ACME can represent using pragmatic weights. Accordingly, in a further run the mappings between propositions sl and ml and between the elements of those propositions (i.e., sl = ml, Socrates = obj _ midwife, and philosopher = mid-wife) were marked as PRESUMED; and proposition s4 and its elements (i.e., s4, obj _ idea, and idea) were marked as IMPORTANT. The right column on [Table 10.2] reports the results for the nonisomorphic version of the metaphor after these pragmatic weights are introduced. The pragmatic information was sufficient to allow almost complete re-covery of the abstract metaphoric mappings. The network settled after 83 cycles. Socrates again maps to the midwife, and the partner to the father; almost all of the appropriate predicate mappings, such as those between idea and child and between introduces and conceives, are also recovered. Note that some of the more superficial mappings of objects, such as between Socrates' wife and the mother, also emerge. *The behavior of the program across these versions of the metaphor thus dramatically illustrates both the power and the limitations of purely structural constraints, and the crucial role of pragmatic knowl-edge in finding abstract mappings in the face of misleading information.* (Holyoak and Thagard, 1989, pp. 344–347; italics added)

PHILOSOPHICAL AND PSYCHOLOGICAL IMPLICATIONS OF ANALOGICAL REASONING SYSTEMS

The abstract component process model of analogical reasoning is an impor-tant contribution to cognitive science. Its abstract character encompasses both human and artificial cognition; its componential structure enables differentiation and clarification of the global process of analogical reasoning. Although Hall (1989) concluded his review of computational and psychological studies on the note of ''problems of scale and generality,'' two points need to be made. First, as new studies appear, the abstract component model can continue to deserve its systematizing function. Second, many more studies will need to be conducted before integrated trends can be discerned.

ACME's mapping performance is algorithmic and, therefore, it is not sur-prising that it should fall short of the flexibility and power found in human analogical reasoning. For example, ACME cannot handle the significant reason-ing operation of the propositional converses. Thus, ACME is unable to map the converse relation between the inscribed proposition and the circumscribed prop-osition in plane and solid geometry.

ACME, as a computational approach to the generation and comprehension of analogies and metaphors, needs to be provided with vast amounts of knowl-edge that would enable it to be useful in complex human exposition of concepts, facts, and illusions. This knowledge requirement can be clearly seen in the following account of metaphor and theories of psychotherapy:

A metaphoric analysis of psychotherapy . . . contributes an understanding that is imme-diate, holistic, and idiographic. Psychoanalysis has a literary, classical, and dramatic metaphor (e.g., the incestuous conflicts of Oedipus, the obsessional struggles of Hamlet). Behavior therapy has a physiological, physicalistic, and mechanistic metaphor (e.g., deconditioning of anxiety responses, systematic training in adaptive behavior). Client-centered therapy has a personalistic, individualistic, and ideational metaphor (e.g., a search for self-identity, the discovery of personal values). Cognitive therapy has a rationalistic, logical, and educative metaphor (e.g., multiple and flexible rather than single and rigid interpretations of the meaning of life events, quality of cognition as precursor to quality of feeling). . . . These metaphors have the advantage of quickly capturing distinctive qualities in systems of psychotherapy. (Wagman, 1988, p. 12)

11

Limitations of Artificial Intelligence

LIMITS IN PHYSICS

Limits of the Transistor

The physical embodiment of artificial intelligence will, for the foreseeable future, depend on the continuous miniaturization of the transistor and on increasing the density of electronic components and their connections on a computer chip. The prospect of open-ended transistor miniaturization may falter because of limits in theoretical knowledge and manufacturing procedures.

Several kinds of physical limitations might emerge if the size of the transistor continues to shrink. The task of connecting minute elements to one another might, for example, become impossible. Declining circuit size also means that researchers must cope with ever stronger electric fields which can affect the movement of electrons in several ways. In the not too distant future, the transistor may span only hundreds of anxtroms. At that point, the presence or absence of individual atoms, as well as their behavior, will become significant. Diminishing size leads to increasing density of transistors on a chip which raises the amount of waste heat that is thrown off. Today's chips shed about ten times as much heat as does a cooking surface of comparable size, a flux that can rise at least 10-fold without exceeding the cooling capacity of known designs. As the size of circuit elements drops below the wavelength of usable forms of radiation, existing manufacturing methods may reach their limits. (Keyes, 1993, p. 70)

The Quantum Computer

Whereas, as discussed in the previous section, Keyes (1993) eludes to problems of quantum effects as transistor miniaturization proceeds, Lloyd (1993) describes the possibility of a quantum computer that would be ultrasmall and ultrafast. The quantum computer would store binary digits as quantum energies, up representing one and down representing zero. Moreover, the superposition event in quantum mechanics permits true generation of random numbers since in the superposition state, energies are simultaneously up and down. Lloyd (1993) discusses details of quantum computer construction but recognizes that an error-correction mechanism will be needed to control certain unstable quantum effects, but Landauer (1991) points out that such a mechanism would involve observation that would interfere with the correction process. Lloyd's proposals for an actual quantum computer have important theoretical and practical consequences and, also, philosophical consequences relating to the conjectures of Roger Penrose (1989, 1994) concerning limits of artificial intelligence and the quantum noncomputational nature of human consciousness (discussed below).

LIMITS IN LOGIC

Concepts of Fuzzy Logic

Fuzzy logic theory and applications became significant in artificial intelligence domains during the final decades of the twentieth century (Kosko, 1991; Zadeh, 1979). Applications include industrial and consumer devices, biological and economic research, and medical and financial information services. Fuzzy logic is a multivalued logic responsive to the imprecise character of human experience, judgment, and reasoning.

Gödel's Theorem: Logical Foundations of Artificial Intelligence

Logical implication was central to Gödel's analytical proof of his famous mathematical theorems. Gödel's theorems, which place limits on the logical completeness and consistency of mathematical systems, have sometimes been interpreted as placing unique limits on artificial intelligence.

The equivalence of probability and logical implication was first proved by Gödel (Gödel, 1930); proofs appear in textbooks on logic. The incompleteness of any finite axiomatization of arithmetic also was proved by Gödel (Gödel, 1931). Although this result is extremely important in mathematical logic, it does not (as some people have claimed [Lucas, 1961]) *preclude the possibility that machines will be able to reason as well as people* [italics added]. People cannot prove consistency of complex systems in this way either! [Genesereth and Nilsson, 1987, p. 62]

Mathematical proofs have sometimes been used to demonstrate that there are limits to the powers of artificial intelligence, in general, and of computers in particular (Dreyfus, 1972). For example, Gödel's (1931) theorem demonstrates that for any sufficiently complex logical system, propositions can be stated that can neither be disproved nor proved within that system, without the system itself being logically inconsistent. However, the application of Gödel's theorem to demonstrate theoretical limits of computers equally extends to demonstrate theoretical limits to the powers of human intelligence. In any case, Gödel's theorem has not impeded advances in the field of mathematics, nor should it impede advances in the field of artificial intelligence. (Wagman, 1988, p. 11)

PHILOSOPHICAL AND PSYCHOLOGICAL IMPLICATIONS OF THE LIMITATIONS OF ARTIFICIAL INTELLIGENCE

In *The Emperor's New Mind: Concerning Computers, Minds, and Laws of Physics*, the mathematician-physicist Roger Penrose (1989) proclaims that the human mind excels over artificial intelligence because its creativity and complexity rests on the indeterminacy of quantum mechanics phenomena at the most basic level of the brain, whereas artificial intelligence is confined to the boundaries of classical mechanics and is thus barred from the discovery of proofs of elegant mathematical truths such as Gödel's theorem.

Penrose's thesis is devastated because of the work of Seth Lloyd (discussed above under the section heading "The Quantum Computer") directed toward the construction of an actual quantum computer. The potential of this technological advance would be to have a computer that is quantum mechanical, whereas Penrose contends that only the human brain is quantum mechanical. Therefore, the putative limitations of artificial intelligence that derive from its non-quantum mechanical character are potentially refutable.

In *Shadows of the Mind: The Search for the Missing Science of Consciousness*, Roger Penrose (1994) asserts that consciousness cannot be simply the result of the computations of electrochemical neural processes, that noncomputational quantum gravitation effects result in consciousness and that neural microtubules in human neurons possess quantum mechanical characteristics. Noncomputational quantum gravity effects and quantum mechanical neurotubules are unsupported speculations in physics and neurology, and Penrose falls back on his entirely refutable contention that because he can see the truth of Gödel's theorem he is a non-formal system, a system that goes beyond what he declares to be inherent in the limitations of artificial intelligence.

One may wonder at Penrose's prodigious intellectual efforts in *The Emperor's New Mind* and *Shadows of the Mind* to establish that the human mind goes beyond limitations of artificial intelligence. It would appear, in part, that Penrose's pride as a mathematical Platonist and his psychological pride in possessing the acumen of an outstanding mathematical physicist are involved.

Penrose holds himself to be a Platonist in mathematics; that is, he believes that mathematical concepts have a physical reality, that they are objects that have always existed independently and await discovery in the brain of the human mathematician. In this view, mathematics is discovered, not invented. Penrose writes:

I have made no secret of the fact that my sympathies lie strongly with the Platonistic view that mathematical truth is absolute, external, and eternal, and not based on man-made criteria; and that mathematical objects have a timeless existence of their own, not dependent on human society nor on particular physical objects. (Penrose, 1989, p. 116)

Plato's world consists not of tangible objects, but of "mathematical things." This world is accessible to us not in the ordinary physical way but, instead, via the *intellect*. One's mind makes contact with Plato's world whenever it contemplates a mathematical truth, perceiving it by the exercise of mathematical reasoning and insight. This world was regarded as distinct and more perfect than the material world of our external experiences, but just as real. (Penrose, 1989, p. 158)

Penrose admits that his theories are tentative and concedes that his Platonistic philosophy is not shared by all, or even by a majority of mathematicians. Penrose's Platonistic position rests, of course, on his own vivid introspective feelings that accompany his mathematical imagination and mathematical creativity. Penrose's holistic view of creative thought is in opposition to the analytic approach to creative thought and consciousness generally. Penrose's holistic consciousness, as opposed to its scientific analysis into discrete component structures, is in essence poetical and metaphysical.

Penrose takes a curious position in that he is a mathematical physicist who posits quantum effects as determinative of the mind's holistic creativity. Thus, at once, he is giving an analytic (i.e., a scientific) basis for the human mind as opposed to artificial intelligence. Creativity, inspiration, intuitiveness, and theoretical discovery are the product of a physical process (quantum mechanics), but Penrose's psychological experience (consciousness) is mystical and Platonistic.

Penrose in a way is like Descartes, who exempted the soul (mind) from the category of physical space, yet asserted a physical explanation for the nonphysical mystical soul as having a basis in the actions of the pineal gland.

Penrose and Descartes, both mathematical physicists, both Platonists, believe that mathematical ideas have an *a priori*, independent, and eternal existence and await discovery by the creative, mystical, and intuitive mind within a brain driven by classical mechanics (Descartes) or by quantum physics (Penrose).

Penrose emphasizes that the holistic creative human mind rests ultimately on a brain that takes advantage of its subatomic quantum mechanics and whose behavior is nonalgorithmic, nonfixed, nondeterministic, and probabilistic. In that sense, it has the potential for combinatory effects and protean structures. Penrose's mentalistic account is strikingly similar to that given by the mathematical physicist Poincaré of his own mathematical imagination and creativity.

[T]he privileged unconscious phenomena, those susceptible of becoming conscious, are those which . . . affect most profoundly our emotional sensibility. . . . Now, what are the mathematic entities to which we attribute this character of beauty and elegance . . . ?

They are those whose elements are harmoniously disposed so that the mind without effort can embrace their totality while realizing the details. This harmony is at once a satisfaction of our aesthetic needs and an aid to the mind, sustaining and guiding. . . . *Figure the future elements of our combinations as something like the unhooked atoms of Epicurus. . . . They flash in every direction through the space . . . like the molecules of a gas in the kinematic theory of gases. Then their mutual impacts may produce new combinations.* (Poincaré, 1913; italics added)

It is of interest that Poincaré's account of his own mental experience—since it is characterized by the simultaneous processing of data—is in that respect holistic. It is not dependent on algorithms but on a kind of creative emergence of numerous mathematical units into meaningful cognitive wholes. Poincaré's description resembles the account of parallel distributed processing given by Rumelhart, McClelland, and the PDP Research Group (1986).

It may be that Penrose would be more satisfied with the Rumelhart and McClelland position than with the traditional serial processing position of fixed algorithms. A reaching for quantum effect explanations may not be necessary, although he, as a mathematical physicist, would probably think that it is important for a complete understanding of the human brain. Poincaré (1913) in his physical explanations reaches for the science of his day, thermodynamic theory, as Penrose (1989) reaches for the science of his day, quantum mechanics theory, to explain in both cases their own personal experience and feelings accompanying their holistic discovery of mathematical truths.

Penrose's emotional reaction to construing the creative processes of the human mind in computational terms, as a problem-solving mechanism is set forth in the following self-revelatory passage:

Over the past few decades, electronic computer technology has made enormous strides. . . . There is something almost frightening about the pace of development. Already computers are able to perform numerous tasks that had previously been the exclusive province of human thinking, with a speed and accuracy which far outstrip anything that a human being can achieve. We have long been accustomed to machinery which easily out-performs us in *physical* ways. *That* causes us no distress. . . . These achievements do not worry our pride. But to be able to *think*—that has been a very human prerogative. It has, after all, been that ability to think which translated into physical terms, has enabled us to transcend our physical limitations and which has seemed to set us above our fellow creatures in achievement. If machines can one day excel us in that one important quality in which we have believed ourselves to be superior, shall we not then have surrendered that unique superiority to our creations? (Penrose, 1989, p. 3)

That machines may one day exceed us in the ability to think apparently worried Penrose's pride and motivated in part his complex intellectual critique of artificial intelligence. Penrose admits that the validity of his critique and his theories will require substantive research, but the emotional threat of a new science to unique human superiority has been met before in the form of Copernican, Darwinian, and Freudian theories. Research concerned with the psychological implications of the computer for the individual and society is discussed elsewhere (Wagman, 1983); the intellectual achievements of artificial intelligence are considered in Wagman (1988, 1991a).

12

Epilogue

KOANS OF HUMAN INTELLECT AND ARTIFICIAL INTELLIGENCE

Human intellect embraces both general knowledge and technical knowledge. In any given profession (psychology, medicine, law, librarianship, engineering, etc.), the solution of problems typically involves both types of knowledge.

However, professional status is often equated with technical knowledge. Computers that possess technical knowledge and that can perform technical problem solving are often viewed as a threat to human professionals (Wagman, 1983).

Computers that employ algorithms to solve problems in psychological counseling or medical diagnosis, legal research, or engineering design may equal or surpass human experts in speed, precision, and power. Professionals may well need to remind themselves, as stated above, that human intellect embraces general knowledge (judgment and discernment) and not just technical knowledge (formulas and decision rules).

From a psychological point of view, the reaction of most modern professionals to the introduction of technology that encroaches, duplicates, and surpasses their technical skills (guarded as zealously as medieval gilds of silversmiths guarded their skills) is no different than the reaction of ancient Greek philosophers (especially Plato) who warned against the introduction of technology of written symbols as constituting a threat to their orally based intellectual powers of memory and reasoning. In reality, the technology of written symbols and the technology of computers augment human intellect, permitting the expansion of human discovery, knowledge, and application, while earlier stages in these developments become mere algorithmic formalisms.

In summary, human intellect and professional problem-solving behavior, at any given time, embrace both general and technical competencies. Artificial intelligence has succeeded in giving only technical competence to computers.

Moreover, within any stream of problem-solving behavior, there is a conical process that begins with general knowledge, comprehension, and approach, and that terminates with the application of a computational formalism. For example, medical problem solving may begin with a general evaluation of the patient's overall status and a consideration of the range of possible diseases and terminate with the application of a computer-controlled specific biochemical diagnosis. Over time, new knowledge and methods are introduced that are initially applied by the human professionals, but that steadily become computable, requiring a psychological readjustment by human professionals as they relinquish the performance of mere technical procedures to computers and strive to revalue themselves as originators of new theory, method, and knowledge.

These psychological koans of human intellect and artificial intelligence may be clarified by geometric cones. Conical sections with wide diameters represent general intellectual knowledge, judgment, and discernment, and conical sections with increasingly narrower diameters represent technical competencies. In problem solving by a professional engineer, physician, or psychologist, the cone is traversed from regions of wide diameter to regions of narrow diameter and algorithms are increasingly applied as the vertex of the cone is approached.

At one point in the development of a profession, it is the professional who applies the algorithm, but with further sophistication in the profession, at a later time, the algorithm is incorporated into and used by the computer program. In the cycle, the professional's algorithmic behavior is replaced by the computer, but the development of new knowledge in the wide regions of the cone is a result of the professional's human intellect.

SPHERES OF HUMAN INTELLECT AND ARTIFICIAL INTELLIGENCE

Whereas the sphere of artificial intelligence rests solely on algorithmic intelligence, the sphere of human intellect rests both on algorithmic intelligence and creative intelligence. Indeed, the enormous increase in the sphere of human intellect in the course of history, and especially in the course of recent scientific history, may be accounted for by the successive and complementary contribution of algorithmic and creative intelligence. *In recent decades, the form of this interaction of types of intelligence is most clearly seen in the moving line phenomenon that characterizes temporal and synergistic relationships between human intellect and artificial intelligence.*

THE MOVING LINE OF INTELLIGENCE

The moving line phenomenon is summarized in Table 12.1. As shown in Table 12.1, the moving line of intelligence is cyclic across both spheres of human intellect and artificial intelligence and interactive between the spheres. The time series of the moving line of intelligence is recapitulated in the final row of Table 12.1.

AUTONOMY AND INTELLIGENCE

The Moving Line of Intelligence and the Spheres of Human Intellect and Artificial Intelligence

The concept of autonomy has different meanings in different contexts. In the human context, autonomy of action may refer to consciously directed behavior, to intentional behavior, to behavior that is independent of compulsion by a political or social organization or by an intellectual or religious ethos. In the artificial intelligence context, autonomy of action may refer to solution search behavior that is independent of continuous human control, to theorem-proving procedures that are independent of content, to self-corrective (cybernetic) behavior.

In general contexts, autonomy of action is often considered as an aspect or an index of creative behavior and intellectual performance. In according intelligence to behavior of entities (human or computer), the relationship between autonomy of action and perceived intelligence is not simple. The reasons for the complexity of this relationship between autonomy of action and perceived intelligence will now be discussed.

The first reason is that neither autonomy of action nor perceived intelligence is an all or none value. Rather, each is a composite of several multi-value variables. The second reason is that the values of the variables change as a function of time (the moving line phenomena).

Regarding the first reason, consider the variables of purpose, consciousness, and knowledge as they enter into the composites of autonomy of action and perceived intelligence of four entities: a statue of horse and rider, an expert system of horse and rider, artificial intelligence, and human intellect. For these entities, consider the variables of algorithmic intelligence and creative intelligence as aspects of the composite of perceived intelligence.

Regarding the entity of the bronze statue of horse and rider, we must assign a value of zero to the variables of autonomy of action (purpose, consciousness, knowledge) and to the variables of perceived intelligence (algorithmic, creative). All of these variables are assignable to the sculptor, and none of the variables is assignable to the statue.

Consider next the entity of a bronze expert system of horse and rider. As

Table 12.1
The Moving Line of Intelligence for the Spheres of Human Intellect and Artificial Intelligence

	Sphere	
	Human Intellect	Artificial Intelligence
Time 1	Theoretical knowledge (the nature of DNA)	Expert System not constructable
Time 2	Specific applied knowledge (gene splicing)	Expert System constructed
Time 3	Expert System substituted for the specific applied knowledge	Expert System in regular use (gene splicing)
Time 4	New theoretical knowledge (the nature of the genome)	New Expert System not constructable
Time 5	New specific applied knowledge (genome mapping)	New Expert System constructed
Time 6	New Expert System substituted for the specific applied knowledge	New Expert System in regular use (genome mapping)
Time 7 ... n	Continuation of series: new theoretical knowledge, new specific applied knowledge, new Expert System substituted for the new specific applied knowledge, . . .	Continuation of series: new Expert System not constructable, new Expert System constructed, new Expert System in regular use, ...

The table depicts temporal and interactive relationships within and between the spheres of human intellect and artificial intelligence. An example from molecular biology is provided.

compared with the statue, we may ascribe a higher level of intelligence as the expert system adaptively maneuvers to a changing terrain of level and sloping ground, trenches, and barriers. The cybernetic quality of its actions suggests a value greater than zero for the variables of purpose and knowledge but not for the variable of consciousness (the expert system possessing the knowledge that it is the agent of its cybernetic performance). Although we may be psychologically intrigued with its apparent intelligent behavior, we, at the same time, recognize that although it has a value greater than zero for the variable of algorithmic intelligence, the value of zero must be assigned to it for the variable of creative intelligence.

Compared with the expert system of horse and rider, the entity of artificial intelligence must be ascribed higher intelligence because it has higher values on the variables of purpose (multiple complex problem-solving goals, intricately patterned) and knowledge (complex representations of multiple types and levels of information about the world of objects, events, and symbols). However, like the expert system, it probably cannot be given a value greater than zero on the variable of consciousness, as consciousness was defined above. As compared with the expert system, artificial intelligence can be ascribed a substantially higher value on the variable of algorithmic intelligence (speed, power, and level of automatic problem solving). Artificial intelligence, as compared with the expert system, must also be assigned a higher value on the variable of creative intelligence (e.g., applications of artificial intelligence directed toward elementary aspects of the process of scientific discovery).

Regarding the entity of human intellect, it is in many respects incommensurate with artificial intelligence, although comparable, to some extent, in other respects. The variable of purpose, except for its cybernetic meaning, contains subtleties of intentionality, freedom of choice, and degrees and levels of determinism uniquely associated with the human condition. Consciousness, self-reflections of consciousness, and self-reflections of self-reflections belong to the sphere of human intellect. Regarding the variable of knowledge, artificial intelligence in selected areas (e.g., advanced expert systems) may equal or surpass human capacity for speed, power, and reliability. We are impressed with these productive performances of artificial intelligence, but we recognize that algorithmic and not creative intelligence is responsible for the product and that algorithmic intelligence is fundamentally the creation of human intellect.

THE ABSTRACT VALIDITY OF LOGIC AND MATHEMATICAL STRUCTURES

From the standpoint of artificial intelligence concepts, a general theory of intelligence would be based on the logic and mathematics of symbolic structures and operations. The human mind and the computer mind would be viewed as manifestations of this general theory. Conceivably, there might be other manifestations of mind that would also derive from the logical and mathematical structures of the general theory. The logical and mathematical structures, themselves, have an abstract validity that is not altered by their technological use as descriptive accounts of the information processing performance of human and computer minds. *At the most abstract and fundamental level*, the concepts of logic and mathematics would provide any validity that current or future general theories of human and artificial intelligence may have.

CRITIQUES OF PURE REASON

The Ultimate Nature of Cognition

Philosophical approaches to the ultimate nature of cognition have their pre-eminent source in the works of Plato (1956) and derivative advances in the works of Descartes (1951), Hobbes (1651), Locke (1975), and Kant (1958).

Plato believed in a world of ideas beyond sense perception. Plato's world possessed ultimate truth, absolute certainty, and undisturbed permanence. This pristine and abstract world could be approached by the study of mathematics, because its truths were permanent, certain, and universal. The Platonic faith in the absolute truth and purity of mathematical reason dominated the later philosophical thought of Descartes, Hobbes, Locke, and Kant, for whom Euclidean geometry possessed a body of truth and a method of reasoning that constituted a bulwark against error and an unassailable paragon of philosophical investigation into the nature of cognition.

Descartes agreed with Plato that mathematics was the key to understanding the universe, itself a colossal mathematical machine. Scrupulous deductive reasoning like that in Euclidean mathematics would disclose the laws of the universe.

Hobbes, like Plato, affirmed that mathematics and only mathematics reveals true knowledge of reality. All knowledge, except mathematical knowledge, is imperfect.

Locke, impressed with the power of mathematics displayed in the Newtonian description of the physical world, was convinced that the human mind was part of physical nature and could be accounted for in mathematical terms. The human mind creates propositions about reality, and the truth about these propositions can be determined by systematically comparing them for consistency or contradiction.

Kant's philosophy of cognition posited pure categories of space and time. These categories were innate, embedded in the brain's structure, independent of personal experience, and provided formal dimensions in which all empirical knowledge was bound and constrained. The pure categories of rationality provide the necessary conditions for logical thought and are normative for human reasoning. The pure categories of space, time, and formal logic are a priori templates into which all cognition is fitted.

We can say with confidence that certain pure *a priori* synthetical cognitions, pure mathematics and pure physics, are actual and given; for both contain propositions which are thoroughly recognized as absolutely certain . . . and yet as independent of experience. (Kant, 1781)

Our intellect does not draw its laws from nature but imposes its laws on nature. (Kant, 1781)

The linchpin in Kant's universally admired philosophy was his deep belief that Euclidean geometry was not derived from experience, but, rather, was an a priori intuition regarding the true nature of physical space. Kant's philosophical edifice was devastated by the development of non-Euclidean geometries that lead to curious theorems, at variance with Euclidean theorems but appropriate to the description of many types of physical space for which the Euclidean system was inapplicable or inadequate. Kant's confident assertion that Euclidean geometry was an a priori truth and the only true empirical geometry collapsed following Riemann's (1953) development of differential geometry. Riemann demonstrated that Euclidean geometry was only a special case derivable from a general equation whose variables and functions could embrace a very large set of possible geometries applicable to possible sets of physical space.

Artificial Intelligence and Naive Physics

Logical approaches to artificial intelligence have demonstrated the power of axioms and deductive systems in the domains of scientific and mathematical reasoning, but the domain of commonsense reasoning contains formidable difficulties in that people do not employ theoretical knowledge of physics or psychology in their everyday reasoning about the physical or social world. Yet, people appear to have a satisfactory working knowledge of events and processes in the physical world, and, according to Turing's thesis (Turing, 1936), this knowledge does fall under the aegis of computational logic. The Turing thesis has been supported by the work of Hayes (1985), who has demonstrated that everyday concepts embedded in naive physics and naive psychology can be stated in the predicate calculus and can be expressed as logical theorems that lead to true or false deductive inferences. This axiomatization includes people's commonsense knowledge and reasoning concerning cause and effect, velocity and acceleration, weight and balance, height and support, path and boundary, and inside and outside.

Artificial Intelligence and Logicism

The logicism of the Hayes research program has been criticized by Mc-Dermott (1990) on the grounds that pure deductive reasoning as a set of formal axioms is not applicable to human thinking, which is largely nondeductive. McDermott (1990) points out that human reasoning is typically nonmonotonic, that it easily takes account of changes in premises, context, and conditions, whereas the monotonic logicism of axiomatic deduction is rigid. McDermott concludes that only when the logicism approach can be extended to cover nonmonotonic everyday thinking will a valid science of intelligence be possible, and pending that development, only an applied technology of computer programs that do makeshift nondeductive reasoning will persist.

To summarize: the logicist project of expressing "naive physics" in first-order logic has not been very successful. One reason may be that the basic argument was flawed. You cannot write down axioms independent of a program for manipulating them if the inferences you are interested in are not deductions. Unfortunately, very few interesting inferences are deductions, and the attempts by logicists to extend logic to cover more territory have been disappointing. Hence we must resign ourselves to writing programs, and viewing knowledge representations as entities to be manipulated by the programs. (McDermott, quoted in Boden, 1990, p. 227)

Conclusion

Mathematics and mathematical logic have been largely responsible for advances in the physical sciences. Whether mathematical logic can serve an analogous role in the development of the sciences of cognition remains to be seen. It may be that nonstandard forms of mathematical logic will have to be created to capture human thinking, which is more often finesse than ratiocination: "Life is the art of drawing sufficient conclusions from insufficient premises" (Butler, quoted in Kline, 1985, p. 210).

Appendix A:
Characteristics of a General
Theory of Intelligence

A general theory of intelligence that would include both human and artificial intelligence must, at the present state of knowledge, rest on the common theme of symbolic logic. The "present state of knowledge" is intended to remind us that the science of symbolic logic is a nineteenth-and twentieth-century development and that Aristotelian logic remained preeminent for two millennia, up until the time of Boolian algebra (Boole, 1854). The trilogy of symbolic logic, Boolian algebra, and electronic circuits (the von Neumann computer (Taube, 1961–1963)) may be revised, expanded, or completely replaced by creative intellectual development. Electronic circuits may be replaced by optical circuits and the von Neumann computer by parallel distributed processing computers by the close of the twentieth century (Grimson and Patil, 1987). Research in theoretical logic and mathematics may replace current formulations of symbolic logic and its representation in binary notations with more powerful conceptions (Fikes and Nilsson, 1971).

THE FOUR CHARACTERISTICS OF A GENERAL THEORY OF INTELLIGENCE

Insofar as these future conceptions are examples of general formal systems, they will share the characteristics of formal systems as understood in current terms. Formal systems are (a) symbolic, (b) autonomous, (c) discrete, and (d) finite.

As such a formal system, a general theory of intelligence would possess the system's characteristics. Intuitively, the formal theory would seem to fit the nature of artificial intelligence more easily than the nature of human intellect. The problem is that, up until about the middle of the twentieth century, formal systems of symbolic logic were abstruse lacunae in general Western intellectual thought. Much of this intellectual tradition was content rather than form oriented; and where there were formal orientations, they tended to use language that was rich in connotative significance rather than symbols that were devoid of connotative meaning. The four characteristics of a general theory of intelligence will now be discussed.

Symbolic and Finite Characteristics

Symbols and their organization into a system of logic are essential to a theory of artificial intelligence. Are symbols and systems of logic equally essential for a theory of human intellect?

At an intuitive level, the answer would appear to be negative; but at a formal level, the answer would seem to be affirmative. Words are symbols, and a system of words depends on alphabetic representation (symbols) and logical (at least, not chaotic) connectives and inferences in order to support any level of human intellect that may range from everyday activity to abstruse research and creative endeavor.

The metasymbol is the binary digit. Sequences of zeros and ones are the ultimate universal representatives of knowledge in artificial intelligence. Has a theory of artificial intelligence, then, come down to this: a finite permutation of binary digits that corresponds to truth values of logic functions that represent the real world of knowledge?

We can more clearly ascertain the validity of this theory because artificial intelligence is an invention. On the other hand, a theory of human intellect is a discovery. Arbitrary permutations of binary digits are required for the electronic basis of the computer (the twentieth-century representative of artificial intelligence). That the neural basis of human intellect requires or is even simply compatible with such a binary digit substrate has not been discovered.

The Discrete Characteristic

The theoretical description of cognitive processes in artificial intelligence as consisting of binary-coded theorem-proving operations requires discreteness in two senses. The sequences of steps in the theorem-proving process are discrete, and the coded representations of the content of the theorem-proving process are discrete.

Would a theoretical description of cognitive processes in human intellect entail such discreteness? Clearly, it is easier to demonstrate the presence of discreteness of content and operation in the terminal cognitive product of human intellect than in the cognitive processes that precede the cognitive product. Our ideas may come to us in a continuous flow, but the critical self-examination or

communication of these ideas requires a discreteness in organization and pres-
entation that may range from everyday verbal behavior to the formal demonstration of a mathematical or logical proof.

The phrase "ideas come to us" reminds us of the seemingly spontaneous
and nondiscrete solutions that appear with vivid conviction in the literary and
mathematical imagination (Poincaré, 1929; Sternberg, 1988). One could argue
that these creative problem solutions are highly accelerated discrete processes
that give to our conscious minds the illusion of continuity. The analogy would
be made with the illusory perception of continuity in digitally produced pho-
tographs that are, in reality, composed of closely packed discrete dots.

Once again, as discussed above, the distinction is the binary code as the
universal medium of artificial intelligence, and the yet-to-be-discovered discrete
code that would provide a universal medium for both conscious systematic
thought and communication and unconscious creative and continuous imagination (Langley and Jones, 1988) that are characteristic of human intellect.

The Autonomous Characteristic

Formal systems are said to be *autonomous*. Autonomous is used here in the
sense of self-contained propositions and operations. A formal system is responsive only to its own internal sets of axioms and logic functions.

Autonomy in the formal systems of artificial intelligence is a dramatic resolution method in theorem proving relentlessly obeying their own internal logic,
through which the establishment of a proof is guaranteed (if a proof, indeed,
does exist). However, the axioms and goals on which the autonomous internal
logic operates in the general resolution method are fundamentally the choice of
creative human intellect.

Conclusion

In conclusion, whether the creative intelligence that marks human intellect
and the algorithmic intelligence that characterizes artificial intelligence can be
bracketed by a common formal theory of general intelligence remains to be
seen. Symbolic logic appears to be the necessary condition in such a general
theory but does not appear, by itself, to constitute as well the sufficient condition.

Appendix B:
A Factor Analytic Study of the Psychological Implications of the Computer for the Individual and Society

The consequences of the expansion of computer presence had led Simon (1977) to refer to the changes in society resulting from the introduction of computers as "the information revolution" (p. 1186). Others (Abelson and Hammond, 1977; Davis, 1977) refer to the "information revolution" as comparable to the earlier Industrial Revolution. The impact of computers upon society has been extensive. The increasing presence of the computer and of electronics has also led to debates and disputes, sometimes extremely vociferous.

The impact of the computer upon man and upon various sectors of society has caused some to rejoice (see Sagan, 1977; Negroponte, 1995) and some to advise caution (see Weizenbaum, 1976; Roszak, 1994). In general, there is agreement that the introduction of electronics and computers into society has had and will have many consequences. Simon (1977) sees four major areas in which the consequences will be felt:

First, there are the economic consequences that follow an innovation that increases human productivity.... Second, there are consequences for the nature of work and leisure—for the quality of life. Third, the computer may have special consequences for privacy and individual liberty. Fourth, there are consequences for man's view of himself, for his picture of the universe and of his place and goals in it. (Simon, 1977, p. 1,189)

Reactions to computers have spawned a vast literature that argues both for and against their presence and usage. The general points made in each specific context are often repeated in numerous other contexts. In each context, the debate is between those in favor of computers and those against their introduction into that specific sector. In any sector, there is the question of the nature of the computer, and the consequences of its presence.

In general terms, those who are against the introduction of the computer decry its dehumanizing effects. Often they point to the limits and boundaries of its applicability. Weizenbaum (1976) points to the necessity of recognizing its limitations.

In an earlier study (Wagman, 1976), the general literature concerned with the impact of the computer on man and society was concisely analyzed in each of ten sectors of society. In each sector, the contrasting viewpoints of behavioral and social scientists advocating or criticizing the use of computers in that sector were analyzed with respect to their major differences. Analyses of these major issues were presented for the following sectors: (1) society, (2) values, (3) cognition, (4) education, (5) medicine, (6) counseling, (7) mathematics, (8) banking, (9) politics, and (10) the criminal justice system. Thus, in the earlier study (Wagman, 1976), an attempt was made to clarify and reduce the general literature by a summary analysis of contending viewpoints within specific sectors.

In the present article, a further clarification and reduction is achieved by representing, insofar as feasible, the specific contending viewpoints as sets of attitude scale items, each set representing advocacy or criticism of the use of computers in a specific sector of society.

METHOD

Subjects

Sixty-three male and fifty-eight female undergraduate students at the University of Illinois served as subjects in connection with course requirements.

Materials

The Cybernetics Attitude Scale (Wagman, 1977) comprises 100 items, 10 items on each of the 10 subscales. Each subscale is designed to measure attitudes toward computers in a specific sector of society. A subscale is composed of five statements representing positive attitudes toward computers. For each of these five statements, there is a converse statement that expresses a negative attitude toward computers. The complete Cybernetics Attitude Scale is arranged to depict groupings of items under each of the subscales (see Table B.1). (As administered to subjects, items are not grouped with respect to subscales.)

Responses are scored on a 7-point Likert scale (1 = strongly agree with the favorable items; 7 = strongly disagree with the converse items). A high score represents negative attitudes toward computers; a low score represents positive attitudes.

Table B.1
The Cybernetics Attitude Scale (100 items)

Statements	Converse

Society

1. The complexity of the problems of modern society require computers for their solutions. (69)
2. There is really no reason to fear computers. (39)
3. Computers increase human freedom and allow us to become more human. (72)
4. Compared with the industrial revolution, the computer is less threatening to society. (47)
5. What is threatening to society is not the computer, but people's use of the computer. (77)

6. Computers increase the complexity of modern life. (60)
7. Computers are justifiably feared. (94)
8. Computers are beginning to make us less human. (37)
9. The widespread use of computers in society threatens civilization more than any other innovation. (81)
10. The most threatening thing about computers is their very existence. (98)

Values

1. It is good that computers do only what they are programmed to do. (61)
2. It is not important that computers do not exercise discretionary judgment over the purpose that may have been intended. (78)
3. The dependability that a computer provides is more important than the human flexibility that is lost. (86)
4. It does not matter that computers cannot reflect upon the meaning of their personal experience. (53)
5. Computers can never change the value of being human. (95)

6. It would be nice if computers didn't always do only what they are programmed to do. (21)
7. Even computers should use discretionary judgment in solving social problems. (38)
8. A computer cannot replace man's flexibility in solving problems. (13)
9. The ability to reflect upon personal experience separates man from computers. (26)
10. The more we use computers the more we will devalue people's worth. (87)

Statements	Converse

Cognition

1. Computers are valuable because they save people from mental drudgery. (23)
2. Just because people use a computer for arithmetic problems does not mean that people will forget how to do arithmetic problems. (65)
3. It is a good idea to use computers to teach concepts to grade-school children. (1)
4. People's mental abilities are actually increased by interacting with the computer. (99)
5. No matter how much society uses computers, the mental capacity of society will remain as good as ever. (17)

6. People have begun to rely too heavily upon computers. (31)
7. If people do all of their math problems on a computer, people will forget how to do these problems by hand. (5)
8. Learning concepts on the computer sacrifices children's grasp of the meaning of these concepts. (63)
9. A computer simply cannot increase a person's mental abilities. (71)
10. If society uses computers too often and too much, the mental capacity of society will begin to decrease. (89)

Counseling

1. I would feel more at ease solving a personal problem with a computer than with a counselor. (45)
2. I would feel more independent solving a personal problem on a computer than with a counselor. (55)
3. I think a computer could have more information to help me solve my problems than a counselor could have. (6)
4. Compared with a counselor, a computer would be more patient and reliable in helping to solve a personal problem. (41)
5. As compared with a counselor, a computer could generate a greater number of solutions to my personal problems. (80)

6. I would rather talk to a counselor than try to solve my personal problems with a computer. (40)
7. I would feel more in control discussing my problems with a counselor than with a computer. (18)
8. A counselor could know me better than a computer ever could. (44)
9. Too many things could go wrong with a computer that couldn't go wrong with a counselor as I try to solve my personal problems. (22)
10. A counselor could help me more than a computer could with my personal problems because a counselor would have more experience with my type of problem. (9)

Statements	Converse

Education

1. I would feel more at ease learning from a computer than from a teacher. (59)
2. I would feel more independent learning from a computer than learning from a teacher. (100)
3. I would like learning with a computer because I can work at my own pace. (97)
4. I would like learning from a computer because I wouldn't feel embarrassed when I didn't know the answer. (35)
5. I would like working with a computer because it doesn't play favorites as a teacher might. (8)

6. I would rather learn from a teacher than from a computer. (82)
7. A computer can never match the human contact a teacher provides. (20)
8. A computer structures the learning situation too much. (88)
9. I would not like to feel that a computer is smarter than I am. (91)
10. Learning from a computer would be a cold and impersonal experience. (56)

Medicine

1. I would be more at ease answering health questions from a computer than from a doctor. (68)
2. I could be more frank and open when answering a computer's health questions than questions from a doctor.
3. I feel that a computer health survey would be more systematic than a health survey taken by a doctor. (49)
4. I think that personal answers to a computer health survey would be kept in stricter confidence than answers to a doctor's survey. (14)
5. In medical diagnosis, I believe that computers are faster and more accurate than a doctor. (4)

6. I would be more comfortable talking to a doctor than to a computer about my health problems. (3)
7. I would be more honest when answering questions about my health from a doctor than from a computer.
8. A doctor would be less likely to miss important facts about my health than would a computer. (96)
9. I could not be sure who would see my answers to a computer health survey. (46)
10. A computer can never replace the experience and intuition of a good doctor. (62)

Statements	Converse

Politics

1. I think it is valuable to have computers to forecast the outcomes of elections. (25)
2. When computers report the outcomes of elections, the democratic process is made more effective. (74)

3. I have more confidence when votes are counted by computer than when they are counted by an election official. (34)
4. When a computer keeps records of contributions to politicians, elections are made fairer. (52)
5. When a computer, instantaneously reports public opinion, both citizens and government benefit. (50)

6. Forecasting the outcomes of elections by computers interferes with the election process. (27)
7. When computers report the outcomes of elections instantaneously, the possibility of naming the wrong person as a winner increases. (2)
8. An election official would be less likely to make a mistake in counting ballots than a computer would. (1)
9. Keeping a computer accounting of political contributions does not deter illegal contributions. (75)
10. Reporting public opinion by computer may interfere with the functioning of the government. (54)

Criminal Justice System

1. I think it is desirable to have information about criminals stored in computers. (12)
2. The use of computers in keeping crime statistics benefits the public. (15)

3. I feel safer knowing the police can use the computer's high speed and extensive memory to help in the apprehension of criminals. (51)
4. I do not think my freedom is reduced by the widespread use of computers in the justice system. (64)
5. There is really no way in which innocent citizens can be harmed by the wide use of computers in the justice system. (76)

6. I don't think computers have a place in the justice system. (85)
7. The crime statistics kept on computers are too misleading to be much good. (36)
8. The use of the speed and memory of computers to help apprehend criminals does not really help to deter crime. (90)
9. The widespread use of computers in the justice system violates my rights. (70)
10. It is too easy to make a mistake and harm an innocent person when computers are used in the justice system. (67)

Statements	Converse

Finance and Banking

1. As compared with people, computers are more accurate in keeping records of personal financial transactions. (57)
2. Credit and other financial transactions are faster when done through a computer than when done through people. (32)
3. Personal credit card information can be kept just as private and confidential on computers as through any other medium. (24)
4. I do not think that personal credit information stored in computers will interfere with my rights to privacy. (83)
5. The danger of theft of personal funds is not increased by the use of computers in banking and credit operations. (92)

6. Computers can never match the accuracy of trained people in keeping records of financial transactions. (66)
7. There are more important things to consider about financial transactions than the speed a computer can give. (16)
8. The use of computers to record personal credit information increases the possibility of other people getting hold of personal information about me. (29)
9. My rights are more easily violated when computers store personal credit information about me. (33)
10. Theft of personal funds has greatly increased since computers were introduced into credit and banking operations. (7)

Mathematics and Statistics

1. The computer's lightening swift calculating ability and nearly infinite memory are entirely desirable. (19)
2. It would be desirable to learn statistics from a computer because most statistics are calculated on computers. (30)
3. It is better to solve math or statistics problems by computer than by hand. (73)
4. I would have more trust in statistics processed by a computer than by hand. (93)
5. I would feel more comfortable doing math or statistics by computer than by hand. (79)

6. Inaccuracy is often the price paid for the speed and memory of a computer. (48)
7. Statistics should be learned and understood before a computer is used for their calculation. (58)
8. Solving statistics or math problems by hand is often better than using the computer to solve these problems. (84)
9. I would use more caution in using computer-calculated statistics than hand-calculated statistics. (43)
10. All in all, I would prefer to do math or statistics myself than use a computer. (28)

Procedure

The Cybernetics Attitude Scale was administered to subjects in groups of twenty or thirty. The subjects were allowed up to one hour to complete the scale. Responses were coded and anonymous. Following completion of the study, the subjects were fully debriefed.

RESULTS

Descriptive Statistics

Means and standard deviations were computed for the total scale score and for each of the ten subscale total scores. These statistics were computed for the total sample and for men and women separately. Analyses were performed on the CYBER 170 at the University of Illinois at Urbana-Champaign. The FREQUENCIES program of the Statistical Package for the Social Sciences (Nie et al., 1975) was employed.

The mean (M) and the standard deviation (SD) for all subjects (N = 121) on the total Cybernetics Attitude Scale (100 items) were 404.36 and 56.80, respectively. The mean and standard deviation for each subscale (ten items) of the Cybernetics Attitude Scale, ranked in order from most favorable attitudes, were criminal justice system (M = 32.66, SD = 7.32); mathematics and statistics (M = 34.31, SD = 7.83); politics (M = 34.36, SD = 7.35); society (M = 35.60, SD = 9.18); finance and banking (M = 35.86, SD = 7.56); cognition (M = 42.72, SD = 8.78); values (M = 44.05, SD = 6.80); medicine (M = 45.73, SD = 7.20); education (M = 47.05, SD = 9.23); counseling (M = 51.84, SD = 8.74).

Five subscales—society, values, cognition, education, and criminal justice— yielded significant differences between men and women. For each of these subscales, men had more favorable attitudes toward computer applications in that sector of society. Specific attitude scale scores were (1) for the society subscale, men (M = 33.11, SD = 8.61), women (M = 38.31, SD = 9.04) (p<.01); (2) for the values subscale, men (M = 42.40, SD = 6.50), women (M = 45.85, SD = 6.71) (p<.01); (3) for the cognition subscale, men (M = 40.98, SD = 8.34), women (M = 44.60, SD = 8.93) (p<.05); (4) for the education subscale, men (M = 45.03, SD = 9.38), women (M = 49.24, SD = 8.61) (p<.05); and (5) for the criminal justice system subscale, men (M = 31.25, SD = 7.02), women (M = 34.19, SD = 7.40) (p<.05). The total scale scores were also different across sex: The mean equaled 392.52 (SD = 53.62) for men versus 417.22 (SD = 57.79) for women (p<.05).

Before one concludes that each of the subscales is truly different across sex, one must consider the correlations between the subscales. If the subscales are highly related, then the *t* tests might be measuring the same variance several times.

The correlations between subscales ranged between .23 for criminal justice and counseling to .67 for society and values. The average correlation was .45. Most correlations were above .40.

Principal-Components Analysis

To further test for the independence of the subscales, two principal-components analyses were conducted on the subscale total scores. SPSS was again used. The first analysis revealed three factors.

Factor 1 had high loadings on two subscales: values (loading = .79) and cognition (loading = .82). Society and education also had highest loadings on Factor 1 compared with loadings on other factors. Society had a loading of .76 on Factor 1 and a loading of .35 on Factor 2. Education loaded .70 on Factor 1 and .44 on Factor 3.

Factor 2 included the politics subscale (with a loading of .76). Criminal justice and finance also had their highest loadings on Factor 2. Criminal justice loaded .34 on Factor 1 and .74 on Factor 2; finance loaded .79 on Factor 2 and .35 on Factor 3.

Medicine loaded .81 on Factor 3. The counseling and mathematics subscales had split loadings: Counseling loaded .84 on Factor 3 and .34 on Factor 1. Mathematics loaded .57 on Factor 1, .37 on Factor 2, and .33 on Factor 3. The criterion used for identifying a subscale with a particular factor was a loading above .4 on that factor and loadings below .3 on all other factors. The subscales that showed sex differences also tended to have high loadings of Factor 1. The only exception was criminal justice.

The second principal-components analysis included sex as a variable. Sex had a loading of .85 on Factor 3. So the third factor in this analysis was virtually identical to the sex variable. This analysis had the effect of separating the variance shared by the society, values, cognition, and education subscales into two parts: (1) variance shared by those variables, and also shared with the sex variable; and (2) variance shared by those variables due to reasons other than the sex variable (such as content similarity). All of the subscales of interest (except for criminal justice) still had moderate factor loadings on Factor 1. But they also showed high loadings on the sex factor (Factor 3). These results suggest that some of the sex differences found by the t tests were reflecting common variance.

Differences between Subscales

Dependent t tests were computed (using SPSS) within the three samples. Each of these revealed that most of the subscale means were significantly different from one another. These subscales did not appear to group together on the basis of the principal-components analysis.

For the total sample, the t values ranged in absolute magnitude from .33 for society versus finance (not statistically significant) to 20.05 for counseling versus mathematics (p < .001). For men, the absolute values range from .18 for the *t* test comparing subscales medicine and education (not significant) to 17.25 for counseling versus criminal justice (p < .001). For women, the lowest *t* value in absolute magnitude occurred between the pair finance and mathematics (t = .08, n.s.). The largest absolute *t* value was 13.42, between education and criminal justice (p < .001).

Factor Analysis

A factor analysis was conducted on the 100 items constituting the Cybernetics Attitude Scale. Oblique rotation using DAPPER (hyperplane fitting—Tucker, 1980) and parallel analysis (Humphreys and Montinelli, 1975) suggested the presence of five major factors. The same criterion for identifying an item with a factor was used with this analysis that had been used with the principal-components analysis. Recall that this criterion was a factor loading above .4 on one factor and loadings below .3 on all other factors. The factor analysis revealed thirty-two items with loadings on only one factor. These items, their factor loadings, and the subscales for which they were written are presented below.

Factor 1. The first factor was a general dimension. Computers were seen as servants of man. Four of the five items are from the values and society subscales. The fifth item (with the lowest loading) was a general mathematics item.

For Factor 1, items, subscales, and factor loadings were "The more we use computers the more we will devalue people's worth" (values, .70); "Computers increase human freedom and allow us to become more human" (society, .64); "Compared with the Industrial Revolution, the computer is less threatening to society" (society, .56); "Computers can never change the value of being human" (values, .49); "I would feel more comfortable doing math or statistics by computer than by hand" (mathematics and statistics, .45).

Factor 2. The second factor had three items. This factor contains items from values and counseling subscales. It appears to emphasize the difference between computers and humans.

For Factor 2, items, subscales, and factor loadings were "The ability to reflect upon personal experience separates man from computer" (values, .60); "Too many things could go wrong with a computer that couldn't go wrong with a counselor as I try to solve my personal problems" (counseling, .44); "I would feel more at ease solving a personal problem with a computer than with a counselor" (counseling, .43).

Factor 3. Two areas contributed items to the third factor: (1) items based on affective reactions, and (2) items dealing with health (mental and physical) and education. The affective items often use phrases such as "I would feel more *at ease* learning from a computer than from a teacher," and "I would like learning from a computer because I wouldn't feel embarrassed when I didn't know the answer." Items also appear to be similar in content. This factor actually consisted of items from the counseling, education, and medicine subscales.

For Factor 3, items, subscales, and factor loadings were "I would like learning with a computer because I can work at my own pace" (education, .62); "I would be more at ease answering health questions from a computer than from a doctor" (medicine, .60); "Compared with a counselor, a computer would be more patient and reliable in helping to solve a personal problem" (counseling, .57); "I would feel more in control discussing my problems with a counselor than with a computer" (counseling, .55); "I would like learning from a computer because I wouldn't feel embarrassed when I didn't know the answer" (education, .53); "I would feel more independent solving personal problems on a computer than with a counselor" (counseling, .51); "As compared with a counselor, a computer could generate a greater number of solutions to my personal problems" (counseling, .48); "I think a computer could have more information to help me solve my problems than a counselor could have" (counseling, .46); "I would be more comfortable talking to a doctor than to a computer about my health problems" (medicine, .41); "I would like working with a computer because it doesn't play favorites as a teacher might" (education, .41).

Factor 4. The accuracy of computers is reflected in the fourth factor. Although items come from subscales as diverse as finance, politics, and mathematics, all deal with the speed and accuracy computers offer.

For Factor 4, items, subscales, and factor loadings were "Computers can never match the accuracy of trained people in keeping record of financial transactions" (finance and banking, .61); "I would have more trust in statistics processed by a computer than by hand" (mathematics and statistics, .61); "I have more confidence when votes are counted by a computer than when they are counted by an election official" (politics, .52); "Inaccuracy is often the price paid for the speed and memory of a computer" (mathematics and statistics, .52); "When computers report the outcomes of elections instantaneously, the possibility of naming the wrong person as a winner increases" (politics, .42); "I would use more caution in using computer-calculated statistics than hand-calculated statistics" (mathematics and statistics, .41).

Factor 5. The fifth factor might be considered a "memory" factor. Four of the eight items pertain to the ability of a computer to store large quantities of information. However, computer memory is not all that is reflected in Factor 5. The use of computers to benefit society could also be found in almost all of the items. This is also shown in the fact that six of the items came from the criminal justice and political subscales.

For Factor 5, items, subscales, and factor loadings were "I feel safer knowing the police can use the computer's high speed and extensive memory to help in the apprehension of criminals" (criminal justice, .63); "The use of computers in keeping crime statistics benefits the public" (criminal justice, .56); "When a computer instantaneously reports public opinions, both citizens and government benefit" (politics, .55); "I do not think that personal credit information stored in computers will interfere with my rights to privacy'' (banking and finance, .51); ''I think it is valuable to have computers forecast the outcomes of elections'' (politics, .47); ''Forecasting the outcomes of elections by computers interferes with the election process'' (politics, .47); ''I think it is desirable to have information about criminals stored in computers'' (criminal justice, .46); ''A computer simply cannot increase a person's mental abilities'' (cognition, .42).

DISCUSSION

The data can be used to examine the question of whether, among the ten sectors of society, there exist generally differentiable rankings of advocacy or criticism of the use of computers. It appears from the data that there is advocacy for the use of computers in such sectors as the criminal justice system and mathematics and statistics, and criticism of the use of computers in such sectors as counseling and medicine. There are a number of possible explanations for the differences: there is a historical hypothesis, a sociological hypothesis, and, finally, a psychological hypothesis.

With respect to the historical hypothesis (Goldstine, 1972; Randall, 1979), the development of the analog computer and the subsequent development of the modern digital computer had as their goal the execution of complex mathematical and statistical analyses that, without the aid of computers, would be exceedingly difficult or impossible. Begun during World War II and, because of their expense, initially restricted to only a few scientific, university, and government settings, digital computer applications in mathematics, science, and statistics have become highly prevalent and, indeed, indispensable. Thus, in the mathematics and statistics sector of society, computers have the longest history and represent a functional use that is equivalent to their definition, that is, a computing function. This computing function was early extended beyond scientific systems to social and government systems such as the criminal justice system and to business organizations such as financial and banking systems, in each of which there is a continuity of the historical use for statistical and data-processing purposes. On the other hand, the uses of computers in psychiatry and psychology, and especially in the areas of counseling and medical diagnosis, depart from the historical purpose of computers (numerical analysis) and represent much more recent applications and, by comparison, are probably still pioneering efforts.

A sociological hypothesis for the slow acceptance of or, indeed, resistance to the use of computers in medical history taking and diagnosis, psychiatry, and counseling might include the concept of cultural lag (Ogburn, 1922), which states that the symbolic acceptance of technological innovation requires a time delay for the overcoming of the strain induced in customary behavior patterns in a particular cultural enterprise. Related sociological hypotheses are those of vested interest and social evolution (Parsons and Smeller, 1956). As pointed out

by Parsons and Smeller (1956, pp. 246–249), a vested interest within a social system may require the rejection of innovative threats to its customary behavior patterns by institutionalized rationalizations (Parsons, 1951, pp. 505–520).

A psychological hypothesis is the threat computers offer in the fields of medical diagnosis (Bleich, 1979; Card, Nicholson, and Crean, 1974; Grossman et al., 1979), psychiatry (Erdman et al., 1981; Lucas et al., 1977), psychotherapy (Colby, 1980; Greist, 1980; Slack and Slack, 1977), and counseling (Harris, 1974; Wagman, 1980a, 1982, 1984 a, 1984b; Wagman and Kerber, 1980, 1984). The threat is to professionals' pride in possessing unique intellectual and judgmental abilities (Blois, 1980; McDonald, 1976). This psychological hypothesis of injury to professional pride has been offered as a more general explanation of the initial resistance to the Copernican heliocentric theory, the Darwinian evolutionary theory of the descent of man, and the Freudian psychodynamic theory of unconscious determination of behavior, which initially were considered to be an insult to mankind's unique dignity and significance (Mazlish, 1993).

The results of the factor analysis indicate clusters of attitudes that cut across several subscales or sectors of society. One such cluster is Factor 3, which represents similarity of attitudes toward computers in the medicine, education, and counseling sectors. This cluster appears to represent affective reactions toward the use of the computer in traditional professional roles, such as those of physician, teacher, psychologist, and psychiatrist. This clustering of items represents highly personal and ego-involved reactions. Whereas Factor 3 cut across the education, medicine, and counseling sectors, Factor 5 represents a cluster of attitudes that cut across the criminal justice system and the politics sectors. It would appear that attitudes toward the use of computers in these sectors of society reflect storage and retrieval functions in which the computers' memories are used for the benefit of society. However, as may be seen from the converse items of the Cybernetics Attitude Scale (Table B.1) for these sectors, these positive uses may imply possible deleterious uses that result in intrusion into privacy and threats to personal freedom in these sectors of society.

In Factor 4, there is a cluster of attitudes that cut across the mathematics and statistics and the finance and banking sectors. Common to this attitude cluster is the recognition of the fundamental hallmarks of the computer, namely, its speed and accuracy in data processing. This efficiency cluster represents the power of the computer's contributions to mathematical, scientific, and engineering applications.

In contrast to Factors 4 and 5, which seem to refer to the specific technical uses of the computer, such as its speed, accuracy, and memory, Factors 1 and 2 search out the meanings of these technical functions of the computer with respect to values and society in general. These factors seem to reflect the concern that, somehow, the intelligent functions of the computer threaten an eventual possible control, in an undesirable direction (Postman, 1992), of the human social system, or at least, a diminution (Slouka, 1995) in the uniqueness of those higher cognitive processes by which the humanistic and scientific disciplines have been advanced (Wolfe, 1993). It is of interest that scholars in the humanities are beginning to relate themselves to the computer in such a way that its mere technical functions become an adjunct to the scholars' inquiries and judgments. Contemporary examples might include proving the authorship of poems, plays, or religious tracts by identifying common elementary features present in a set of written productions, tracing etymological changes in classical languages over several centuries (Dilligan, 1982) and computer-aided investigations by art historians and conservators into the restoration of paintings by old masters (Cherlin, 1982).

Bibliography

Abelson, P. and Hammond, A. (1977). The electronics revolution. *Science, 195*, 1087–1092.

Achinstein, P. (1965). Theoretical models. *The British Journal for the Philosophy of Science, 16(62)*, 102–120.

Anderson, A. and Belnap, N. (1975). *Entailment*. Princeton, NJ: Princeton University Press.

Anderson, J. R. (1983). *The architecture of cognition*. Cambridge, MA: Harvard University Press.

Anderson, J. R., Farrell, R., and Sauers, R. (1984). Learning to program LISP. *Cognitive Science, 8*, 87–129.

Austin, J. L. (1962). *How to do things with words*. Oxford: Oxford University Press.

Baldwin, E. (1947). *Dynamic aspects of biochemistry*. New York: Macmillan.

Bartlett, F. C. (1932). *Remembering: A study in experimental and social psychology*. Cambridge: Cambridge University Press.

Becker, J. D. (1973). A model for the encoding of experimental information. In R. C. Schank and K. M. Colby (Eds.), *Computer models of thought and language* (pp. 396–435). San Francisco: Freeman.

Birnbaum, L. (1991). Rigor mortis: A response to Nilsson's "Logic of artificial intelligence." *Artificial Intelligence, 47*, 57–77.

Bleich, H. L. (1979). The computer as a consultant. *New England Journal of Medicine, 284*, 141–147.

Blois, M. S. (1980). Clinical judgement and computers. *New England Journal of Medicine, 303*, 192–197.

Bobrow, D. G. and Winograd, T. (1977). Experience with KRL—One cycle of a knowledge representation language. *International Joint Conferences on Artificial Intelligence, 5*, 213–222.

Boden, M. A. (1990). *The philosophy of artificial intelligence*. Oxford: Oxford University Press.

Bonjour, L. (1985). *The structure of empirical knowledge*. Cambridge, MA: Harvard University Press.

Boole, G. (1854). *An investigation of the laws of thought*. New York: Macmillan.

Broadbent, D. (1985). A question of levels: Comment on McClelland and Rumelhart. *Journal of Experimental Psychology: General, 114*, 189–192.

Brooks, R. A. (1986). A robust layered control system for a mobile robot. *IEEE Journal of Robotic Automation, 2*, 14–23.

Brooks, R. A. (1991). Intelligence without representation. *Artificial Intelligence, 47*, 139–159.

Brooks, R. A. and Connell, J. H. (1986). Asychronous distributed control system for a mobile robot. *Proceedings SPIE* (pp. 77–84), Cambridge, MA.

Brown, A. L. and Campione, J. C. (1985). Three faces of transfer: Implications for early competence, individual differences, and instruction. In M. Lamb, A. L. Brown, and B. Rogoff (Eds.), *Advances in developmental psychology*. Hillsdale, NJ: Erlbaum.

Brown, R. (1977). Use of analogy to achieve new expertise. Cambridge, MA: The MIT Press.

Brownston, L., Farrel, R., Kant, E., and Martin, N. (1985). *Programming expert systems in OPS5: An introduction to rule-based programming*. Reading, MA: Addison-Wesley.

Buchanan, B. G. and Feigenbaum, E. A. (1978). DENDRAL and meta-DENDRAL: Their application dimension. *Artificial Intelligence, 11*, 5–24.

Burstein, M. H. (1986). A model of learning by incremental analogical reasoning and debugging. In R. Michalski, J. G. Carbonell, and T. M. Mitchell (Eds.), *Machine learning: An artificial intelligence approach (Vol. 2)*. Los Altos, CA: Kaufmann.

Carbonell, J. G. (1981). Invariance hierarchies in metaphor interpretation. *Proceedings of the Third Annual Meeting of the Cognitive Science Society*, Berkeley, CA.

Carbonell, J. G. (1982). Metaphor: An inescapable phenomenon in natural-language comprehension. In W. G. Lehnert and M. H. Ringle (Eds.), *Strategies for natural language processing*. Hillsdale, NJ: Erlbaum.

Carbonell, J. G. (1983). Learning by analogy: Formulating and generalizing plans from past experience. In R. Michalski, J. G. Carbonell, and T. M. Mitchell (Eds.), *Machine learning: An artificial intelligence approach (Vol. 1)*. Los Altos, CA: Tioga.

Carbonell, J. G. (1986). Analogy in problem solving. In R. S. Michalski, J. G. Carbonell, and T. M. Mitchell (Eds.), *Machine learning: An artificial intelligence approach (Vol. 2)*. Los Altos, CA: Kaufmann.

Card, W. I., Nicholson, M., and Crean, G. P. (1974). A comparison of doctor and computer interrogation of patients. *International Journal of Biomedicine and Computers, 3*, 175–187.

Carey, S. (1985). *Conceptual change in childhood*. Cambridge, MA: The MIT Press.

Chapman, D. (1987). Planning for conjunctive goals. *Artificial Intelligence, 32*, 333–377.

Charniak, E., Riesbeck, C. K., and McDermott, D. V. (1980). *Artificial intelligence programming*. Hillsdale, NJ: Erlbaum.

Chase, W. G., and Simon, H. A. (1973). Perception in chess. *Cognitive Psychology, 4*, 55–81.

Fodor, J. A. and Pylyshyn, Z. W. (1981). How direct is visual perception? *Cognition, 9,* 139–196.

Fodor, J. A. and Pylyshyn, Z. W. (1988). Connectionism and cognitive architecture: A critical analysis. *Cognition, 28,* 3–71.

Foster, M. and Martin, M. (Eds.). (1966). *Probability, confirmation, and simplicity.* New York: Odyssey Press.

Fruton, J. S. (1972). *Molecules and life.* New York: Wiley-Interscience.

Gardner, H. (1988). Creative lives and creative works: A synthetic scientific approach. In R. J. Sternberg (Ed.), *The nature of creativity* (pp. 288–324). Cambridge, MA: Cambridge University Press.

Gasser, L. (1991). Social conceptions of knowledge and action: DAI foundations and open systems semantics. *Artificial Intelligence, 47,* 107–138.

Genesereth, M. R. and Nilsson, N. J. (1987). *Logical foundations of artificial intelligence.* Los Altos, CA: Kaufmann.

Gentner, D. (1983). Structure-mapping: A theoretical framework for analogy. *Cognitive Science, 7,* 155–170.

Gentner, D. (1987). Analogical inference and analogical access. In A. Prieditis (Ed.), *Analogica: The first workshop on analogical reasoning.* London: Pittman.

Gentner, D. and Toupin, C. (1986). Systematicity and surface similarity in the development of analogy. *Cognitive Science, 10,* 277–300.

Gholson, B., Eymard, L. A., Long, D., Morgan, D., and Leeming, F. C. (1988). Problem solving, recall, isomorphic transfer, and non-isomorphic transfer among third-grade and fourth-grade children. *Cognitive Development, 3,* 37–57.

Gibson, J. J. (1979). *The ecological approach to visual perception.* Boston: Houghton-Mifflin.

Gick, M. L. and Holyoak, K. J. (1980). Analogical problem solving. *Cognitive Psychology, 12,* 306–355.

Gödel, K. (1930). Die Vollständigkeit des axiome des logischen funktionenkaküls. *Monatshefte für Matheematik und Physik, 37,* 349–360.

Gödel, K. (1931). Uber formal unentscheidbare Satz der Principia Mathematica und verwandter System, I. *Monatshefte für Matheematik und Physik, 37,* 173–189.

Goldstine, H. (1972). *The computer from Pascal to von Neumann.* Princeton, NJ: Princeton University Press.

Gould, J. L. and Marler, P. (1986). Learning by instinct. *Scientific American,* 74–85.

Greiner, R. (1985). Learning by understanding analogies. Ph.D. dissertation, Stanford University.

Greiner, R. (1988). Learning by understanding analogies. *Artificial Intelligence, 35,* 81–125.

Greist, J. H. (1980). Computer therapy. In R. Herenk (Ed.), *The Psycho-therapy handbook.* New York: New American Library.

Grice, H. P. (1975). Logic and conversation. In D. Davidson and G. Harmon (Eds.), *The logic of grammar* (pp. 41–58). New York: Dickenson.

Grimson, E. H. and Patil, R. S. (Eds.). (1987). *AI in the 1980s and beyond: An MIT survey.* Cambridge, MA: The MIT Press.

Grossman, J., Barnett, G. O., McGuire, M. T., and Swedlow, D. (1979). Computer acquired patient histories. *Journal of the American Medical Association, 215,* 1286–1291.

Gupta, A. and Tambe, M. (1988). Suitability of message passing computers for implementing production systems. *Proceedings of the AAAI-88* (pp. 687–692), St. Paul, MN.

Hadamard, J. (1949). *The psychology of invention in the mathematical field*. Princeton, NJ: Princeton University Press.

Halasz, F. and Moran, T. P. (1982). Analogy considered harmful. *Proceedings Conference on Human Factors in Computer Systems* (pp. 33–36), Gaithersburg, MD.

Halford, G. S. and Wilson, W. H. (1980). A category theory approach to cognitive development. *Cognitive Psychology, 12*, 356–411.

Halford, G. S., Wilson, W. H., Guo, J., Wiles, J., and Stewart, J. E. M. (1993). Connectionist implications for processing capacity limitations in analogies. In K. J. Holyoak and J. A. Barnden (Eds.), *Advances in Connectionist and Neural Computation Theory*. Vol. 2: *Analogical Connections*. Norwood, NJ: Ablex.

Hall, R. P. (1989). Computational approaches to analogical reasoning: A comparative analysis. *Artificial Intelligence, 39*, 39–120.

Harman, G., Ranney, M., Salem, K., Doring, F., Epstein, J., and Jaworksa, A. (1988). A theory of simplicity. *Proceedings of the Tenth Annual Conference of the Cognitive Science Society*. Hillsdale, NJ: Erlbaum.

Harris, H. (1974). The computer: Guidance tool of the future. *Journal of Counseling Psychology, 21*, 331–339.

Hayes, P. J. (1985). The second naive physics manifesto. In J. C. Hobbes and R. C. Moore (Eds.), *Formal theories of the commonsense world*. Norwood, NJ: Ablex.

Hayes-Roth, F. (1978). The role of partial and best matches in knowledge systems. In D. A. Waterman and F. Hayes-Roth (Eds.), *Pattern-directed inference systems* (pp. 557–576) New York: Academic Press.

Hayes-Roth, F., Waterman, D. A., and Lenat, D. B. (Eds.). (1983). *Building expert systems*. Reading, MA: Addison-Wesley.

Hennessey, B. A. and Amabile, T. M. (1988). The conditions of creativity. In R. J. Sternberg (Ed.), *The nature of creativity*. Cambridge, MA: Cambridge University Press.

Hesse, M. B. (1963). Models and analogies in science. In M. A. Hoskin (Ed.), *Newman history and philosophy of science series, vol. 14*. London: Sheed and Ward.

Hewitt, C. (1991). Open information systems semantics for distributed artificial intelligence. *Artificial Intelligence, 47*, 97–106.

Hillis, W. D. (1985). *The connection machine*. Cambridge, MA: The MIT Press.

Hobbes, T. (1651). Leviathan. In Sir William Molesworth (Ed.) (1839–1945), *The English Works of Thomas Hobbes of Mathersbury (vol. 3)*. London: John Bohn.

Hobbs, J. R. (1983a). Metaphor interpretation as selective inferencing: Cognitive processes in understanding metaphor (Part 1). *Empirical Studies of the Arts, 1 (1)*, 17–33.

Hobbs, J. R. (1983b). Metaphor interpretation as selective inferencing: Cognitive processes in understanding metaphor (Part 2). *Empirical Studies of the Arts, 1 (2)*, 125–142.

Hobbs, J. R. and Moore, R. (Eds.). (1985). *Formal theories of the commonsense world*. Norwood, NJ: Ablex.

Holland, J., Holyoak, K. J., Nisbett, R. E., and Thagard, P. (1986). *Induction: Process of learning, inference, and discovery*. Cambridge, MA: The MIT Press.

Holmes, F. L. (1980). Hans Krebs and the discovery of the ornithine cycle. *Federation Proceedings, 39*, 216–225.

Holyoak, K. J. (1985). The pragmatics of analogical transfer. *Psychological Learning and Motivation, 19*, 59–87.

Holyoak, K. J. (1991). Symbolic connectionism: *Toward third-generation theories of expertise.* In K. A. Ericsson and J. Smith (Eds.), *Toward a general theory of expertise: Prospects and limits.* Cambridge, MA: Cambridge University Press.

Holyoak, K. J. and Barnden, J. A. (Eds.) (1993). *Advances in Connectionist and Neural Computation Theory.* Vol. 2: *Analogical Connections.* Norwood, NJ: Ablex.

Holyoak, K. J. and Koh, K. (1987). Surface and structural similarity in analogical transfer. *Memory and Cognition, 15*, 332–340.

Holyoak, K. J., Novick, L. R., and Melz, E. R. (1993). Component processes in analogical transfer: Mapping, pattern completion, and adaptation. In K. J. Holyoak and J. A. Barnden (Eds.), *Advances in connectionist and neural computation theory.* Vol. 2: *Analogical connections.* Norwood, NJ: Ablex.

Holyoak, K. J., and Spellman, B. A. (1993). Thinking. *Annual Review of Psychology, 44*, 265–315.

Holyoak, K. J. and Thagard, P. (1989). Analogical mapping by constraint satisfaction. *Cognitive Science, 13*, 295–355.

Horgan, J. (1993). The death of proof. *Scientific American, 269* (October), 93–103.

Hovy, E. H. (1987). Some pragmatic decision criteria in generation. In G. Kempen (Ed.), *Natural language generation: New results in artificial intelligence* (pp. 3–19). Dordrecht, Netherlands: Kluwer Academic Publishers.

Hovy, E. H. (1988). *Generating natural language under pragmatic constraints.* Hillsdale, NJ: Erlbaum.

Hovy, E. H. (1990). Pragmatics and natural language generation. *Artificial Intelligence, 43*, 153–197.

Hsu, W., Prietula, M., and Steier, D. (1988). MERL-SOAR: Applying SOAR to scheduling. *Proceedings Workshop on Artificial Intelligence Simulation AAAI-88* (pp. 81–84), St. Paul, MN.

Hummel, J. E. and Holyoak, K. J. (1992). Indirect analogical mapping. *Proceedings of the 14th Annual Conference of the Cognitive Science Society* (pp. 510–521). Hillsdale, NJ: Erlbaum.

Humphreys, L. G. and Montinelli, R. G. (1975). An investigation of parallel analysis criterion for determining the number of common factors. *Multivariate Behavioral Research, 10*, 193–205.

Hunt, E. (1989). Cognitive science: Definitions, status, and questions. *The Annual Review of Psychology, 33*, 73–77.

John-Steiner, V. (1985). *Notebooks of the mind.* Albuquerque, NM: University of New Mexico Press.

Johnson-Laird, P. N. (1988). Reasoning by rule or model? *Proceedings of the 10th Annual Conference of the Cognitive Science Society* (pp. 765–771), Montreal, Quebec.

Just, M. A. and Carpenter, P. A. (1980). A theory of reading: From eye fixations to comprehension. *Psychological Review, 87*, 329–354.

Just, M. A. and Carpenter, P. A. (1987). *The psychology of reading and language comprehension.* Boston: Allyn and Bacon.

Kant, I. (1781). *Prolegomena to any future metaphysics.* New York: Random House.

Kant, I. (1958). *Critique of pure reason,* trans. N. Kemp Smith (first published 1781). New York: Random House.

Kedar-Cabelli, S. (1985). Purpose-directed analogy. *Proceedings of the Seventh Annual*

Conference of the Cognitive Science Society. Irvine, CA: Cognitive Science Society.

Keyes, R. W. (1993). The future of the transistor. *Scientific American, 268,* 70–78.

Kintsch, W. (1988). The role of knowledge in discourse comprehension: A construction-integration model. *Psychological Review, 95,* 163–182.

Kirsh, D. (1991). Foundations of AI: The big issues. *Artificial Intelligence, 47,* 3–30.

Kittay, E. (1987). *Metaphor: Its cognitive force and linguistic structure.* Oxford: Clarendon Press.

Kline, M. (1985). *Mathematics and the search for knowledge.* New York: Oxford University Press.

Kling, R. E. (1971). Reasoning by analogy with applications to heuristic problem solving: A case study, Technical Report CS-216. Ph.D. dissertation, Stanford University.

Kolodner, J. L. (1983a). Towards an understanding of the role of experience in the evolution from novice to expert. *International Journal of Man-Machine Studies, 19,* 497–518.

Kolodner, J. L. (1983b). Maintaining order in a dynamic long-term memory. *Cognitive Science, 7,* 243–280.

Kolodner, J. L. (Ed.). (1988). *Proceedings of the DARPA Workshop on Case-Based Reasoning,* Clearwater Beach, FL.

Konolige, K. (1985). Belief and Incompleteness. In J. R. Hobbs and R. Moore (Eds.), *Formal Theories of the Commonsense World.* Norwood, NJ: Ablex.

Kosko, B. (1991). *Neural networks and fuzzy systems.* Englewood Cliffs, NJ: Prentice-Hall.

Kulkarni, D. and Simon, H. A. (1988). The process of scientific discovery: The strategy of experimentation. *Cognitive Science, 12,* 139–175.

Kulkarni, D. and Simon, H. A. (1990). Experimentation in machine discovery. In J. Shrager and P. Langley (Eds.), *Computational models of scientific discovery and theory formation.* San Mateo, CA: Morgan Kaufmann.

Kurzwell, R. (1990). *The age of intelligent machines.* Cambridge, MA: The MIT Press.

Laird, J. E. (1986). *SOAR's user's manual (Version 4),* Technical Report ISL-15. Palo Alto, CA: Xerox Palo Alto Research Center.

Laird, J. E. (1988). Recovery from incorrect knowledge in SOAR. *Proceedings of the AAAI-88* (pp. 618–623), St. Paul, MN.

Laird, J. E. and Newell, A. (1983). A universal weak method. Technical Report 83–141. Pittsburgh, PA: Department of Computer Science, Carnegie-Mellon University.

Laird, J. E., Newell, A., and Rosenbloom, P. S. (1987). SOAR: An architecture for general intelligence. *Artificial Intelligence, 33,* 1–64.

Laird, J. E., Rosenbloom, P. S., and Newell, A. (1984). Towards chunking as a general learning mechanism. *Proceedings of the AAAI-84* (pp. 188–92), Austin, TX.

Laird, J., Rosenbloom, P., and Newell, A. (1986). Chunking in SOAR: The anatomy of a general learning mechanism. *Machine Learning, 1,* 11–46.

Lakoff, G. and Johnson, M. (1980). *Metaphors we live by.* Chicago: University of Illinois Press.

Landauer, R. (1989). Can we switch by control of quantum mechanical transmission? *Physics Today, 42(10),* 119–121.

Langley, P. (1981). Data-driven discovery of physical laws. *Cognitive Science, 5,* 50.

Langley, P. and Jones, R. (1988). A computational model of scientific insight. In R. J.

Sternberg (Ed.), *The nature of creativity* (pp. 177–201). Cambridge, MA: Cambridge University Press.

Langley, P., Simon, H. A., Bradshaw, G. L., and Zytkow, J. M. (1987). *Scientific discovery: Computational explorations of the creative processes*. Cambridge, MA: The MIT Press.

Langley, P. and Zytkow, J. M. (1989). Data-driven approaches to empirical discovery. *Artificial Intelligence, 40*, 283–312.

Larkin, J. H., McDermott, J., Simon, D. P., and Simon, H. A. (1980). Models of competence in solving physics problems. *Cognitive Science, 4*, 317–345.

Lavoisier, A. (1862). *Oeuvres* (6 vols.). Paris: Imprimerie Impèriale.

Lehnert, W. (1983). BORIS—An expert in in-depth understanding of narratives. *Artificial Intelligence, 20*, 15–61.

Lehnert, W. G. (1982). Plot units: A narrative summarization strategy. In W. G. Lehnert and M. H. Ringle (Eds.), *Strategies for natural language processing*. Hillsdale, NJ: Erlbaum.

Lehnert, W. G. and Burstein, M. H. (1979). The role of object primitives in natural language processing. *Proceedings of the 6th International Joint Conference on Artificial Intelligence*, Sofia, Bulgaria.

Lenat, D. B. (1979). On automated scientific theory formation: A case study using the AM program. In J. E. Hayes, D. Michie, and L. Mikulich (Eds.), *Machine Intelligence 9*, 251–286. New York: Halstead Press.

Lenat, D. B. and Feigenbaum, E. A. (1991). On the thresholds of knowledge. *Artificial Intelligence, 47*, 185–250.

Lenat, D. B. and Guha, R. V. (1989). *Building large knowledge-based systems: Representation and inference in the CYC project*. Reading, MA: Addison-Wesley.

Levesque, H. J. (1986). Knowledge representation and reasoning. *Annual Review of Computer Science, 1*. Palo Alto, CA: Annual Reviews.

Lewis, A. C. (1986). Memory constraints and flower choice in pieris rapae. *Science, 232*, 863–865.

Lewis, R. L., Newell, A., and Polk, T. A. (1989). Toward a SOAR theory of taking instructions for immediate reasoning tasks. *Proceedings of the 11th Annual Conference of the Cognitive Science Society*, Ann Arbor, MI.

Lindsey, R. K., Buchanan, B. G., Feigenbaum, E. A., and Lederberg, J. (1980). *Applications of artificial intelligence for organic chemistry: The DENDRAL project*. New York: McGraw-Hill.

Lloyd, S. (1992). *Ideals as interests in Hobbes's Leviathan: The power of mind over matter*. Cambridge: Cambridge University Press.

Locke, J. (1975). *An Essay concerning human understanding*, ed. P. H. Nidditch (first published 1690). Oxford: Clarendon Press.

Lucas, J. R. (1961). Minds, machines, and Gödel. *Philosophy, 36*, 112–127.

Lucas, R. W., Mullin, P. J., Luna, C. D., and McInroy, D. C. (1977). Psychiatrists and a computer as interrogators of patients with alcohol related illnesses: A comparison. *British Journal of Psychiatry, 131*, 160–167.

Luck, J. M. (1932). *Annual review of biochemistry*. Stanford, CA: Stanford University Press.

Malgady, R. G. and Johnson, M. G. (1980). Measurement of figurative language: Semantic feature models of comprehension and appreciation. In R. P. Honeck and R. R. Hoffman (Eds.), *Cognition and figurative language*. Hillsdale, NJ: Erlbaum.

Mannes, S. M. and Kintsch, W. (1991). Routine computing tasks: Planning as under-
    standing. *Cognitive Science, 115*, 305–342.
Markov, A. (1954). *A theory of algorithms*. Moscow: National Academy of Sciences.
Marr, D. (1982). *Vision*. San Francisco: Freeman.
Martindale, C. (1990). *Cognitive psychology: A neural network approach*. Pacific Grove,
    CA: Brooks-Cole.
Mazlish, B. (1993). *The fourth discontinuity*. New Haven, CT: Yale University Press.
McCarthy, J. (1960). Recursive functions of symbolic expressions and their computation
    by machine. *Communications of the Association for Computing Machinery, 7*,
    184–195.
McClelland, J. L., and Rumelhart, D. E. (1980). An interactive activation model of the
    effect of context in perception. Technical Report no. 91. Center for Human In-
    formation Processing, University of California at San Diego.
McClelland, J. L., Rumelhart, D. E., and the PDP Research Group (1986). *Parallel dis-
    tributed processing: Explorations in the microstructure of cognition 2: Psycho-
    logical and biological models*. Cambridge, MA: The MIT Press.
McDermott, J. (1978). ANA: An assimilating and accommodating production system.
    Technical Report CMU-CS-78-156. Pittsburgh, PA: Computer Science Depart-
    ment, Carnegie-Mellon University.
McDermott, J. (1979). Learning to use analogies. *Proceedings IJCAI-79* (pp. 568–576),
    Tokyo, Japan.
McDermott, J. (1990). A critique of pure reason. In M. Boden (Ed.), *The philosophy of
    artificial intelligence* (pp. 206–230). Oxford: Oxford University Press.
McDonald, C. L. J. (1976). Protocol-based reminders—The quality of care and the non-
    perfectability of man. *New England Journal of Medicine, 295*, 1351–1355.
Miller, G. A. (1956). The magical number seven, plus or minus two: Some limts on our
    capacity for processing information. *Psychology Review, 63*, 81–97.
Minsky, M. (1975). A framework for representing knowledge. In P. Winston (Ed.), *The
    psychology of computer vision*. New York: McGraw-Hill.
Minsky, M. (1986). *The society of mind*. New York: Simon and Schuster.
Minsky, M. (1991). Logical versus analogical or symbolic versus connectionist or neat
    versus scruffy. *AI Magazine, 12*, 34–51.
Mitchell, T. M. (1982). Generalization in search. *Artificial Intelligence, 18*, 203–226.
Mitchell, T. M., Keller, R. M., and Kedar-Cabelli, S. T. (1986). Explanation-based gen-
    eralization: A unifying view. *Machine Learning, 1*, 47–80.
Montague, R. (1974). *Formal philosophy: Selected papers of Richard Montague*, ed.
    R. H. Thompson. New Haven, CT: Yale University Press.
Munyer, J. C. (1981). Analogy as a means of discovery in problem solving and learning.
    Ph.D. dissertation, University of California at Santa Cruz.
Negroponte, N. (1995). *Being digital*. New York: Alfred Knopf.
Newell, A. (1980). Reasoning, problem solving and decision processes: The problem
    space as a fundamental category. In R. Nickerson (Ed.), *Attention and perform-
    ance, Vol. 8*. Hillsdale, NJ: Erlbaum.
Newell, A. (1990). *Unified theories of cognition*. Cambridge, MA: Harvard University
    Press.
Newell, A. (1991). Unified theories of cognition: The William James lectures. Unpub-
    lished manuscript.
Newell, A. and Rosenbloom, P. S. (1981). Mechanisms of skill acquisition and the law

of practice. In J. R. Anderson (Ed.), *Cognitive skills and their acquisition*. Hillsdale, NJ: Erlbaum.

Newell, A., Rosenbloom, P. S., and Laird, J. E. (1989). Symbolic architectures for cognition. In M. Posner (Ed.), *Foundations of cognitive science*. Cambridge, MA: Cambridge University Press.

Newell, A. and Simon, H. A. (1972). *Human problem solving*. Englewood Cliffs, NJ: Prentice-Hall.

Newell, A. and Simon, H. A. (1976). Computer science as empirical inquiry: Symbols and search. *Communications of the ACM, 3*, 113–126.

Nie, N. H., Hull, C. H., Jenkins, J. G., Steinbrenner, K., and Bent, D. H. (1975). *Statistical package for the social sciences*, 2nd ed. New York: McGraw-Hill.

Nilsson, N. J. (1980). *Principles of artificial intelligence*. Palo Alto, CA: Tioga.

Nilsson, N. J. (1991). Logic and artificial intelligence. *Artificial Intelligence, 47*, 31–56.

Nordhausen, B. and Langley, P. (1990). An integrated approach to emipirical discovery. In J. Shrager and P. Langley (Eds.), *Computational models of scientific discovery and theory formation* (pp. 97–128). San Mateo, CA: Morgan Kaufmann.

Norman, A. C. (1975). On computing with formal power series. *Association for Computing Machinery Transactions on Mathematical Software, 1*, 346–356.

Nowak, G. and Thagard, P. (1989). Copernicus, Newton, and explanatory coherence. *Minnesota Studies in the Philosophy of Science*.

Nowak, G. and Thagard, P. (forthcoming). Copernicus, Newton, and explanatory coherence. *Minnesota Studies in the Philosophy of Science*.

Ogburn, W. F. (1922). *Social change*. Gloucester, MA: Smith.

Parsons, T. (1951). *The social system*. New York: Free Press of Glencoe.

Parsons, T. and Smeller, N. J. (1956). *Economy and society*. New York: Free Press of Glencoe.

Penrose, R. (1989). *The emperor's new mind: Concerning computers, minds, and the laws of physics*. Oxford: Oxford University Press.

Penrose, R. (1994). *Shadows of the mind: The search for the missing science of consciousness*. Oxford: Oxford University Press.

Pirolli, P. L. and Anderson, J. R. (1985). The role of learning from examples in the acquisition of recursive programming skills. *Canadian Journal of Psychology, 39*, 270–272.

Plato. (1956). Meno. In E. H. Wormington and P. O. Rouse (Eds.), *Great dialogues of Plato*, trans. W. H. D. Rouse. New York: New American Library.

Poincaré, H. (1913). *Foundations of science*, trans. G. B. Halstead. New York: Science Press.

Poincaré (1929). *The foundations of science*. New York: Science Press.

Polk, T. A. and Newell, A. (1988). Modeling human syllogistic reasoning in SOAR. *Proceedings of the 10th Annual Conference of the Cognitive Science Society* (pp. 181–187), Montreal, Quebec.

Post, E. L. (1943). Formal reductions of the general combinatorial decision problem. *American Journal of Mathematics, 65*, 197–268.

Postman, N. (1992). *Technopoly*. New York: Vintage Books.

Powell, L. (1984). Parsing the picnic problem with SOAR3 implementation of DYPAR-1. Pittsburgh: PA: Department of Computer Science, Carnegie-Mellon University.

Quiller-Couch, A. (1969). *The Shakespeare classic series*. Cambridge, MA: Cambridge University Press.

Quillian, M. R. (1968). Semantic memory. In M. Minsky (Ed.), *Semantic information processing*. Cambridge, MA: The MIT Press.

Quine, W. V. O. (1960). *Word and logic*. Cambridge, MA: The MIT Press.

Quine, W. V. O. (1961). *From a logical point of view*, 2nd ed. New York: Harper Torchbooks.

Quinlan, J. R. (1986). Induction of decision trees. *Machine Learning, 1*, 81–106.

Rajamoney, S., Dejong, G. F., and Faltings, B. (1985). Towards a model of conceptual knowledge acquisition through directed expermentation. *Proceedings of the IJCAI-85* (pp. 688–690), Los Angeles, CA.

Randall, B. (1979). Annotated bibliography of the origins of computers. *Annals of the History of the Computer, 1*, 107–207.

Ranney, M. (1987). Changing naive conception of motion. Ph.D. dissertation, Learning, Research, and Development Center, University of Pittsburgh.

Ranney, M. (1993). Explorations in explanatory coherence. In E. Bar-On, B. Eylon, and Z. Schertz (Eds.), *Designing intelligent learning environments: From cognitive analysis to computer implementation*. Norwood, NJ: Ablex.

Ranney, M. and Thagard, P. (1988). Explanatory coherence and belief revision in naive physics. *Proceedings of the Tenth Annual Conference of the Cognitive Science Society*. Hillsdale, NJ: Erlbaum.

Read, S. J. and Marcus-Newhall, A. (1993). The role of explanatory coherence in social explanations. *Journal of Personality and Social Psychology, 65(3)*, 429–447.

Reich, Y. (1988). Learning plans as a weak method for design. Pittsburgh, PA: Department of Civil Engineering, Carnegie-Mellon University.

Riemann, B. (1953). *Gesammelte mathematische werke*, 2nd ed. New York: Dover, 272–287, 391–404.

Roads, C. (1986). The Tsukuba musical robot. *Computer Music Journal* (Summer).

Rogers, C. (1951). *Client centered therapy: Current practice, implications and theory*. Boston: Houghton-Mifflin.

Rolston, D. (1988). *Principles of artificial intelligence and expert systems development*. New York: McGraw-Hill.

Root-Bernstein, R. S. (1989). *Discovering: Inventing and solving problems at the frontiers of scientific knowledge*. Cambridge, MA: Harvard University Press.

Rosenbloom, P. S. (1988). Beyond generalization as search: Towards a unified framework for the acquisition of new knowledge. In G. F. DeJong (Ed.), *Proceedings of the AAAI Symposium on Explanation-Based Learning* (pp. 17–21), Stanford, CA.

Rosenbloom, P. S. (1989). A symbolic goal-oriented prespective on connectionism and SOAR. In R. Pfeifer, Z. Schreter, F. Fogelman-Soulie, and L. Steels (Eds.), *Connectionism in perspective*. Amsterdam: Elsevier.

Rosenbloom, P. S. and Laird, J. E. (1986). Mapping explanation-based generalization into SOAR. *Proceedings of the AAAI-86* (pp. 561–567), Philadelphia, PA.

Rosenbloom, P. S., Laird, J. E., McDermott, J., Newell, A., and Orciuch, E. (1985). R1-SOAR: An experiment in knowledge-intensive programming in a problem-solving architecture. *IEEE Transportation Pattern Analogy Machine Intelligence, 7*, 561–569.

Rosenbloom, P. S., Laird, J. E., and Newell, A. (1987). Knowledge level learning in SOAR. *Proceedings of the AAAI-87* (pp. 499–504), Seattle, WA.

Rosenbloom, P. S., Laird, J. E., and Newell, A. (1988). Meta-levels in SOAR. In P. Maes and D. Nardi (Eds.), *Meta-level architectures and reflection* (pp. 227–240). Amsterdam: North-Holland.

Rosenbloom, P. S., Laird, J. E., Newell, A., and McCarl, R. (1991). A preliminary analysis of the SOAR architecture as a basis for general intelligence. *Artificial Intelligence, 47*, 289–325.

Rosenbloom, P. S. and Newell, A. (1986). The chunking of goal hierarchies: A generalized model of practice. In R. S. Michalski, J. G. Carbonell, and T. M. Mitchell (Eds.), *Machine learning: An artificial intelligence approach* (Vol. 2). Los Altos, CA: Kaufmann.

Rosenbloom, P. S., Newell, A., and Laird, J. E. (1990). Towards the knowledge level in SOAR: The role of the architecture in the use of knowledge. In K. VanLehn (Ed.), *Architectures for intelligence*. Hillsdale, NJ: Erlbaum.

Rosenschein, S. J. and Kaebling, L. P. (1986). The synthesis of machines with provably epistemic properties. In J. Y. Halpern (Ed.), *Proceedings of the 1986 Conference on Theoretical Aspects of Reasoning about Knowledge* (pp. 83–98). Los Altos, CA: Kaufmann.

Roszak, T. (1994). *The cult of information*. Berkeley, CA: University of California Press.

Rumelhart, D. E., Hinton, G., and McClelland, J. L. (1986). A general framework for parallel distributed processing. In D. Rumelhart and J. L. McClelland (Eds.), *Parallel distributed processing, Vol. 1: Foundations*. Cambridge, MA: The MIT Press.

Rumelhart, D. E., McClelland, J. R., and the PDP Research Group. (1986). *Parallel distributed processing: Explorations in the microstructure of cognition*. 2 vols. Cambridge, MA: The MIT Press.

Sacerdoti, E. D. (1974). Planning in a hierarchy of abstraction spaces. *Artificial Intelligence, 5*, 115–135.

Sagan, C. (1977). *The dragons of Eden: Speculations on the evolution of human intelligence*. New York: Ballantine Books.

Saul, R. H. (1984). A SOAR2 implementation of version-space inductive learning. Pittsburgh, PA: Department of Computer Science, Carnegie-Mellon University.

Schank, P. and Carbonell, J. G., Jr. (1979). Re: The Gettysburg Address. Representing social and political acts. In N. Findler (Ed.), *Associative networks*. New York: Academic Press.

Schank, P. and Ranney, M. (1991). The psychological fidelity of ECHO: Modeling an experimental study of explanatory coherence. *Proceedings of 13th Annual Conference of the Cognitive Science Society* (pp. 892–897). Hillsdale, NJ: Erlbaum.

Schank, P. and Ranney, M. (1992). Accessing explanatory coherence: A new method for integrating verbal data with models of on-line brief revision. *Proceedings of the 14th Annual Conference of the Cognitive Science Society* (pp. 599–604). Hillsdale, NJ: Erlbaum.

Schank, P. and Reisbeck, C. (1981). *Inside computer understanding*. Hillsdale, NJ: Erlbaum.

Schank, R. C. (1972). Semantics in conceptual analyisis. *Lingua, 30*, 101–140.

Schank, R. C. (1975). *Conceptual information processing*. Amsterdam: North-Holland.

Schank, R. C. (1982). *Dynamic memory: A theory of reminding and learning in computers and people*. Cambridge, MA: Cambridge University Press.

Schank, R. C. (1985). *Dynamic memory: A theory of reminding and learning in computers and people*. 2nd ed. Cambridge, MA: Cambridge University Press.

Schank, R. and Ableson, R. (1977). *Scripts, plans, goals and understanding.* Hillsdale, NJ: Erlbaum.

Searle, J. R. (1969). *Speech acts.* New York: Cambridge University Press.

Shastri, L. and Ajjanagadde, V. (1993). From simple associations to systematic reasoning: A connectionist representation of rules, variables and dynamic bindings. *Behavioral and Brain Sciences, 16,* 118–129.

Shortliffe, E. H. (1976). *MYCIN: Computer-based medical consultations.* New York: Elsevier.

Simon, H. A. (1969). *The sciences of the artificial.* Cambridge, MA: The MIT Press.

Simon, H. A. (1977). What computers mean for man and society. *Science, 195,* 1186–1190.

Simon, H. A. (1979). Information processing models of cognition. *Annual Review of Psychology, 30,* 363–396.

Simon, H. A. (1990). Invariants of human behavior. *Annual Review of Psychology, 41,* 1–19.

Simon, H. A. and Lea, G. (1974). Problem solving and rule induction: A unified view. In L. Gregg (Ed.), *Knowledge and cognition.* Hillsdale, NJ: Erlbaum.

Simpson, R. L. (1985). A computer model of case-based reasoning in problem solving: An investigation in the domain of dispute mediation, Technical Report GIT-ICS-85/18. Ph.D. dissertation, Georgia Institute of Technology.

Skinner, B. F. (1938). *The Behavior of organisms: Experimental analysis.* New York: Appleton-Century.

Slack, W. V. and Slack, C. L. W. (1977). Talking to a computer about emotional problems: A comparative study. *Psychotherapy Theory, Research, Practice, 14,* 156–164.

Slouka, M. (1995). *War of the worlds: Cyberspace and the high-tech assault on reality.* New York: Basic Books.

Spector, R. D. (1981). *The Scarlett Letter by Hawthorne.* New York: Bantam Books.

Spellman, B. A. and Holyoak, K. J. (1992). If Saddam is Hitler then who is George Bush? Analogical mapping between systems of social roles. *Journal of Personality and Social Psychology, 62,* 913–933.

Sperber and Wilson. (1987). Relevence. In *BBS Multiple Book Review, 10(4).*

Steier, D. M. (1987). Cypress-SOAR: A case study in search and learning algorithm design. *Proceedings IJCAI-87* (pp. 327–330), Milan, Italy.

Steier, D. M., Laird, J. E., Newell, A., Rosenbloom, P. S., Flynn, R., Golding, A., Polk, T. A., Shivers, O. G., Unruh, A., and Yost, G. R. (1987). Varieties of learning in SOAR. In P. Langley (Ed.), *Proceedings of the Fourth International Workshop on Machine Learning* (pp. 300–311), Irvine, CA.

Steier, D. M. and Newell, A. (1988). Integrating multiple sources of knowledge in Designer-SOAR: An automatic algorithm designer. *Proceedings of the AAAI-88* (pp. 8–13), St. Paul, MN.

Stenning, K. and Levy, K. (1988). Knowledge-rich solutions to the binding problem: A simulation of some human computational mechanisms. *Knowledge Based Systems, 1,* 143–152.

Stenning, K. and Oaksford, M. (1993). Rational reasoning and human implementations of logics. In K. I. Manktelow and D. E. Over (Eds.), *Rationality.* London: Routledge.

Stenning, K., Shepherd, M., and Levy, J. (1988). On the construction of representations for individuals from descriptions in text. *Language and Cognitive Processes, 2*, 129–164.

Sterling, L. and Shapiro, E. (1986). *The art of PROLOG*. Cambridge, MA: The MIT Press.

Sternberg, R. J. (1977). *Intelligence, information processing and analogical reasoning: The componential analysis of human abilities*. Hillsdale, NJ: Erlbaum.

Sternberg, R. J. (Ed.). (1988). *The nature of creativity*. Cambridge, MA: Cambridge University Press.

Tambe, M. (1988). *Speculations on the computational effects of chunking*. Pittsburgh, PA: Computer Science Department, Carnegie-Mellon University.

Tambe, M., Acharya, A., and Gupta, A. (1989). *Implementation of production systems on message passing computers: Simulation results and analysis*, Technical Report CMU-CS-89-129. Pittsburgh, PA: Computer Science Department, Carnegie-Mellon University, School of Computer Science.

Tambe, M., Kalp, D., Gupta, A., Forgy, C. L., Milnes, B., and Newell, A. (1988). SOAR/PSM-E: Investigating match parallelism in a learning production system. *Proceedings of the ACM/SIGPLAN Symposium on Parallel Programming: Experience with Applications, Languages, and Systems*, 146–161.

Tambe, M. and Newell, A. (1988). Some chunks are expensive. In J. Laird (Ed.), *Proceedings of the Fifth International Conference on Machine Learning* (pp. 451–458), Ann Arbor, MI.

Tambe, M. and Rosenbloom, P. S. (1989). Eliminating expensive chunks by restricting expressiveness. *Proceedings of the IJCAI-89*, Detroit, MI.

Taube, A. H. (Ed.). (1961–1963). *Collected Works of John von Neumann*, 6 vols. Oxford: Pergamon.

Teitleman, W. (1976). Reasoning with conditional sentences. *Journal of Verbal Learning and Verbal Behavior, 10*, 218–225.

Thagard, P. (1978). The best explanation: Criteria for the theory of choice. *Journal of Philosophy, 75*, 76–92.

Thagard, P. (1988a). *Computational philosophy of science*. Cambridge, MA: The MIT Press/Bradford Books.

Thagard, P. (1988b). The dinosaur debate: Application of a connectionist model of theory evaluation. Princeton, NJ: Princeton University. Unpublished manuscript.

Thagard, P. (in press). The conceptual structure of the chemical revolution. *Philosophy of Science*.

Thagard, P. (1989). Explanatory coherence. *Behavioral and Brain Sciences 12*, 435–502.

Thagard, P. (1992). *Conceptual revolutions*. Princeton, NJ: Princeton University Press.

Thagard, P., Holyoak, K. J., Nelson, G., and Gochfeld, D. (1990). Analog retrieval by constraint satisfaction. *Artificial Intelligence, 46*, 259–310.

Thagard, P. and Nowak, G. (1988). The explanatory coherence of continental drift. In A. Fine and J. Leplin (Eds.), *PSA 1988*. N.p.: Philosophy of Science Association.

Thagard, P. and Nowak, G. (in press). The conceptual structure of the geological revolution. In J. Shrager and P. Langley (Eds.), *Computational models of discovery and theory formation*. Norwood, NJ: Erlbaum.

Torrance, P. E. (1988). The nature of creativity as manifest in its testing. In R. J. Sternberg (Ed.), *The nature of creativity*. Cambridge, MA: Cambridge University Press.

Tucker, L. R. (1980). *DAPPFER: Direct artificial personal probability factor rotations.* University of Illinois at Urbana-Champaign, Department of Psychology. Unpublished manuscript and computer program.

Turing, A. M. (1936). On computable numbers, with an application to Entscheudung's problem. *Proceedings of the London Mathematics Society, 52,* 230–265.

Turing, A. M. (1937). Computing machinery and intelligence. *CT,* 11–35.

Turing, A. M. (1950). Computing machinery and intelligence. *Mind, 59,* 434–460.

Turing, A. M. (1963). Computing machinery and intelligence. In E. A. Feigenbaum and J. Feldman (Eds.), *Computers and thought* (first published 1950). New York: McGraw-Hill.

Tweney, R. D. (1990). Five questions for computationalists. In J. Shrager and P. Langley (Eds.), *Computational models of scientific discovery and theory formation* (pp. 471–484). San Mateo, CA: Kaufmann.

Unruh, A. and Rosenbloom, P. S. (1989). Abstraction in problem solving and learning. *Proceedings of the IJCAI-89,* Detroit, MI.

Unruh, A., Rosenbloom, P. S., and Laird, J. E. (1987). Dynamic abstraction problem solving in SOAR. *Proceedings of the Third Aerospace Applications of Artificial Intelligence Conference* (pp. 245–256), Dayton, OH.

von Neumann, J. (1951). The general and logical theory of automata. In L.A. Jeffress (Ed.), *Cerebral mechanism in behavior* (pp. 77–103). New York: Wiley.

Wagman, M. (1976). *Conceptual analysis of the psychological meaning of the computer in ten sectors of society,* University of Illinois at Urbana–Champaign, Department of Psychology. Unpublished manuscript.

Wagman, M. (1977). *The cybernetics attitude scale.* University of Illinois at Urbana–Champaign, Department of Psychology. Unpublished manuscript.

Wagman, M. (1978). The comparative effects of didactic-correction and self-contradiction on fallacious scientific and personal reasoning. *Journal of General Psychology* (99), 67–80.

Wagman, M. (1980a). PLATO DCS—An interactive computer system for personal counseling. *Journal of Counseling Psychology, 27,* 16–30.

Wagman, M. (1980b). Systematic dilemma counseling: Transition from counselor mode to autonomous mode. *Journal of Counseling Psychology, 27,* 171–178.

Wagman, M. (1982). A computer method of solving dilemmas. *Psychological Reports, 50,* 291–298.

Wagman, M. (1983). A factor analytic study of the psychological implications of the computer for the individual and society. *Behavior Research Methods and Instrumentation, 15,* 413–419.

Wagman, M. (1984a). *The dilemma and the computer: Theory, research, and applications to counseling psychology.* New York: Praeger.

Wagman, M. (1984b). Using computers in personal counseling. *Journal of Counseling and Development, 63,* 172–176.

Wagman, M. (1988). *Computer psychotherapy systems: Theory and research foundations.* New York: Gordon and Breach.

Wagman, M. (1991a). *Artificial intelligence and human cognition: A theoretical intercomparison of two realms of intellect.* New York: Praeger.

Wagman, M. (1991b). *Cognitive science and concepts of mind: Toward a general theory of human and artificial intelligence.* New York: Praeger.

Wagman, M. and Kerber, K. W. (1980). PLATO DCS—An interactive computer system for personal counseling: Further development and evaluation. *Journal of Counseling Psychology, 27*, 31–39.

Wagman, M. and Kerber, K. W. (1984). Computer-assisted counseling: Problems and prospects. *Counselor Education and Supervision, 24*, 147–154.

Waltz, D. L. and Pollack, J. B. (1985). Massively parallel parsing: A strongly interactive model of natural language interpretation. *Cognitive Science, 9 (1)*, 51–74.

Washington, R. and Rosenbloom, P. S. (1988). *Applying problem and learning to diagnosis.* Stanford, CA: Department of Computer Science, Stanford University.

Wiesmeyer, M. (1988). *SOAR I/O reference manual, version 2.* Ann Arbor, MI: Department of EECS, University of Michigan.

Weismeyer, M. (1989). *New and improved SOAR IO.* Ann Arbor, MI: Department of EECS, University of Michigan.

Weizenbaum, J. (1965). ELIZA—A computer program for the study of natural language communication between man and machine. *Communications of the ACM, 9*, 36–45.

Weizenbaum, J. (1976). *Computer power and human reason: From judgement to calculation.* San Francisco: Freeman.

Whewell, W. (1967). *The Philosophy of the Inductive Sciences* (first published 1840). London: Johnson Reprint.

Wilensky, R. (1978). Why John married Mary: Understanding stories involving recurring goals. *Cognitive Science, 2(3)*, 235–266.

Wilson, M. D. (Ed.). (1969). *The essential Descartes.* New York: Mentor.

Winograd, T. (1972). *Understanding natural language.* New York: Academic Press.

Winston, P. H. (1978). Learning by creating and justifying transfer frames. *Artificial Intelligence, 10(2)*, 147–172.

Winston, P. H. (1980). Learning and reasoning by analogy. *Communications of the ACM, 23(12)*, 689–703.

Winston, P. H. (1982). Learning new principles from precedents and exercises. *Artificial Intelligence, 19*, 321–350.

Winston, P. H. (1986). Learning by augmenting rules and accumulating censors. In R. S. Michalski, J. G. Carbonell, and T. M. Mitchell (Eds.), *Machine learning: An artificial intelligence approach* (pp. 45–61). Los Altos, CA: Kaufmann.

Winston, P. H., Binford, T. O., Katz, B., and Lowry, M. (1983). Learning physical descriptions from functional definitions. *Proceedings of the AAAI-83* (pp. 433–439), Washington, DC.

Wolfe, A. (1993). *The human difference: Animals, computers, and the necessity of social science.* Berkeley, CA: University of California Press.

Zadeh, L. A. (1979). A theory of approximate reasoning. In J. Hayes, D. Michie, and L. I. Mikulich (Eds.), *Machine intelligence, Vol. 9* (pp. 149–194). New York: Halstead Press.

Zippel, R. (1976). Univariate power series expansions in algebraic manipulations. *Proceedings of the Association for Computing Machinery Symposium on Symbolic and Algebraic Computation*, New York.

Author Index

Subject Index

About the Author

MORTON WAGMAN is Professor Emeritus of Psychology at the University of Illinois, Urbana–Champaign, and is a Diplomate in Counseling Psychology, American Board of Professional Psychology. He was honored as Distinguished Psychologist by the American Psychological Association in 1990. His most recent books include *The General Unified Theory of Intelligence* (Praeger, 1997), *Cognitive Science and the Symbolic Operations of Human and Artificial Intelligence* (Praeger, 1997), *Human Intellect and Cognitive Science* (Praeger, 1996), *The Sciences of Cognition* (Praeger, 1995), *Cognitive Psychology and Artificial Intelligence* (Praeger, 1993), *Cognitive Science and Concepts of Mind* (Praeger, 1991), *Artificial Intelligence and Human Cognition* (Praeger, 1991), and *The Dilemma and the Computer* (Praeger, 1984).

ISBN 0-275-95910-4

90000>

EAN

9 780275 959104

HARDCOVER BAR CODE